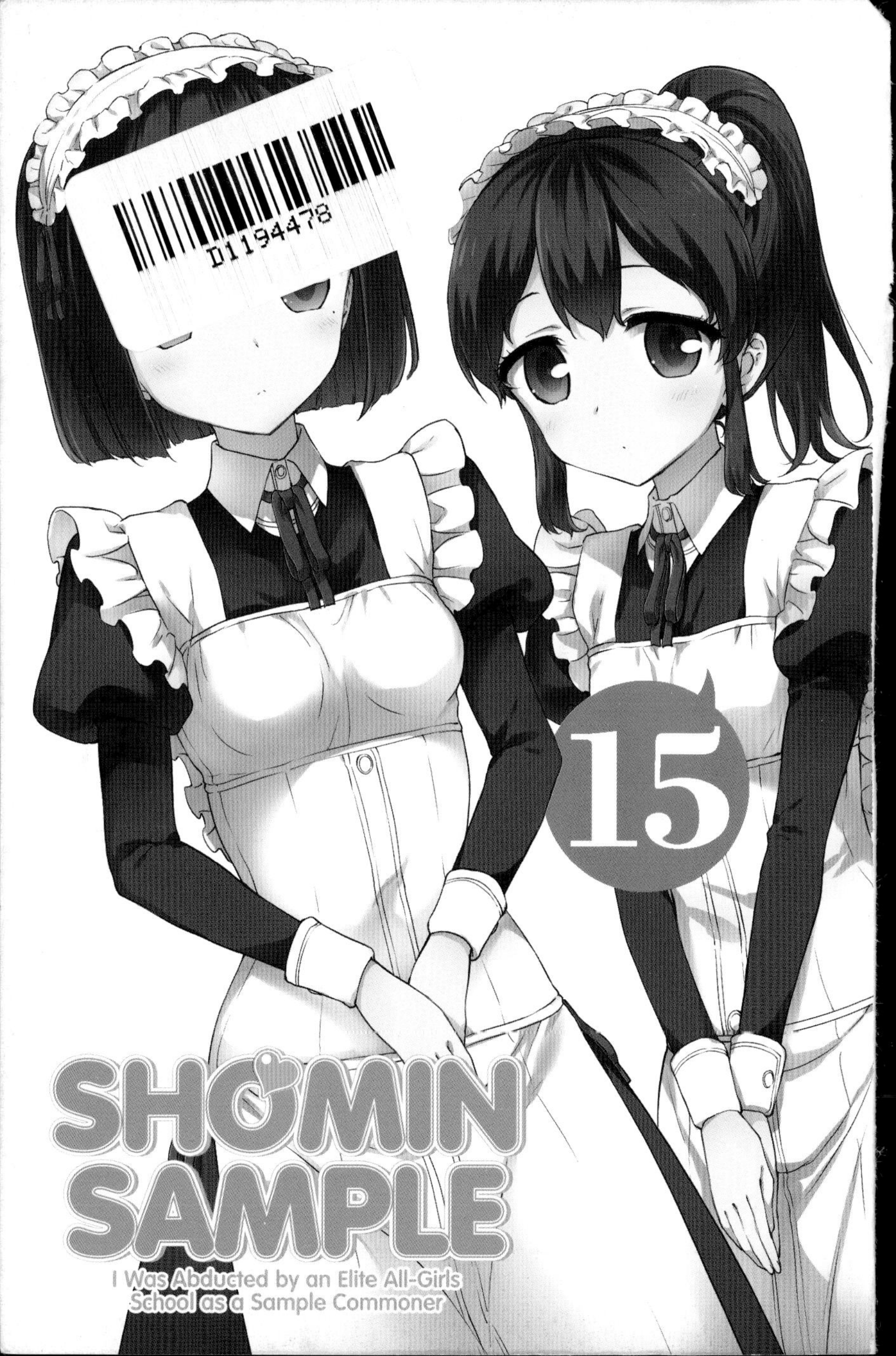
15
SHOMIN SAMPLE
I Was Abducted by an Elite All-Girls School as a Sample Commoner

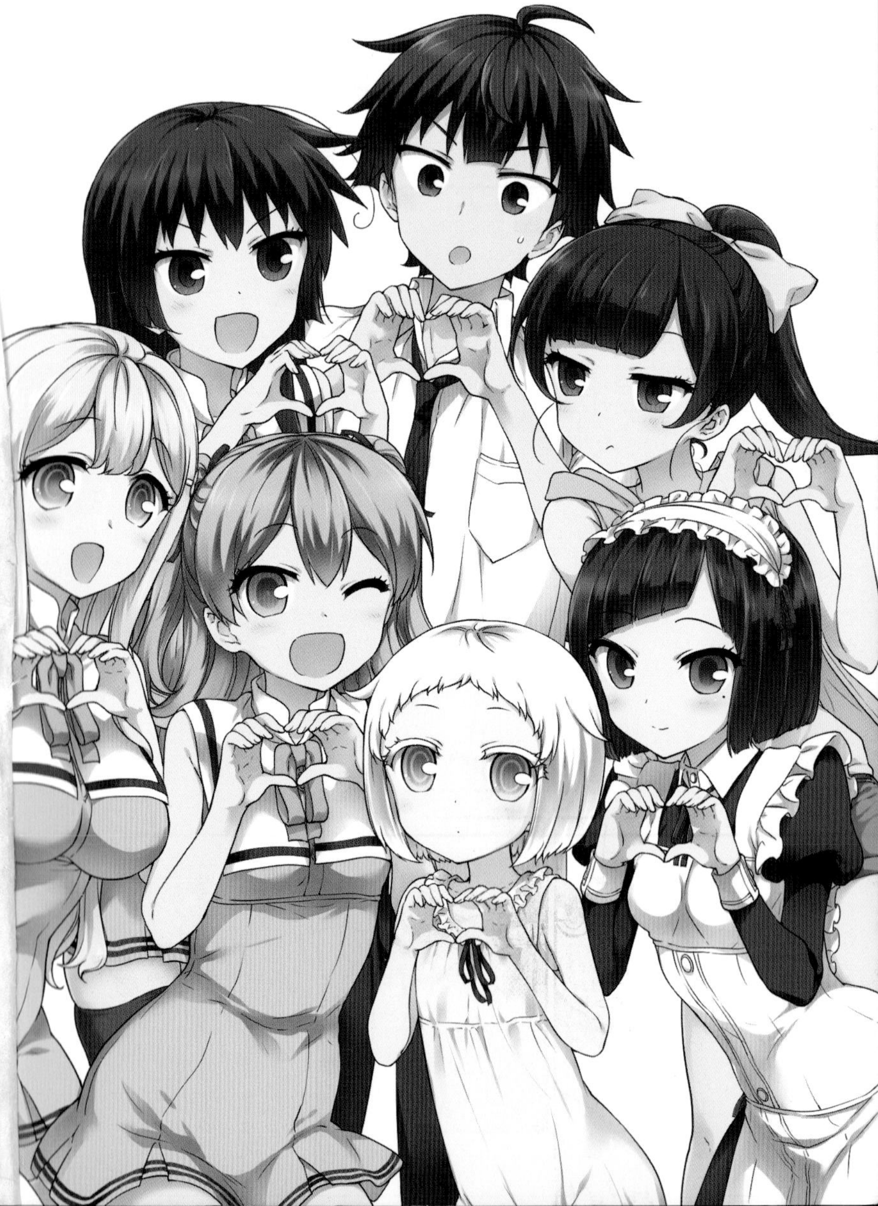

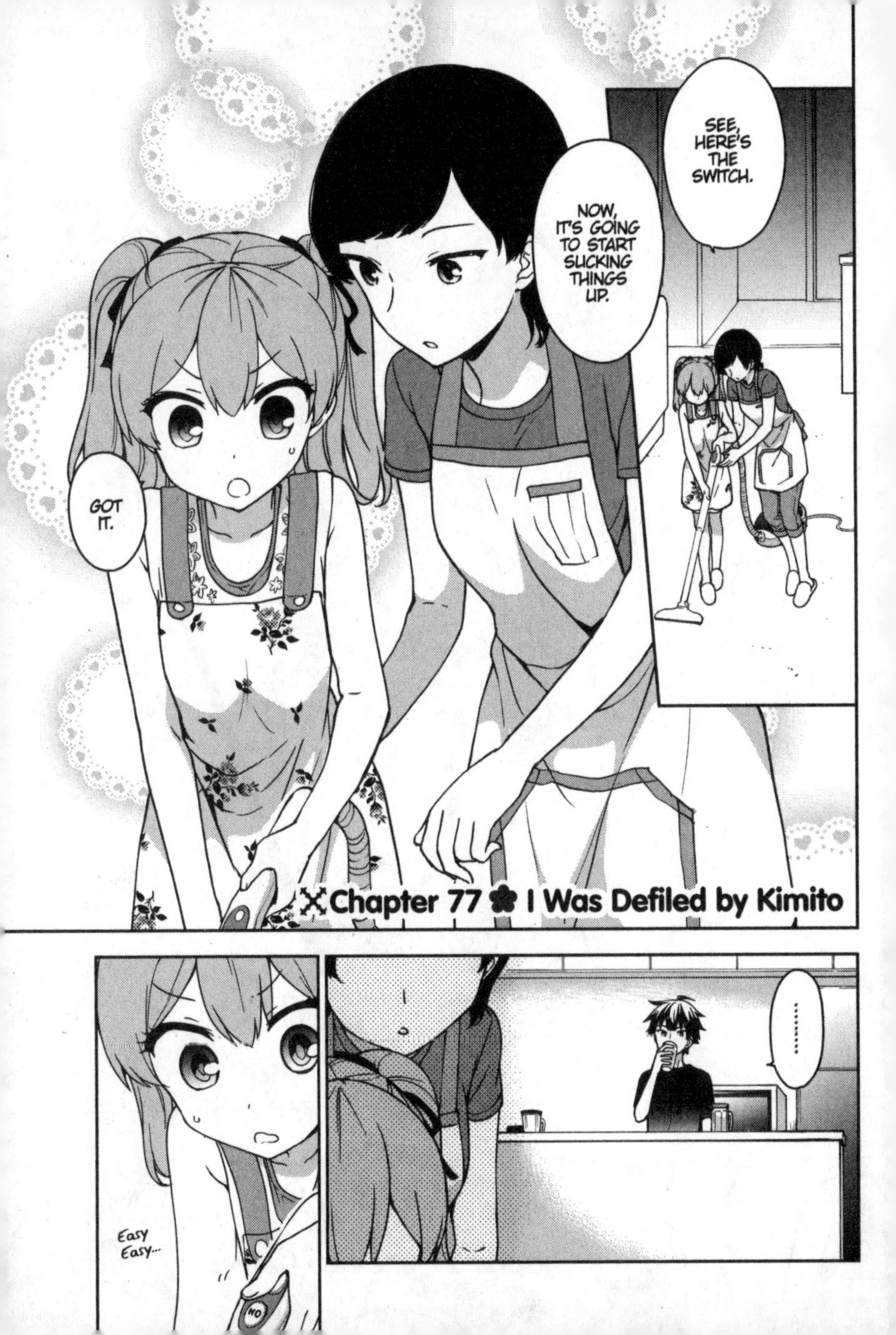
SEE, HERE'S THE SWITCH.
NOW, IT'S GOING TO START SUCKING THINGS UP.
GOT IT.
Chapter 77 I Was Defiled by Kimito
....
Easy Easy...
NO

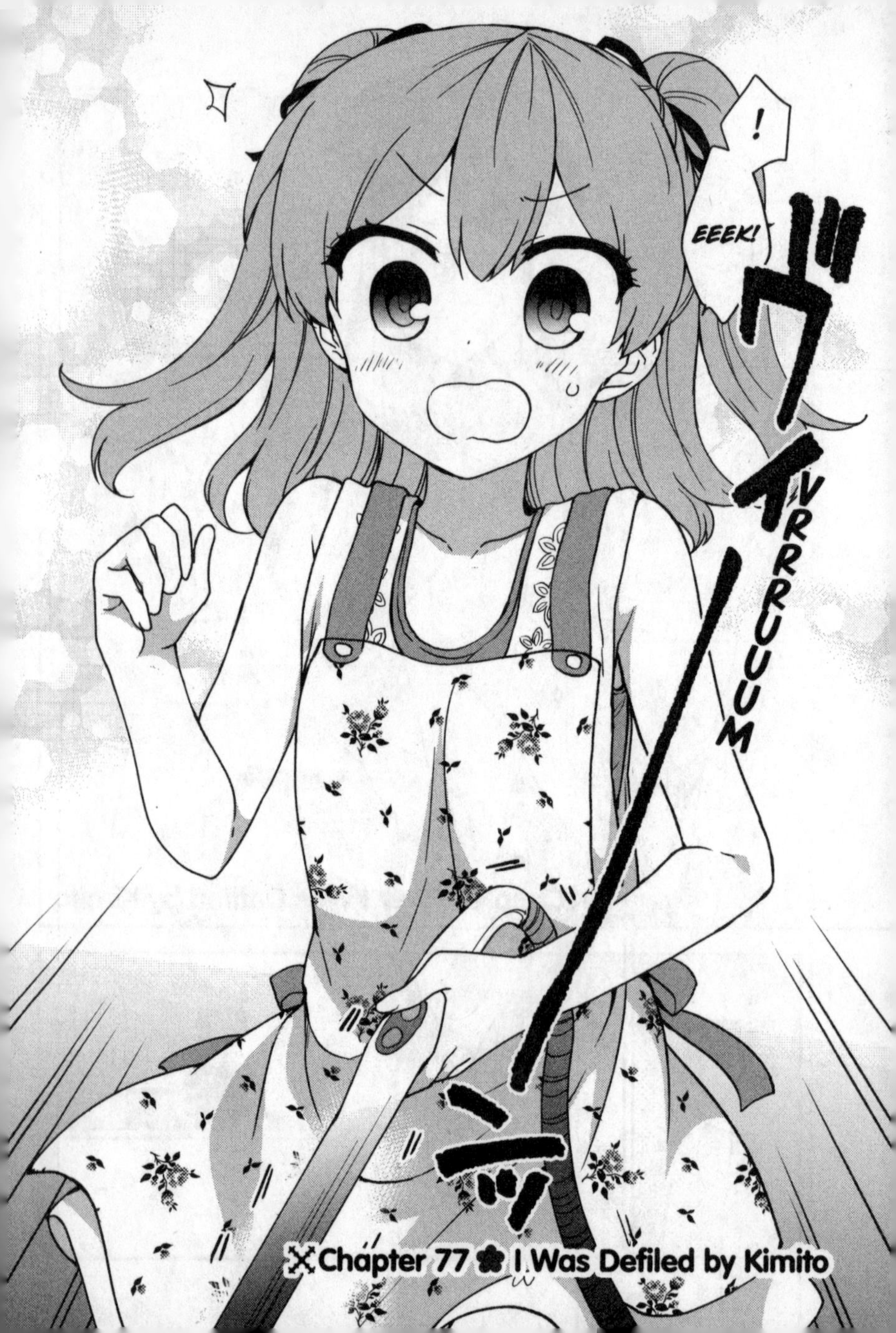
!
EEEK!
VRRRRUUUM
Chapter 77 I Was Defiled by Kimito

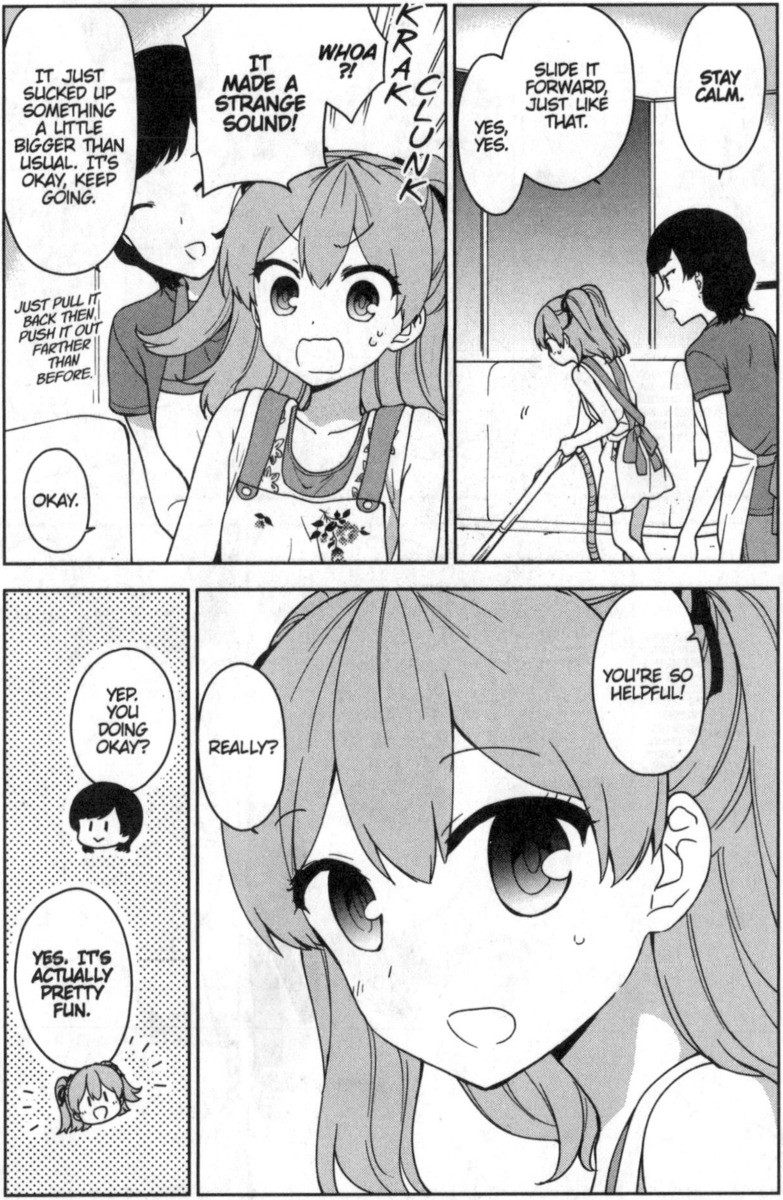
STAY CALM.
SLIDE IT FORWARD, JUST LIKE THAT.
YES, YES.
KRAK
CLUNK
WHOA ?!
IT MADE A STRANGE SOUND!
IT JUST SUCKED UP SOMETHING A LITTLE BIGGER THAN USUAL. IT'S OKAY, KEEP GOING.
JUST PULL IT BACK THEN PUSH IT OUT FARTHER THAN BEFORE.
OKAY.
YOU'RE SO HELPFUL!
REALLY?
YEP. YOU DOING OKAY?
YES. IT'S ACTUALLY PRETTY FUN.

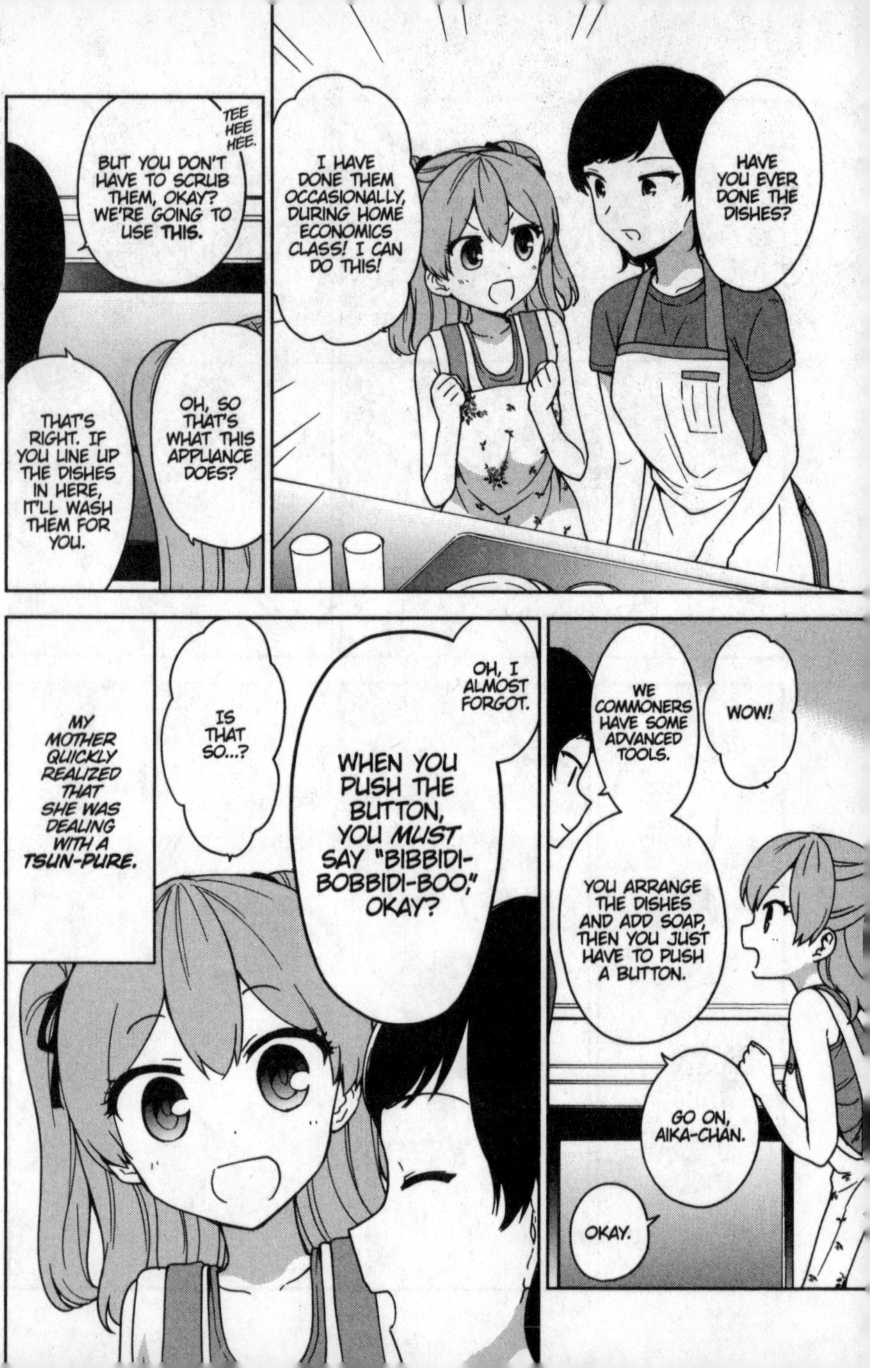
HAVE YOU EVER DONE THE DISHES?
I HAVE DONE THEM OCCASIONALLY, DURING HOME ECONOMICS CLASS! I CAN DO THIS!
TEE HEE HEE.
BUT YOU DON'T HAVE TO SCRUB THEM, OKAY? WE'RE GOING TO USE THIS.
OH, SO THAT'S WHAT THIS APPLIANCE DOES?
THAT'S RIGHT. IF YOU LINE UP THE DISHES IN HERE, IT'LL WASH THEM FOR YOU.
WOW!
WE COMMONERS HAVE SOME ADVANCED TOOLS.
YOU ARRANGE THE DISHES AND ADD SOAP, THEN YOU JUST HAVE TO PUSH A BUTTON.
GO ON, AIKA-CHAN.
OKAY.
OH, I ALMOST FORGOT.
WHEN YOU PUSH THE BUTTON, YOU *MUST* SAY "BIBBIDI-BOBBIDI-BOO," OKAY?
IS THAT SO...?
MY MOTHER QUICKLY REALIZED THAT SHE WAS DEALING WITH A **TSUN-PURE.**

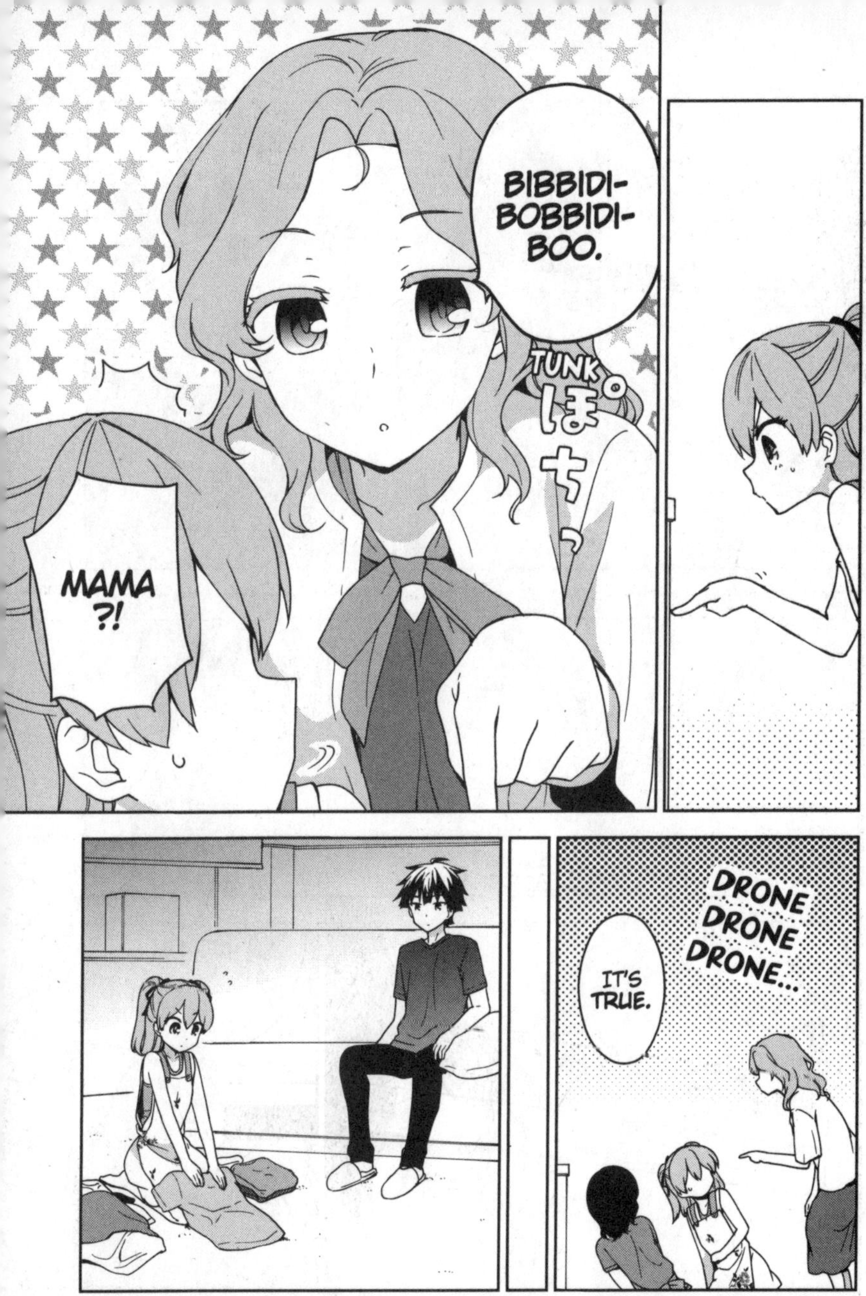
BIBBIDI-BOBBIDI-BOO.
TUNK
ぽちっ
MAMA?!
DRONE DRONE DRONE...
IT'S TRUE.

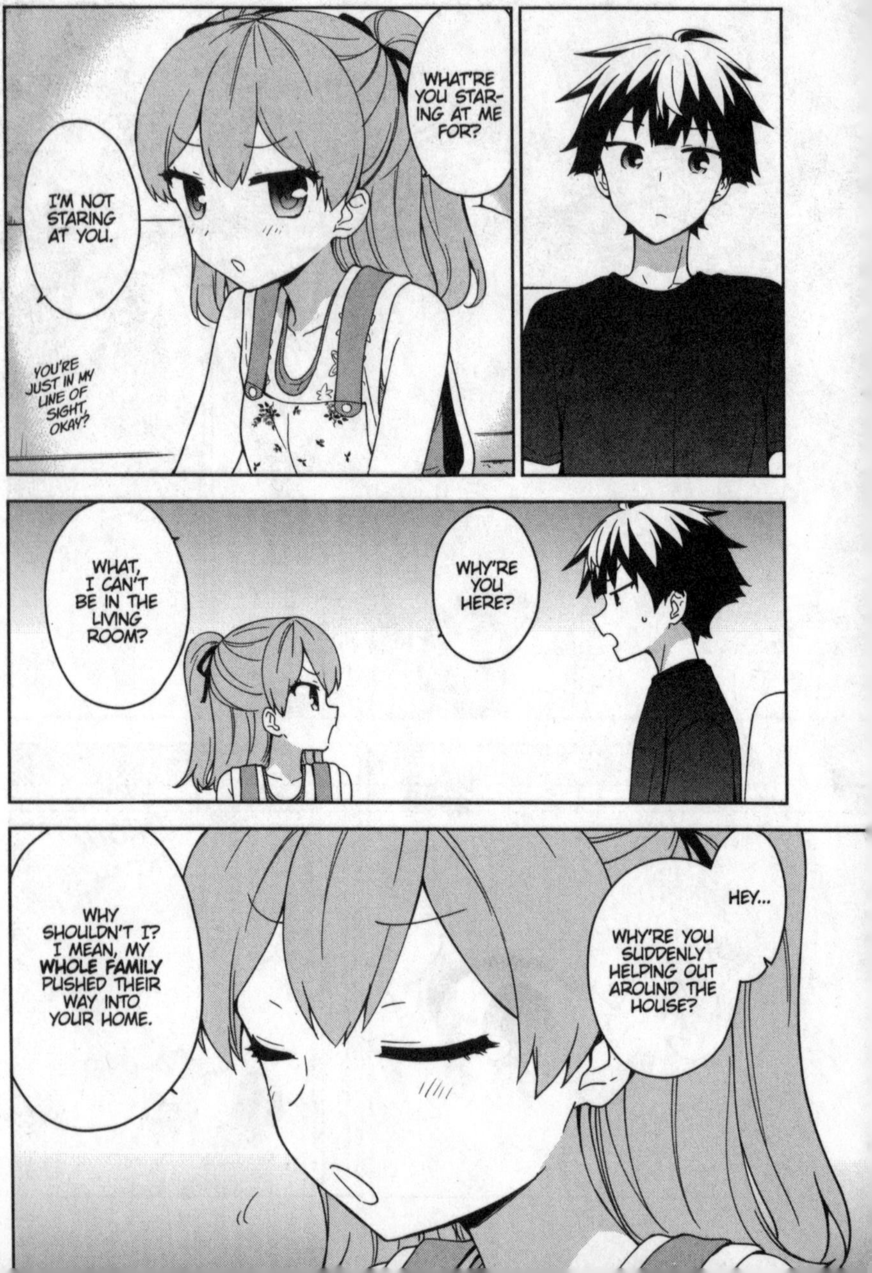
WHAT'RE YOU STARING AT ME FOR?
I'M NOT STARING AT YOU.
YOU'RE JUST IN MY LINE OF SIGHT, OKAY?
WHY'RE YOU HERE?
WHAT, I CAN'T BE IN THE LIVING ROOM?
HEY...
WHY'RE YOU SUDDENLY HELPING OUT AROUND THE HOUSE?
WHY SHOULDN'T I? I MEAN, MY **WHOLE FAMILY** PUSHED THEIR WAY INTO YOUR HOME.

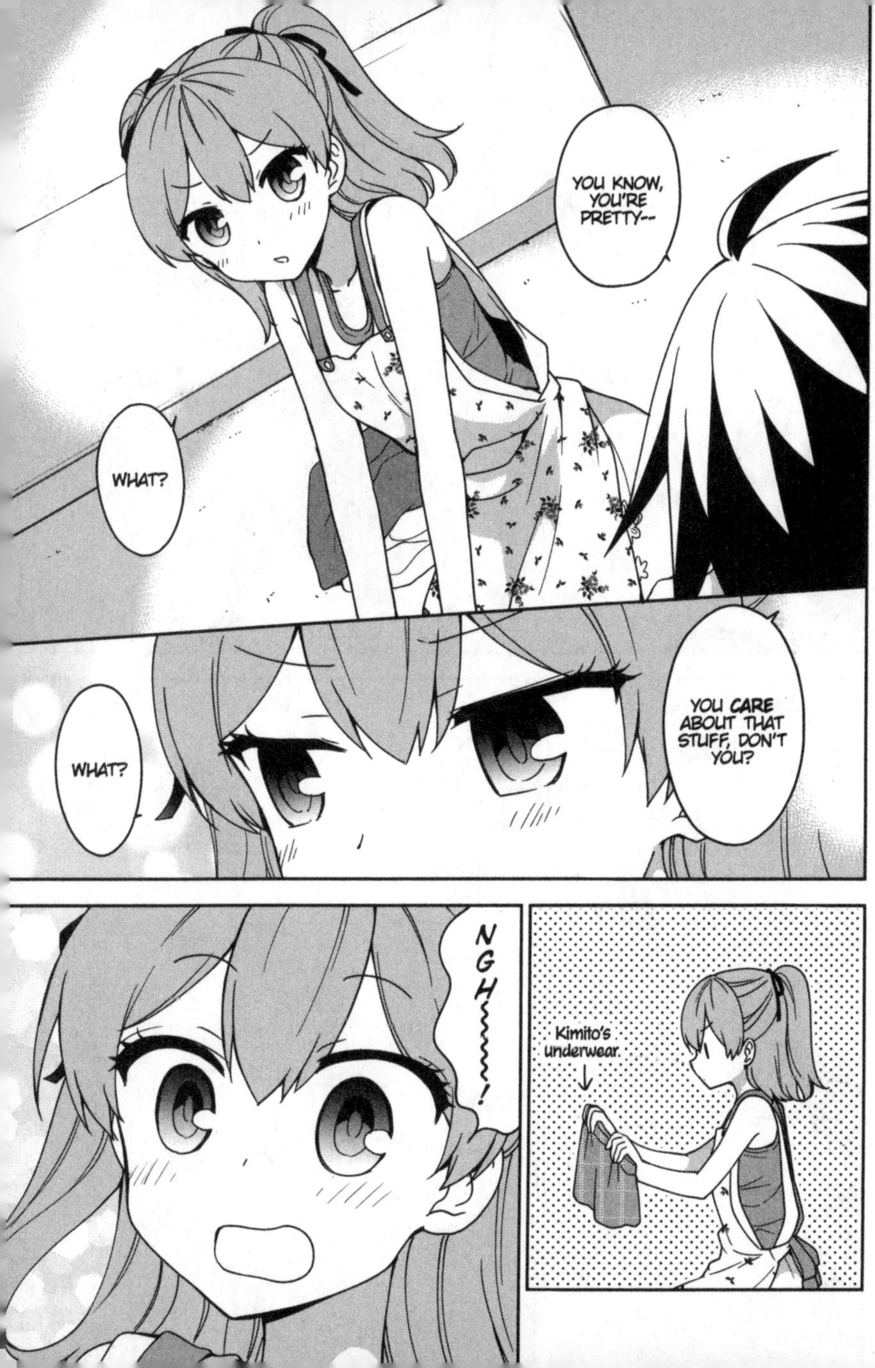
YOU KNOW, YOU'RE PRETTY--
WHAT?
YOU CARE ABOUT THAT STUFF, DON'T YOU?
WHAT?
Kimito's underwear.
NGH~~~!

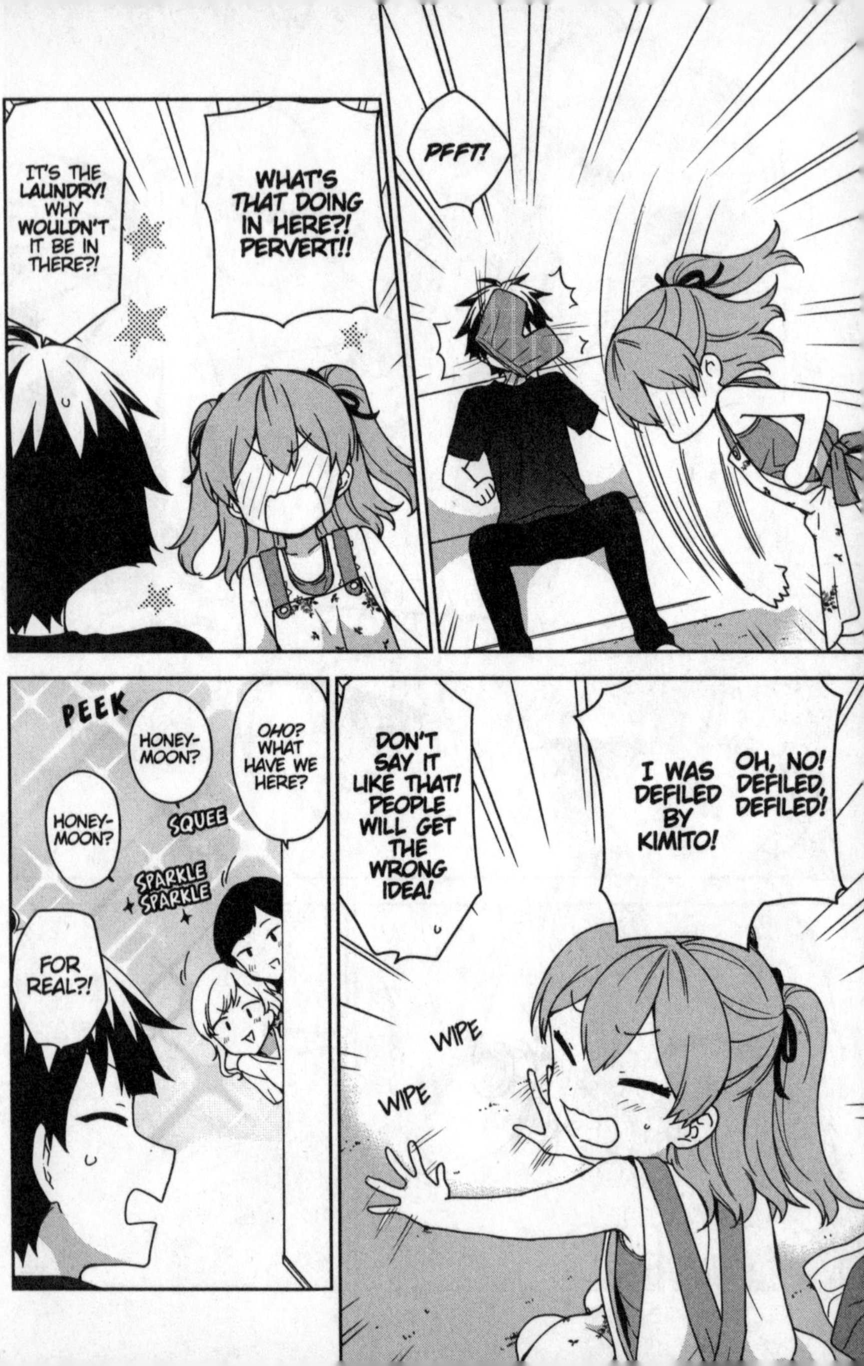
PFFT!
WHAT'S THAT DOING IN HERE?! PERVERT!!
IT'S THE LAUNDRY! WHY WOULDN'T IT BE IN THERE?!
OH, NO! DEFILED, DEFILED!
I WAS DEFILED BY KIMITO!
DON'T SAY IT LIKE THAT! PEOPLE WILL GET THE WRONG IDEA!
WIPE
WIPE
OHO? WHAT HAVE WE HERE?
HONEY-MOON?
PEEK
SQUEE
HONEY-MOON?
SPARKLE SPARKLE
FOR REAL?!

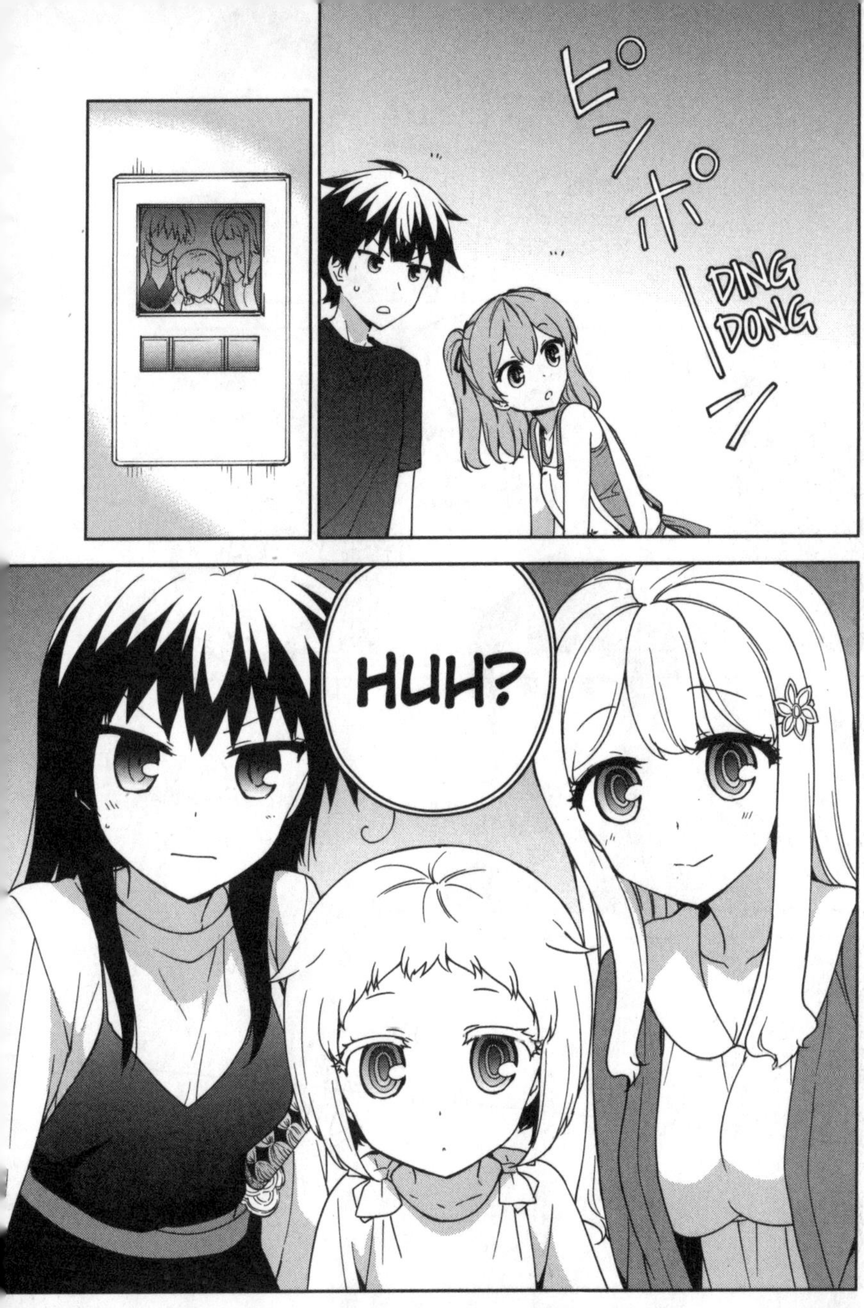
ピンポーン
DING DONG
HUH?

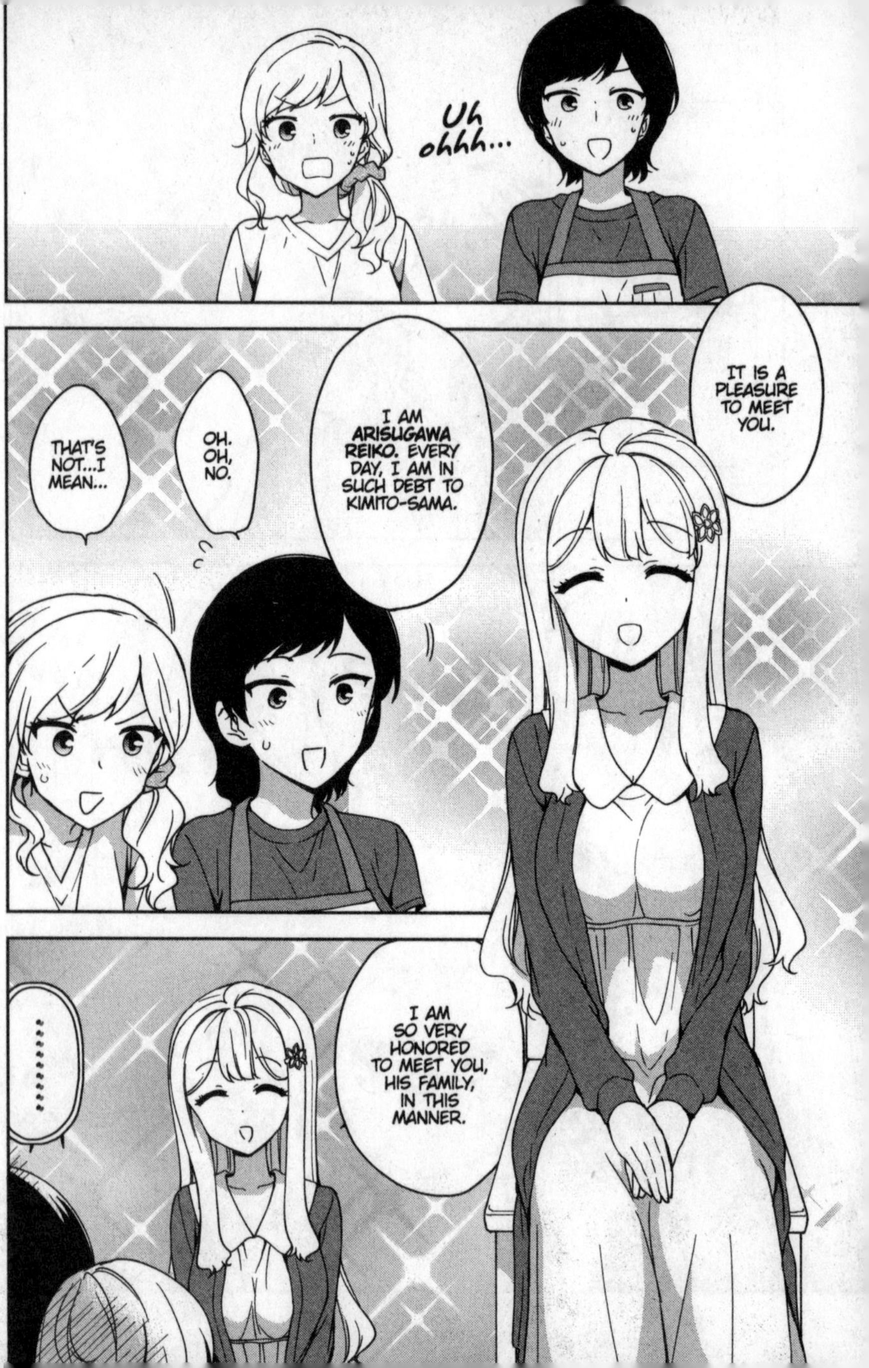
Uh ohhh...
IT IS A PLEASURE TO MEET YOU.
I AM ARISUGAWA REIKO. EVERY DAY, I AM IN SUCH DEBT TO KIMITO-SAMA.
OH. OH, NO.
THAT'S NOT...I MEAN...
I AM SO VERY HONORED TO MEET YOU, HIS FAMILY, IN THIS MANNER.
....

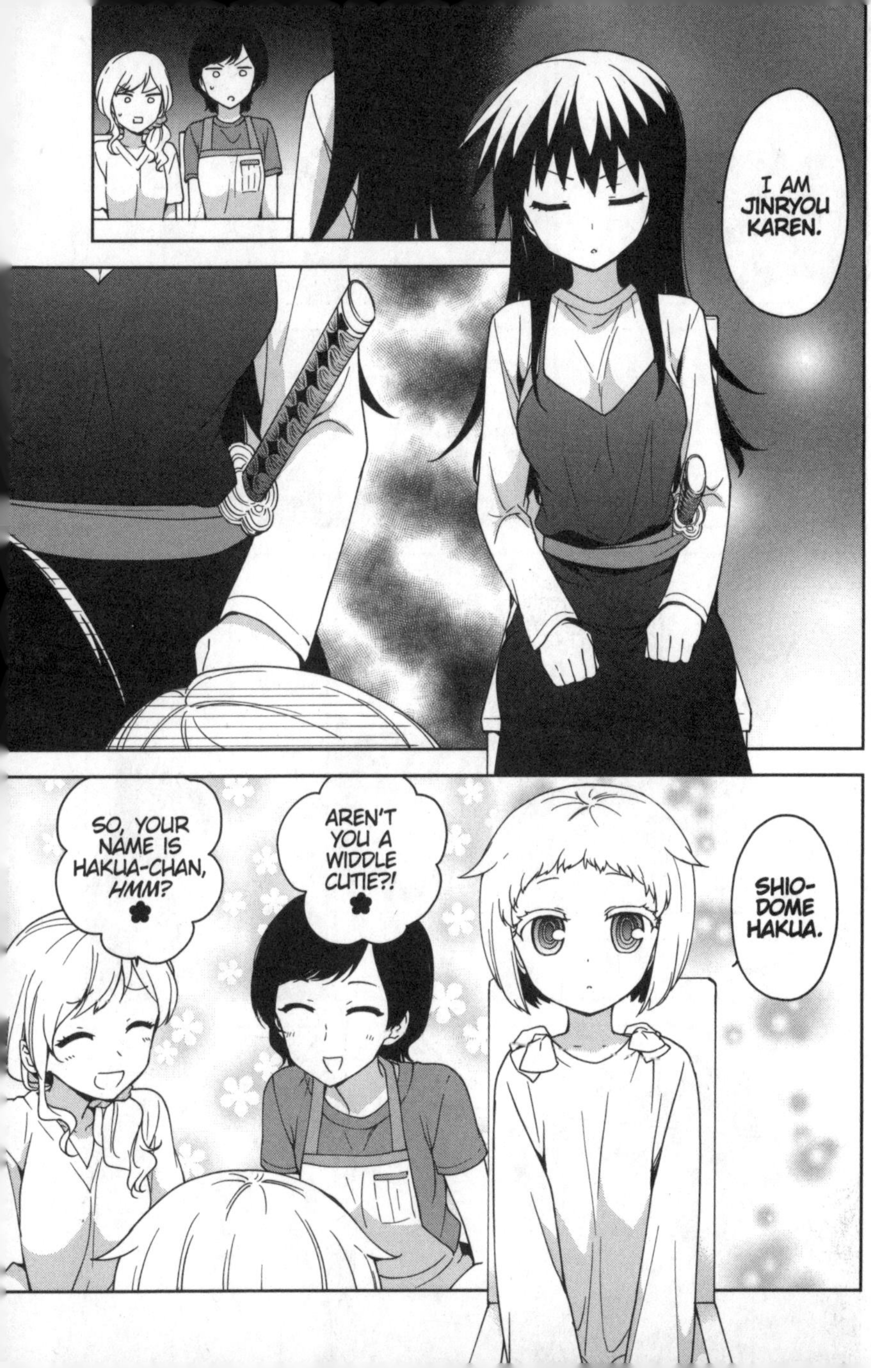
I AM JINRYOU KAREN.
SHIO-DOME HAKUA.
AREN'T YOU A WIDDLE CUTIE?!
SO, YOUR NAME IS HAKUA-CHAN, HMM?

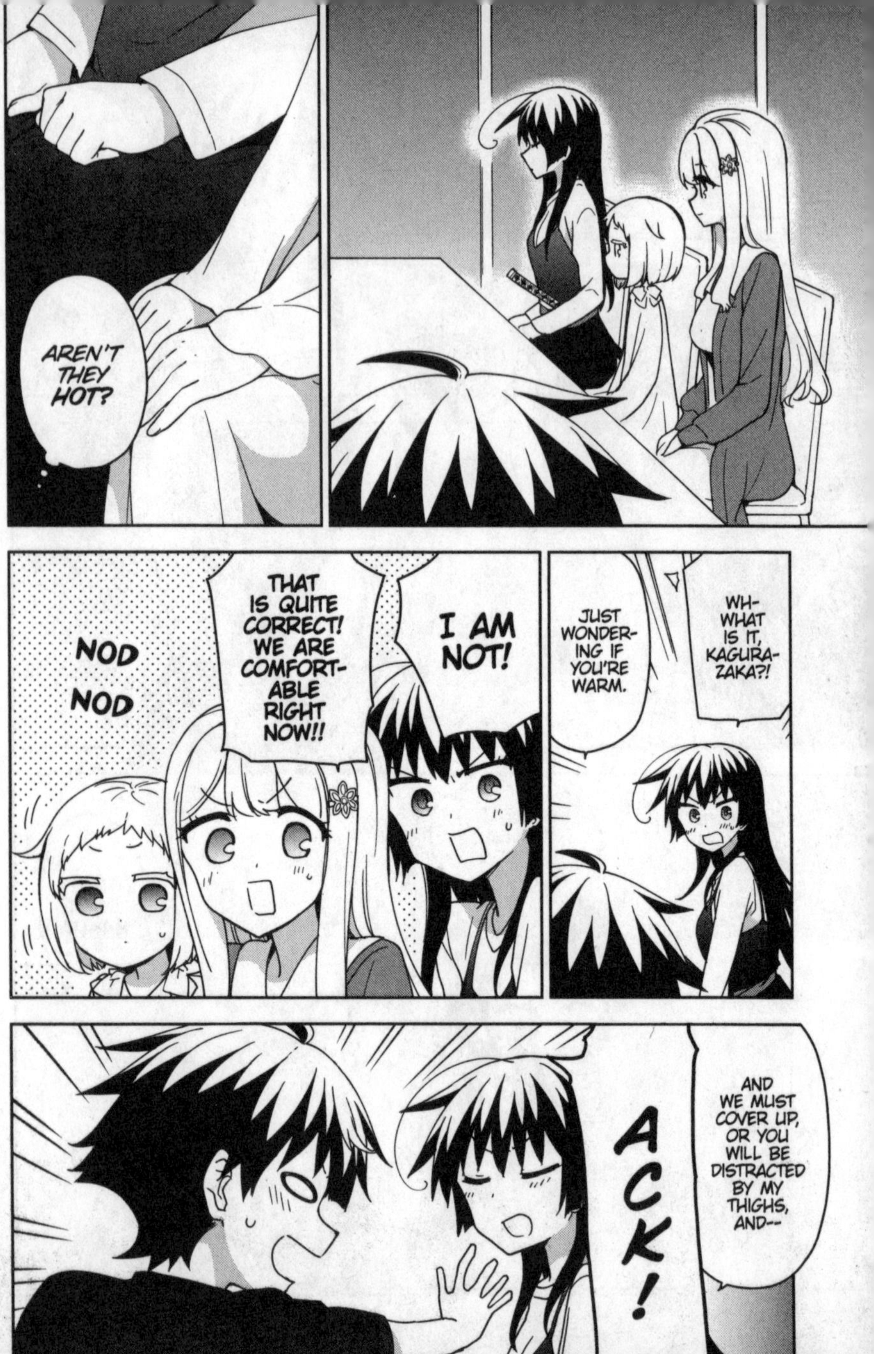
AREN'T THEY HOT?
WH-WHAT IS IT, KAGURAZAKA?!
JUST WONDERING IF YOU'RE WARM.
I AM NOT!
THAT IS QUITE CORRECT! WE ARE COMFORTABLE RIGHT NOW!!
NOD NOD
AND WE MUST COVER UP, OR YOU WILL BE DISTRACTED BY MY THIGHS, AND--
ACK!

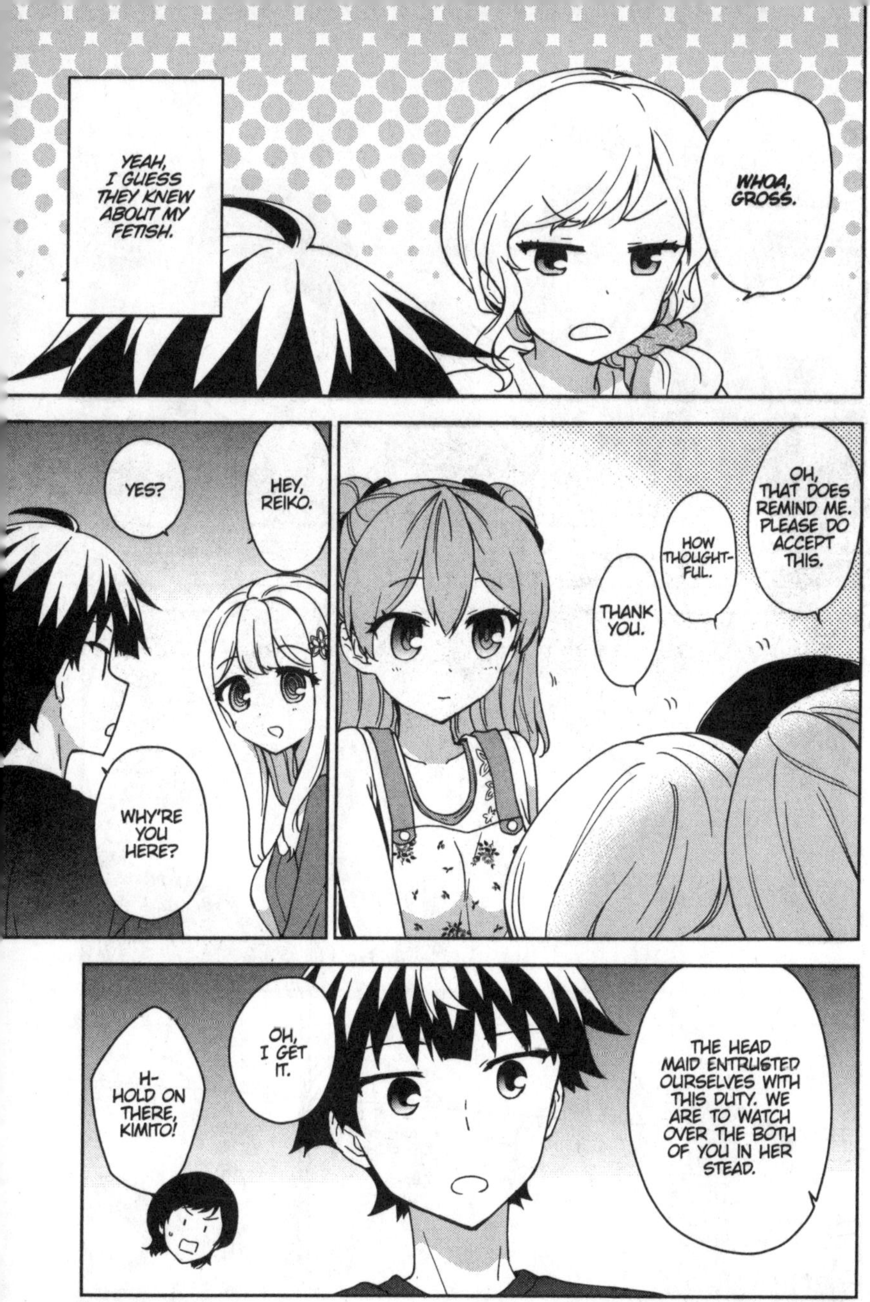
WHOA, GROSS.
YEAH, I GUESS THEY KNEW ABOUT MY FETISH.
OH, THAT DOES REMIND ME. PLEASE DO ACCEPT THIS.
HOW THOUGHTFUL.
THANK YOU.
HEY, REIKO.
YES?
WHY'RE YOU HERE?
THE HEAD MAID ENTRUSTED OURSELVES WITH THIS DUTY. WE ARE TO WATCH OVER THE BOTH OF YOU IN HER STEAD.
OH, I GET IT.
H-HOLD ON THERE, KIMITO!

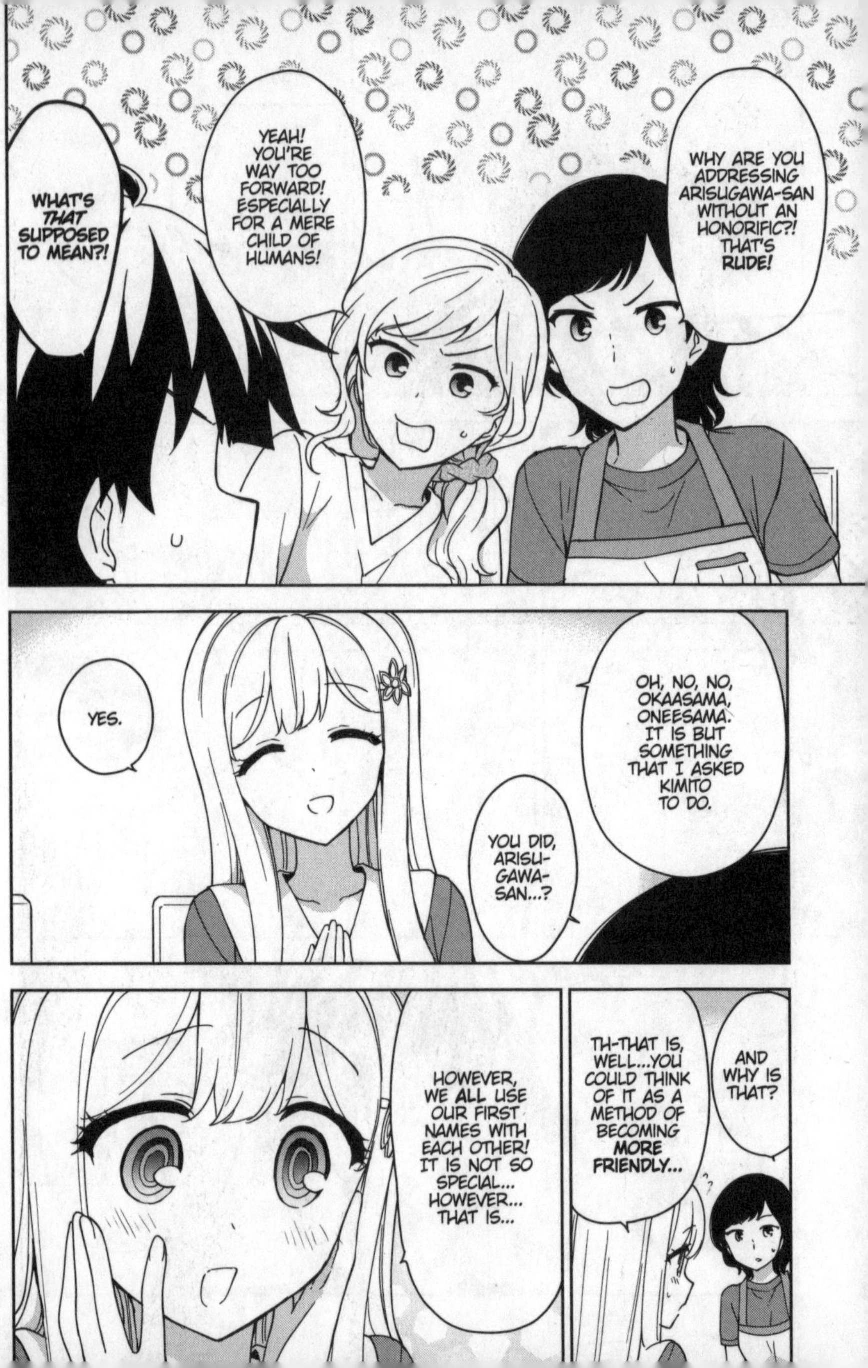
WHY ARE YOU ADDRESSING ARISUGAWA-SAN WITHOUT AN HONORIFIC?! THAT'S RUDE!
YEAH! YOU'RE WAY TOO FORWARD! ESPECIALLY FOR A MERE CHILD OF HUMANS!
WHAT'S THAT SUPPOSED TO MEAN?!
OH, NO, NO, OKAASAMA, ONEESAMA. IT IS BUT SOMETHING THAT I ASKED KIMITO TO DO.
YOU DID, ARISUGAWA-SAN...?
YES.
AND WHY IS THAT?
TH-THAT IS, WELL...YOU COULD THINK OF IT AS A METHOD OF BECOMING MORE FRIENDLY...
HOWEVER, WE ALL USE OUR FIRST NAMES WITH EACH OTHER! IT IS NOT SO SPECIAL... HOWEVER... THAT IS...

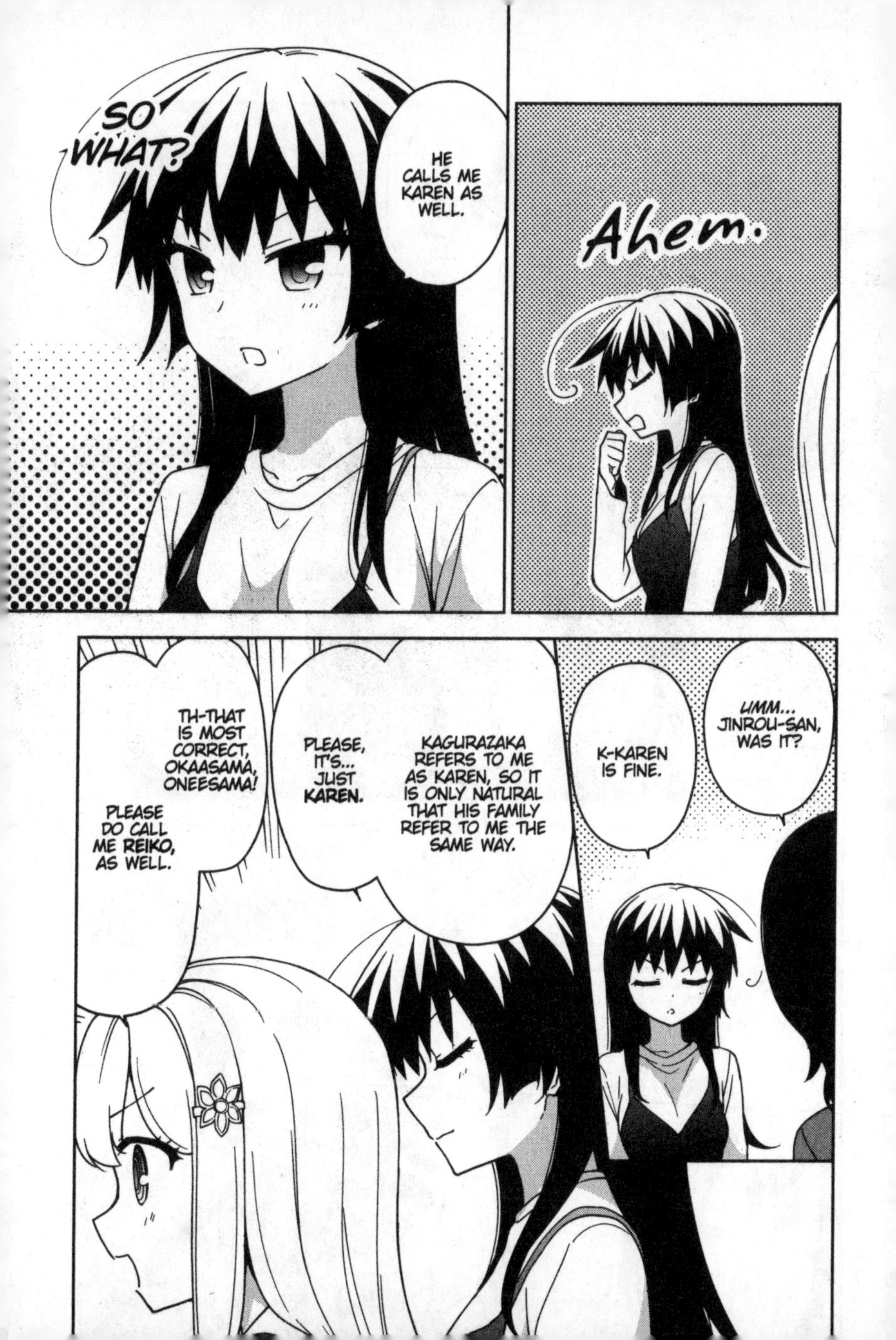
Ahem.
HE CALLS ME KAREN AS WELL.
SO WHAT?
UMM... JINROU-SAN, WAS IT?
K-KAREN IS FINE.
KAGURAZAKA REFERS TO ME AS KAREN, SO IT IS ONLY NATURAL THAT HIS FAMILY REFER TO ME THE SAME WAY.
PLEASE, IT'S... JUST KAREN.
TH-THAT IS MOST CORRECT, OKAASAMA, ONEESAMA!
PLEASE DO CALL ME REIKO, AS WELL.

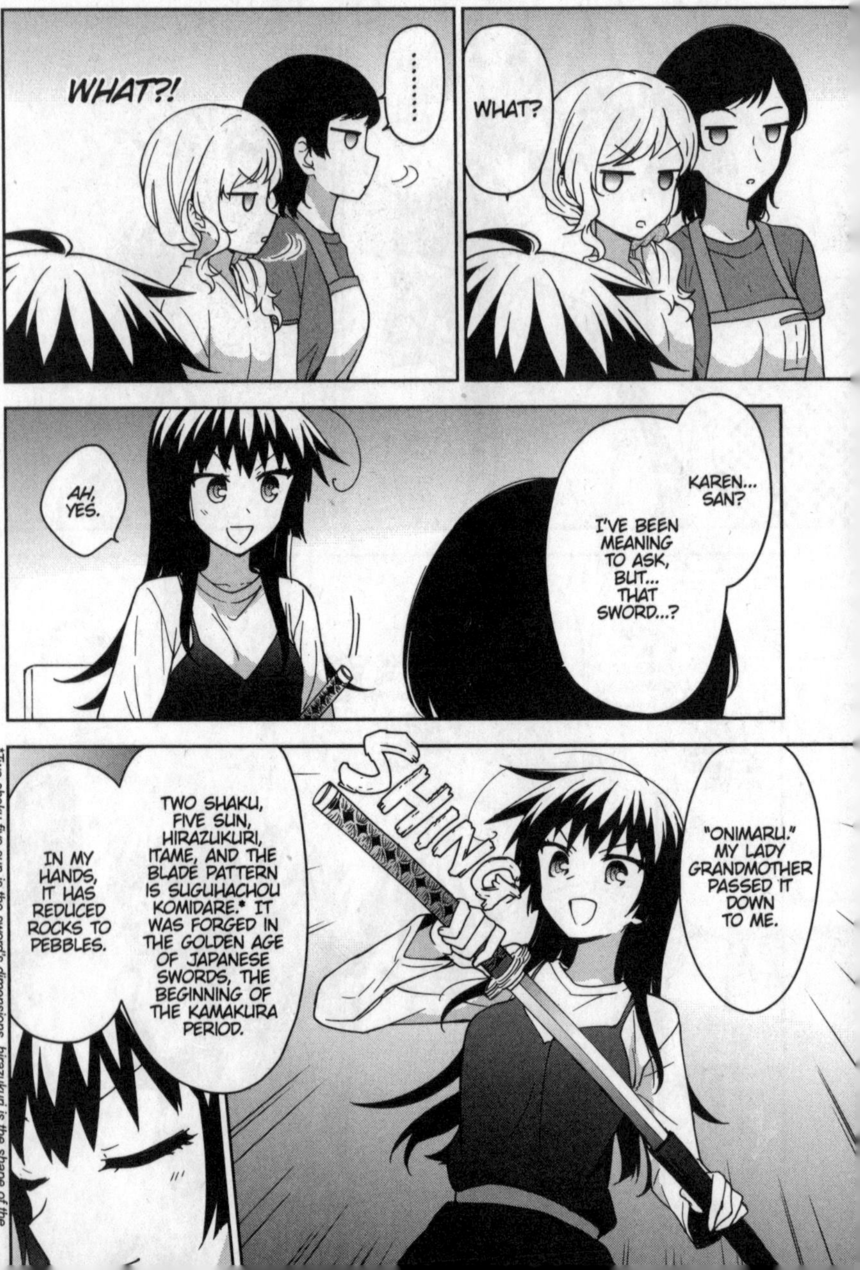
WHAT?
......
WHAT?!
KAREN... SAN?
I'VE BEEN MEANING TO ASK, BUT... THAT SWORD...?
AH, YES.
"ONIMARU." MY LADY GRANDMOTHER PASSED IT DOWN TO ME.
SHING
TWO SHAKU, FIVE SUN, HIRAZUKURI, ITAME, AND THE BLADE PATTERN IS SUGUHACHOU KOMIDARE.* IT WAS FORGED IN THE GOLDEN AGE OF JAPANESE SWORDS, THE BEGINNING OF THE KAMAKURA PERIOD.
IN MY HANDS, IT HAS REDUCED ROCKS TO PEBBLES.

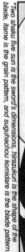

*Two shaku five sun is the sword's dimensions, hirazukuri is the shape of the blade, itame is the grain pattern, and suguhachou komidare is the blade pattern.

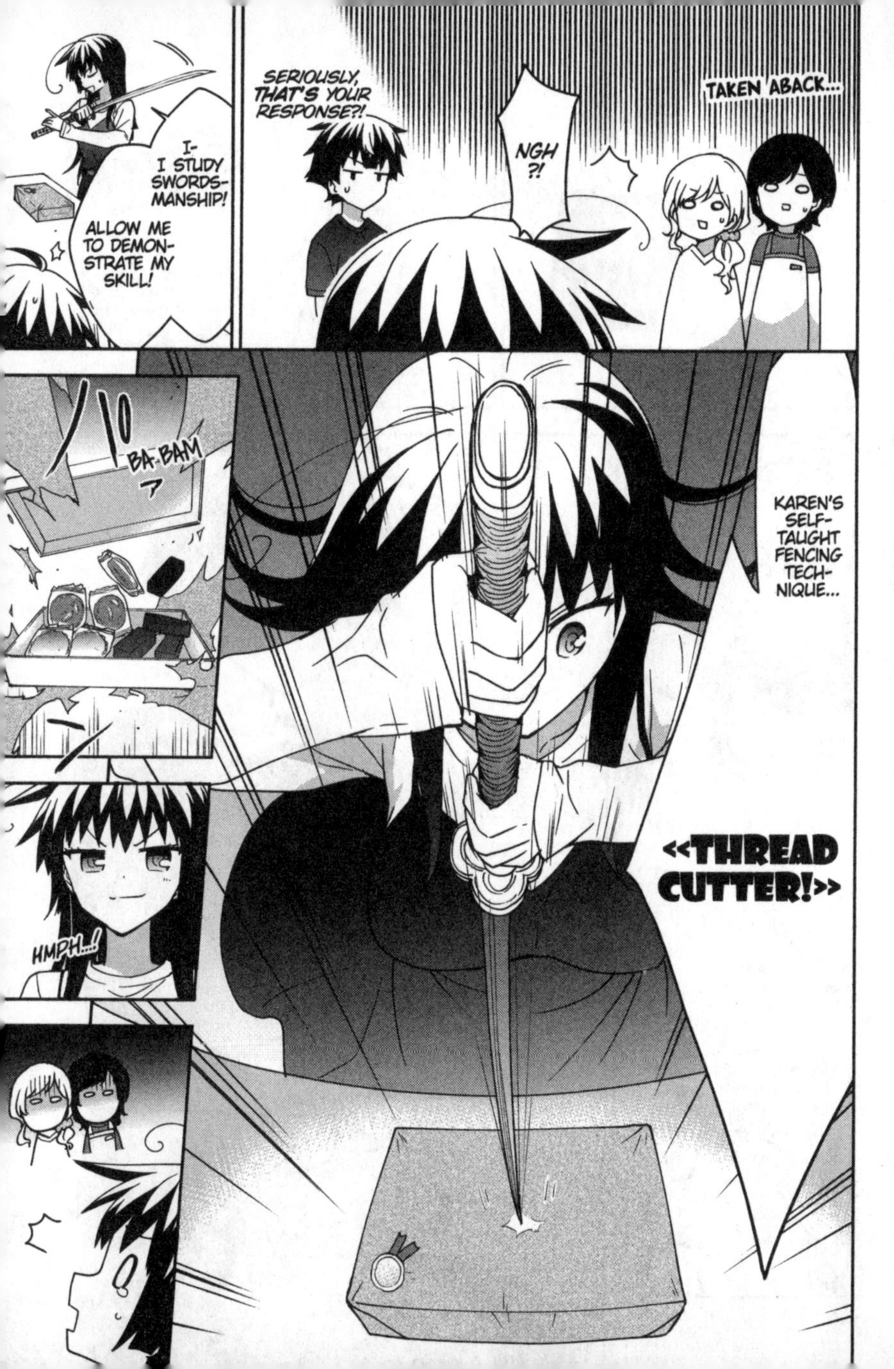
TAKEN ABACK...
NGH ?!
SERIOUSLY, THAT'S YOUR RESPONSE?!
I- I STUDY SWORDS-MANSHIP!
ALLOW ME TO DEMON-STRATE MY SKILL!
KAREN'S SELF-TAUGHT FENCING TECH-NIQUE...
<<THREAD CUTTER!>>
BA-BAM
HMPH...!

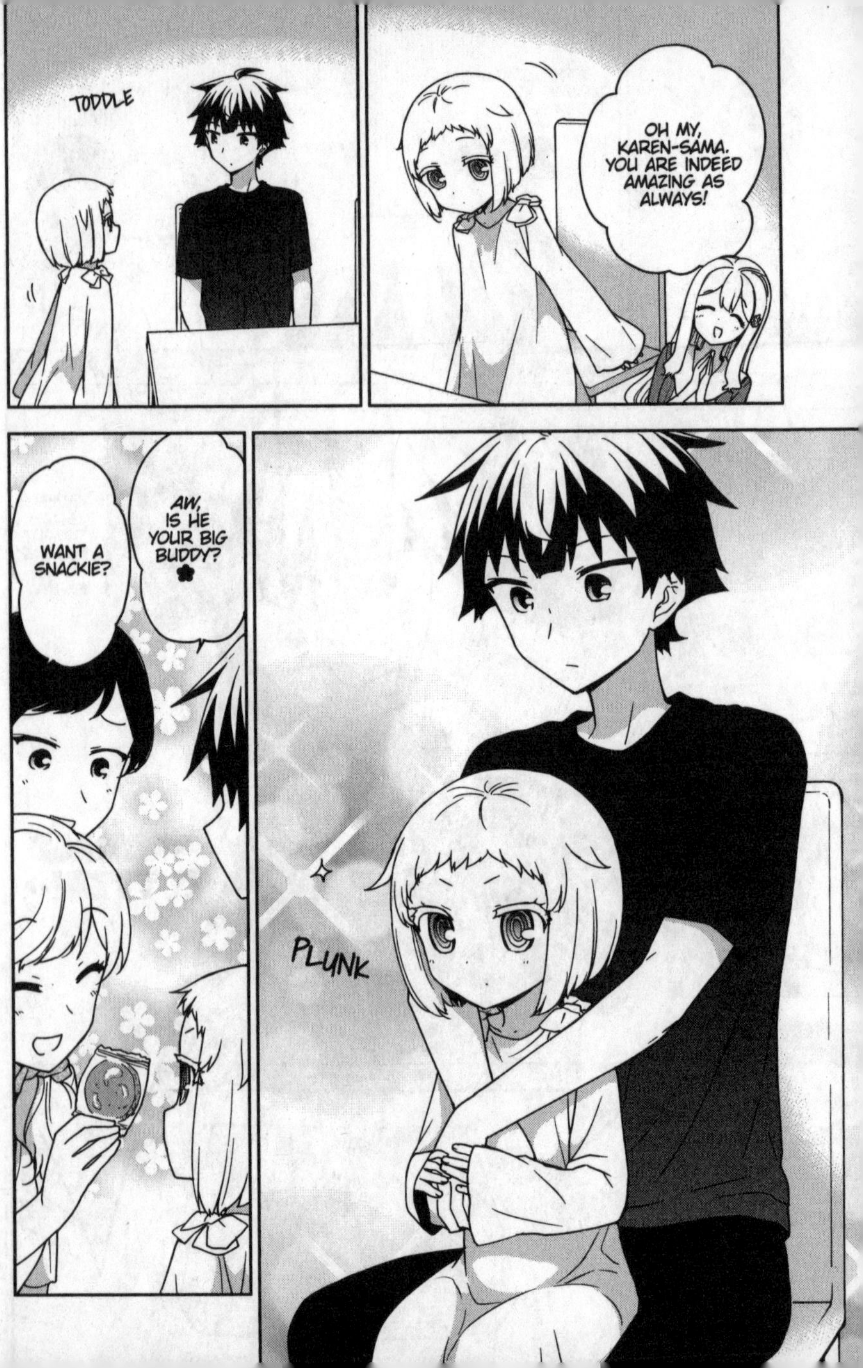
OH MY, KAREN-SAMA. YOU ARE INDEED AMAZING AS ALWAYS!
TODDLE
PLUNK
AW, IS HE YOUR BIG BUDDY?
WANT A SNACKIE?

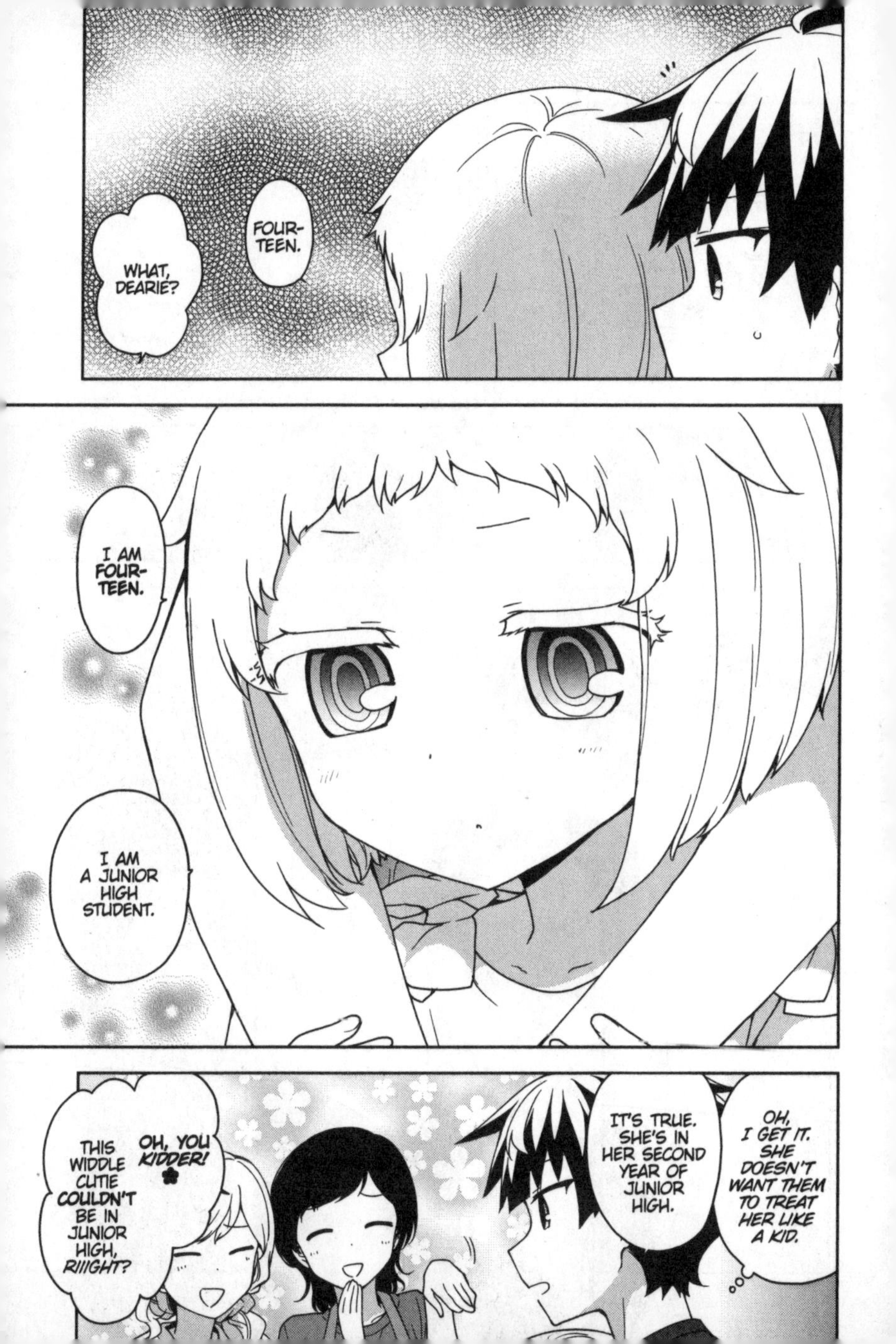
FOUR-TEEN.
WHAT, DEARIE?
I AM FOUR-TEEN.
I AM A JUNIOR HIGH STUDENT.
OH, I GET IT. SHE DOESN'T WANT THEM TO TREAT HER LIKE A KID.
IT'S TRUE. SHE'S IN HER SECOND YEAR OF JUNIOR HIGH.
OH, YOU KIDDER!
THIS WIDDLE CUTIE COULDN'T BE IN JUNIOR HIGH, RIIIGHT?

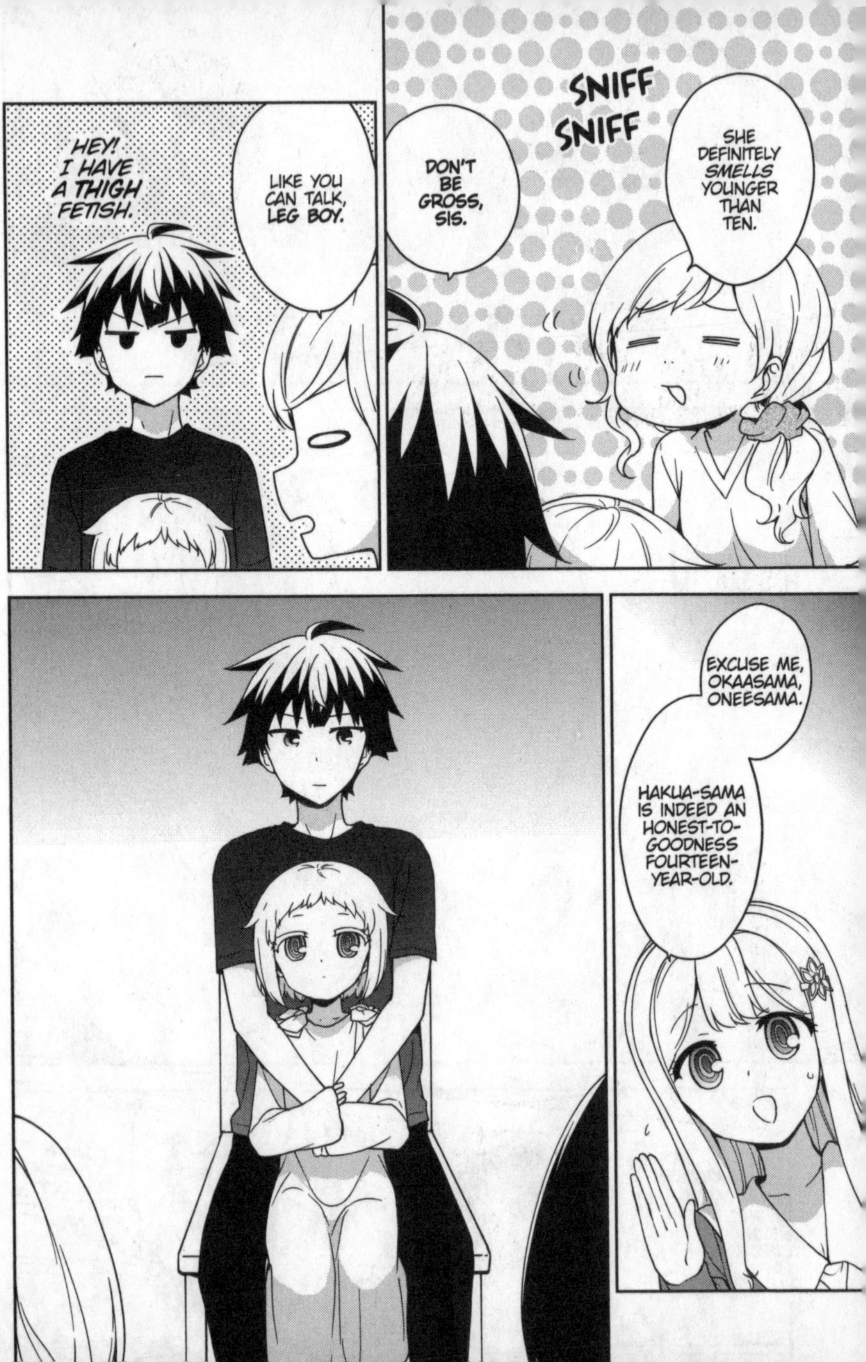
SHE DEFINITELY SMELLS YOUNGER THAN TEN.
SNIFF SNIFF
DON'T BE GROSS, SIS.
LIKE YOU CAN TALK, LEG BOY.
HEY! I HAVE A THIGH FETISH.
EXCUSE ME, OKAASAMA, ONEESAMA.
HAKUA-SAMA IS INDEED AN HONEST-TO-GOODNESS FOURTEEN-YEAR-OLD.

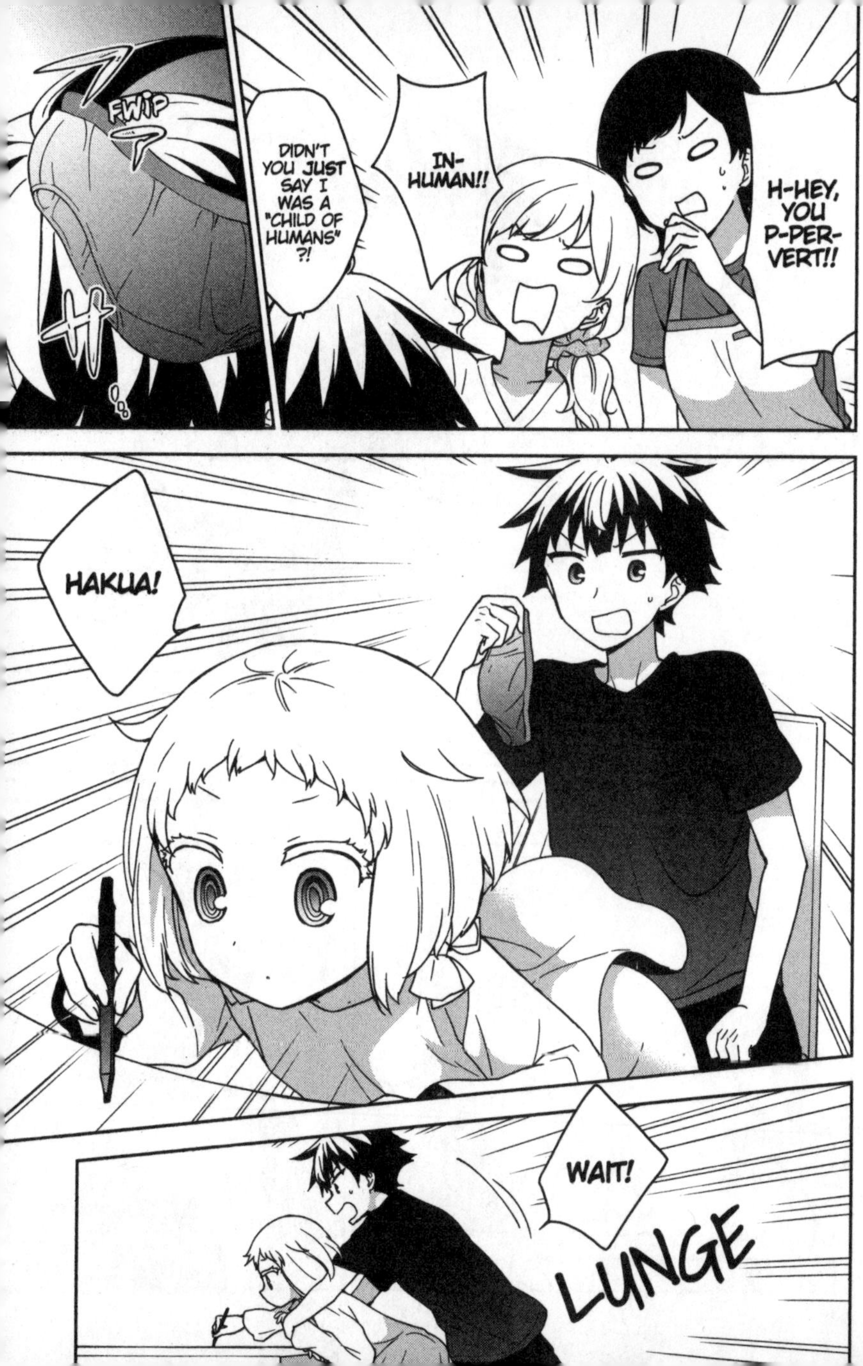
H-HEY, YOU P-PER-VERT!!
IN-HUMAN!!
DIDN'T YOU JUST SAY I WAS A "CHILD OF HUMANS"?!
FWIP
HAKUA!
WAIT!
LUNGE

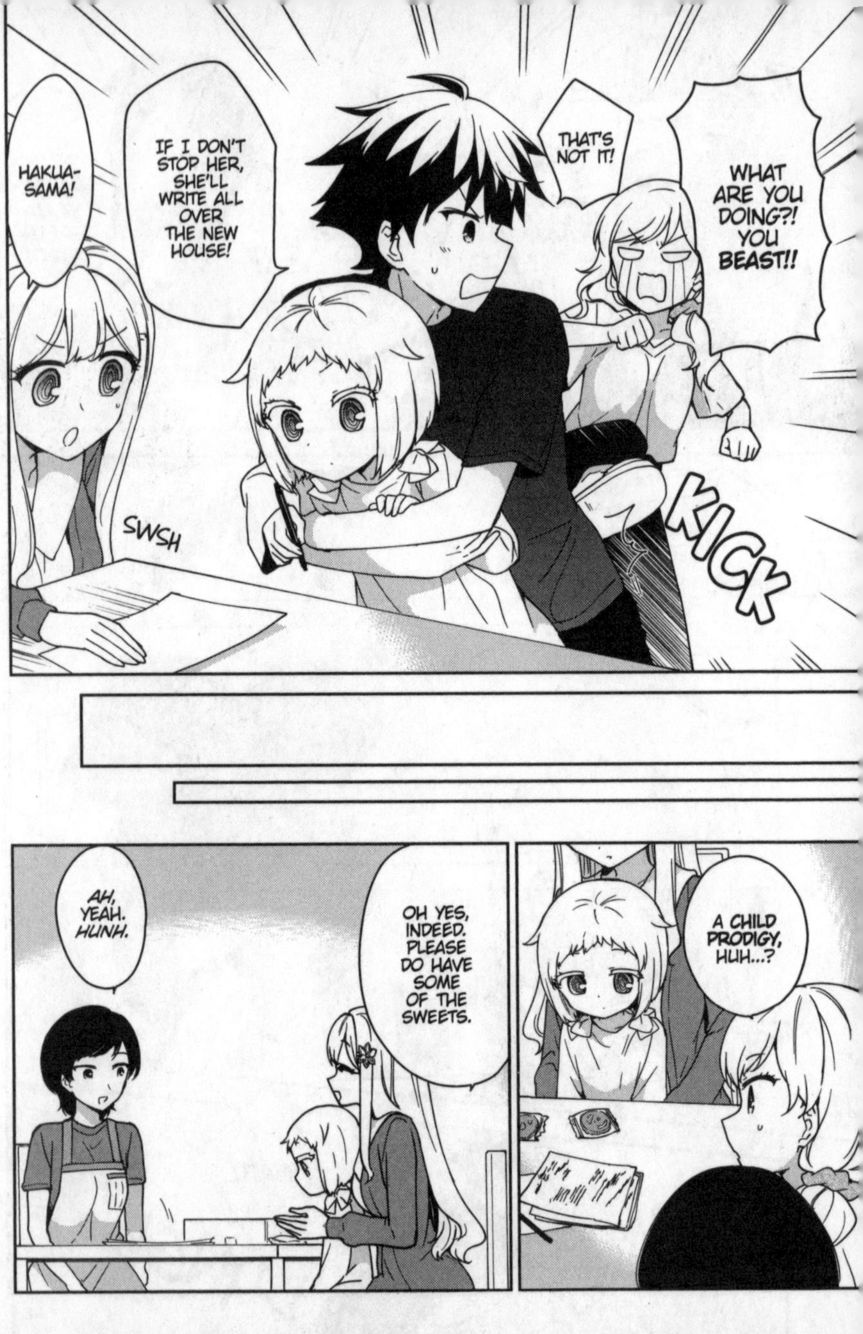
WHAT ARE YOU DOING?! YOU BEAST!!
THAT'S NOT IT!
IF I DON'T STOP HER, SHE'LL WRITE ALL OVER THE NEW HOUSE!
HAKUA-SAMA!
KICK
SWSH
A CHILD PRODIGY, HUH...?
OH YES, INDEED. PLEASE DO HAVE SOME OF THE SWEETS.
AH, YEAH. HUNH.

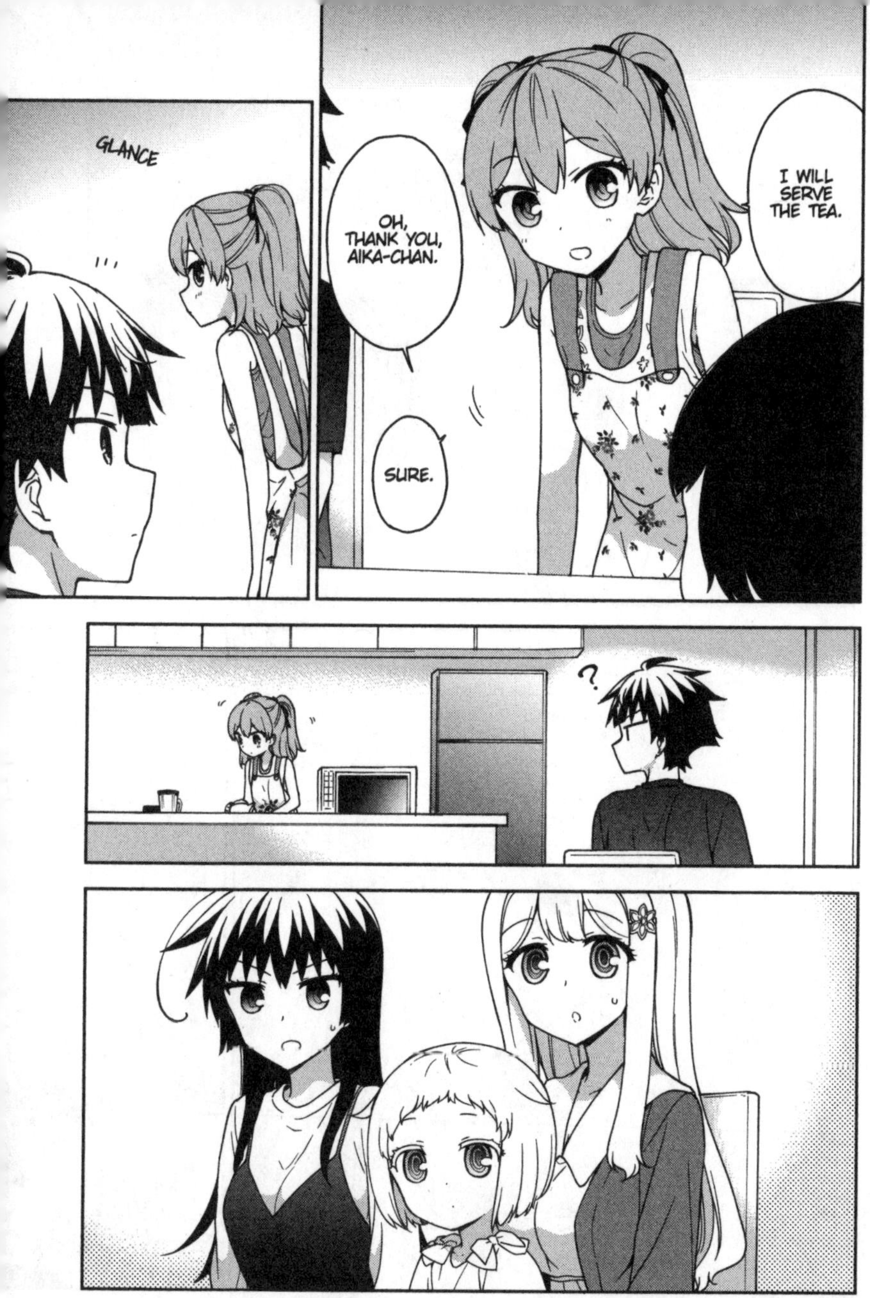
I WILL SERVE THE TEA.
OH, THANK YOU, AIKA-CHAN.
SURE.
GLANCE
?

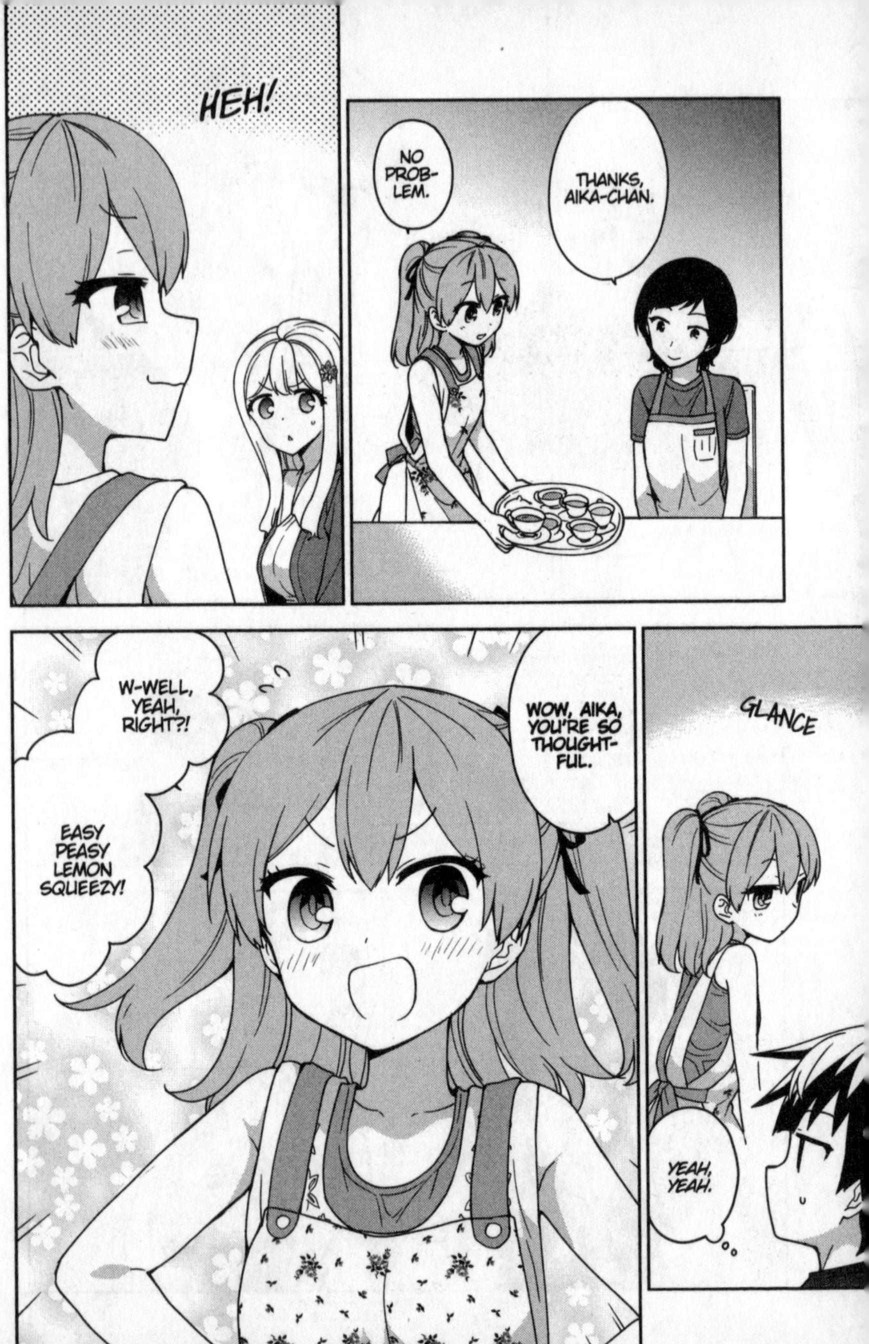
THANKS, AIKA-CHAN.
NO PROB-LEM.
HEH!
GLANCE
YEAH, YEAH.
WOW, AIKA, YOU'RE SO THOUGHT-FUL.
W-WELL, YEAH, RIGHT?!
EASY PEASY LEMON SQUEEZY!

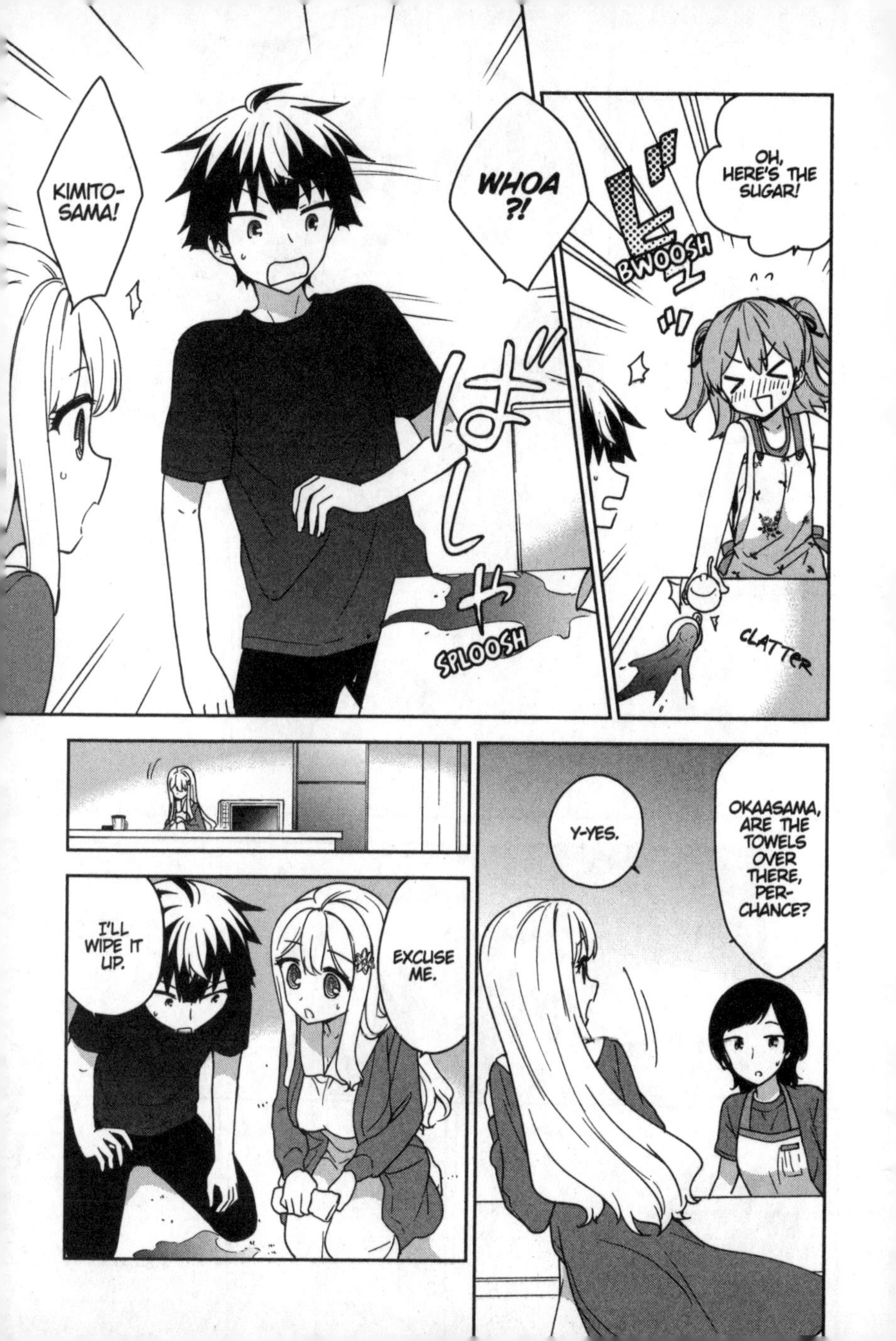

OH, HERE'S THE SUGAR!
BWOOSH
CLATTER
WHOA ?!
KIMITO-SAMA!
ばしゃ
SPLOOSH
OKAASAMA, ARE THE TOWELS OVER THERE, PER-CHANCE?
Y-YES.
EXCUSE ME.
I'LL WIPE IT UP.

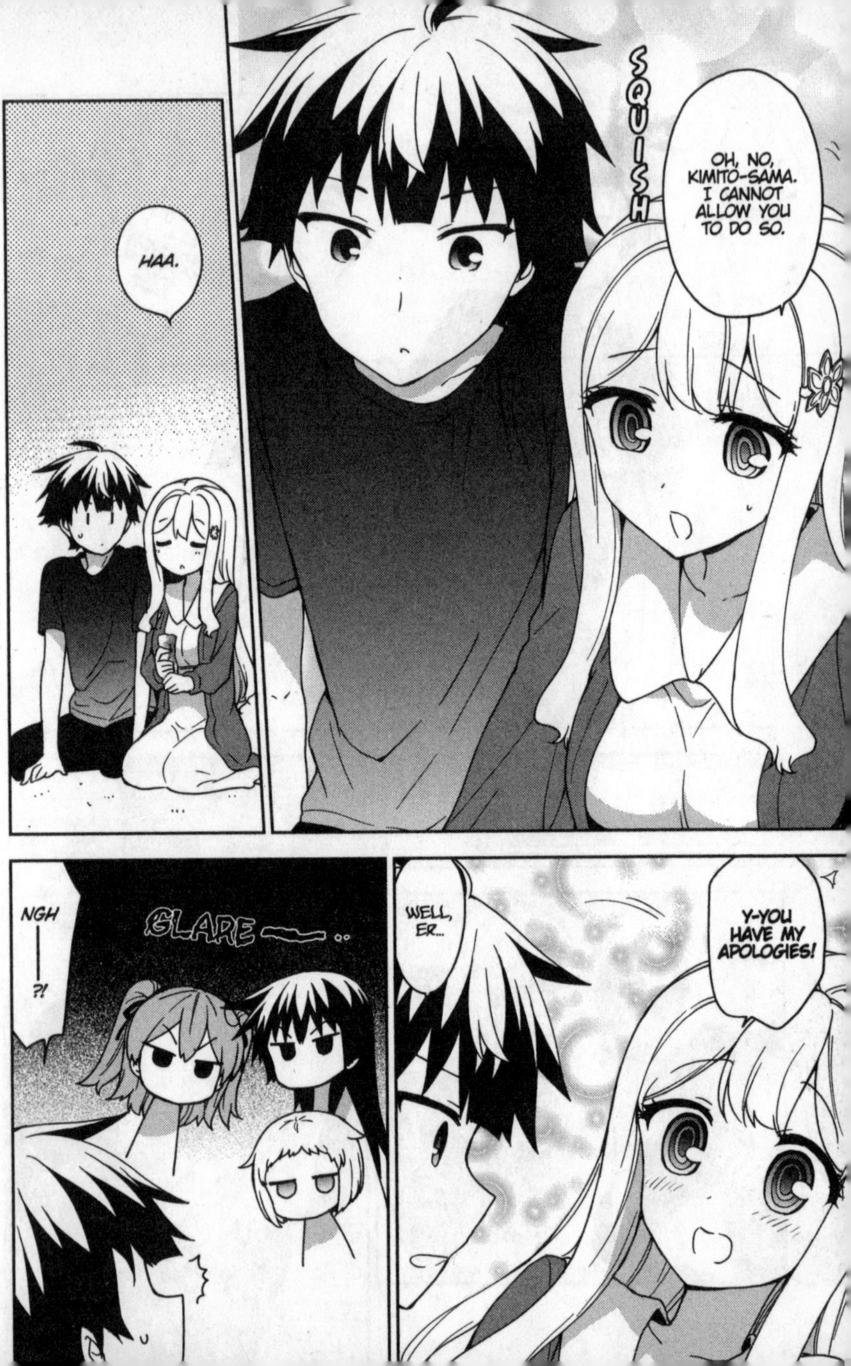
OH, NO, KIMITO-SAMA. I CANNOT ALLOW YOU TO DO SO.
SQUISH
HAA.
Y-YOU HAVE MY APOLOGIES!
WELL, ER...
GLARE
NGH—?!

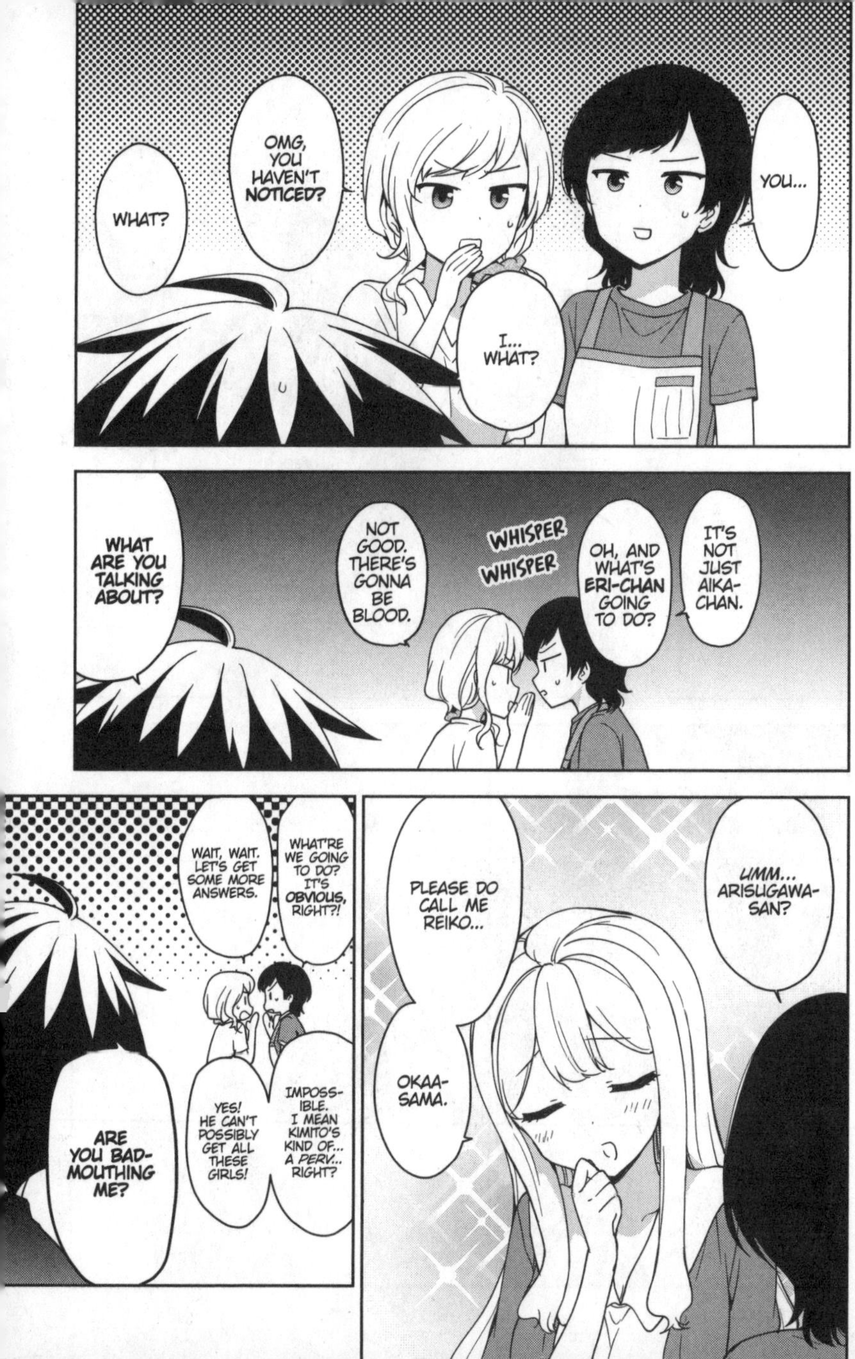
YOU...
I... WHAT?
OMG, YOU HAVEN'T NOTICED?
WHAT?
IT'S NOT JUST AIKA-CHAN.
OH, AND WHAT'S ERI-CHAN GOING TO DO?
WHISPER WHISPER
NOT GOOD. THERE'S GONNA BE BLOOD.
WHAT ARE YOU TALKING ABOUT?
UMM... ARISUGAWA-SAN?
PLEASE DO CALL ME REIKO...
OKAA-SAMA.
WHAT'RE WE GOING TO DO? IT'S OBVIOUS, RIGHT?!
WAIT, WAIT. LET'S GET SOME MORE ANSWERS.
IMPOSSIBLE. I MEAN KIMITO'S KIND OF... A *PERV*... RIGHT?
YES! HE CAN'T POSSIBLY GET ALL THESE GIRLS!
ARE YOU BAD-MOUTHING ME?

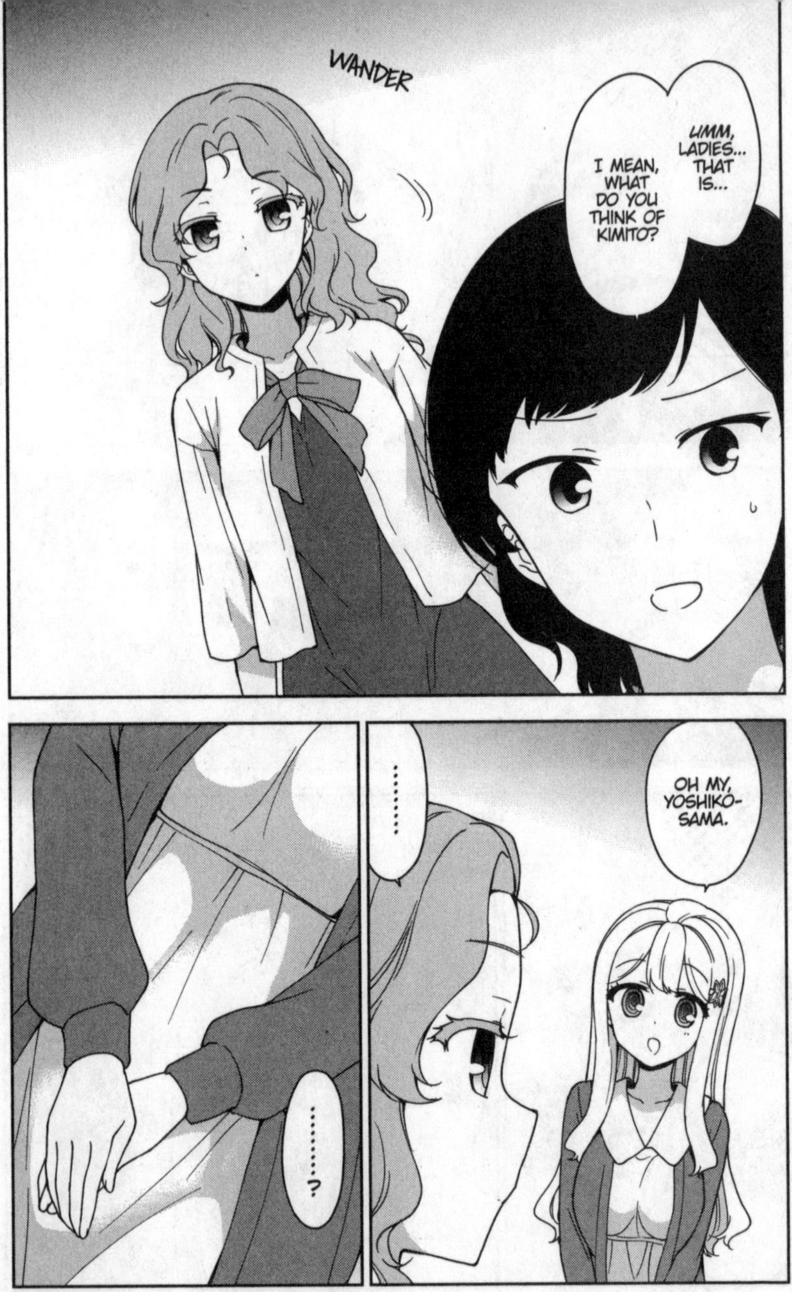
UMM, LADIES... THAT IS... I MEAN, WHAT DO YOU THINK OF KIMITO?
WANDER
OH MY, YOSHIKO-SAMA.
......
......?

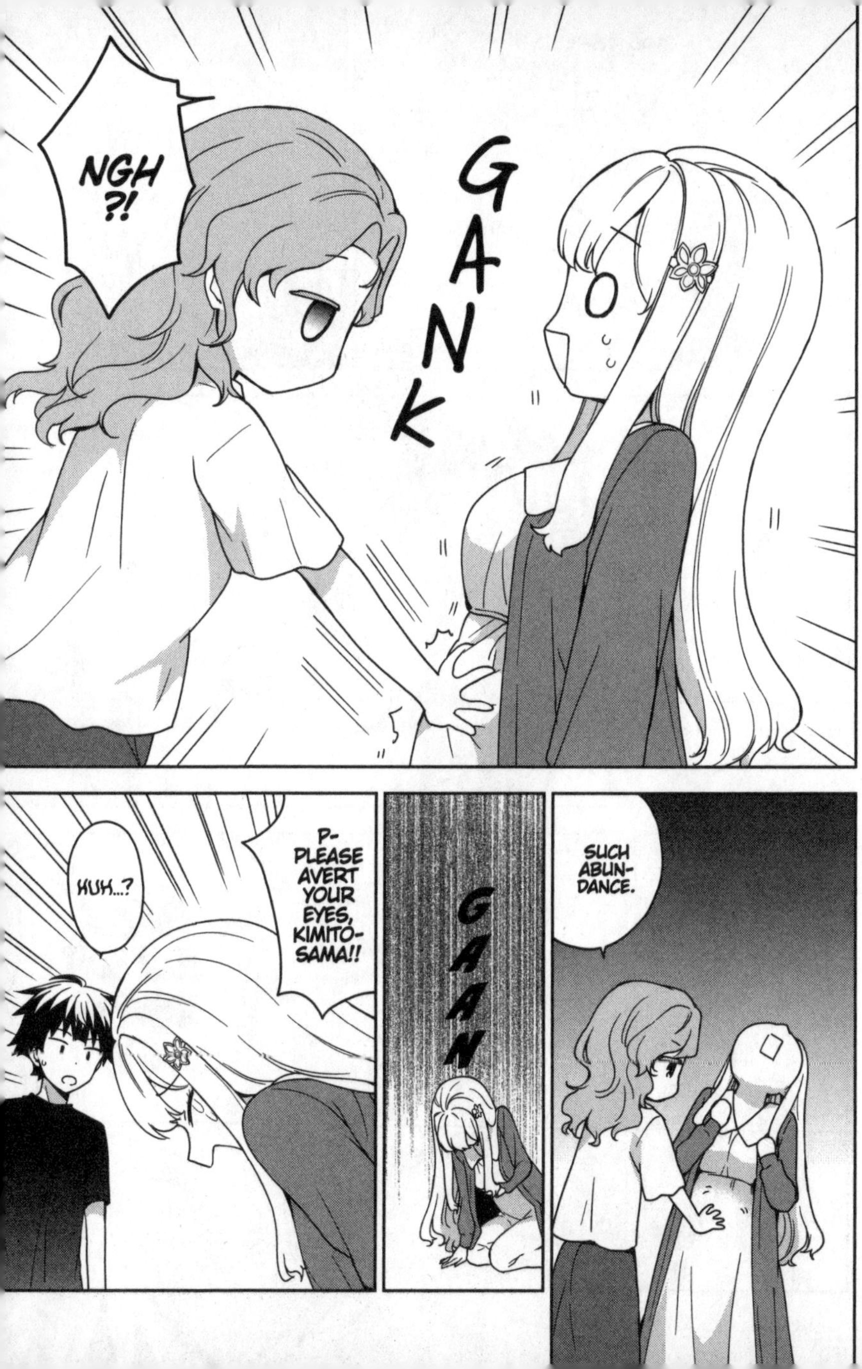
GANK
NGH?!
SUCH ABUN-DANCE.
GAAAN
P-PLEASE AVERT YOUR EYES, KIMITO-SAMA!!
HUH...?

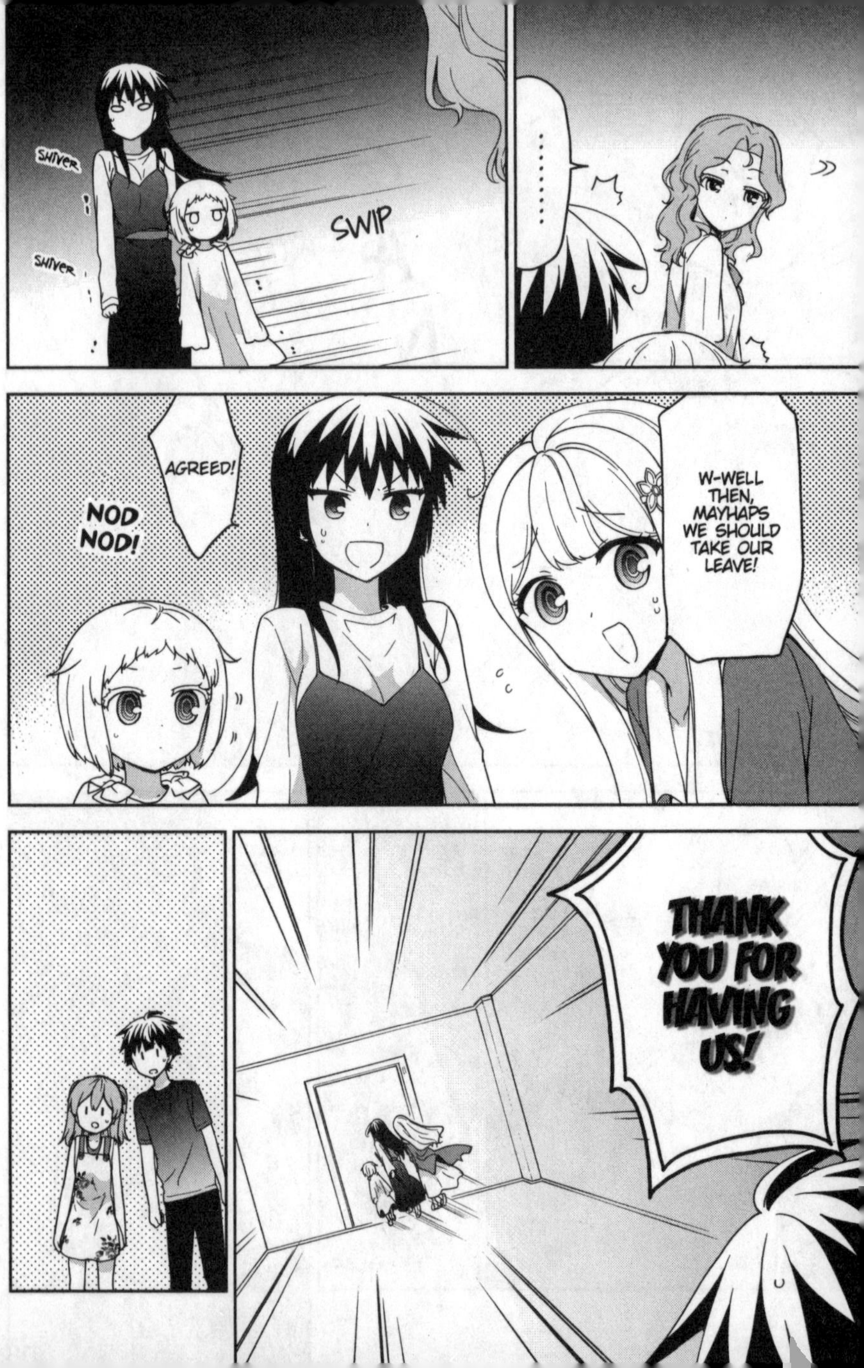
......
SWIP
SHIVER
SHIVER
W-WELL THEN, MAYHAPS WE SHOULD TAKE OUR LEAVE!
AGREED!
NOD NOD!
THANK YOU FOR HAVING US!

SHOMIN SAMPLE 15

I Was Abducted by an Elite All-Girls
School as a Sample Commoner

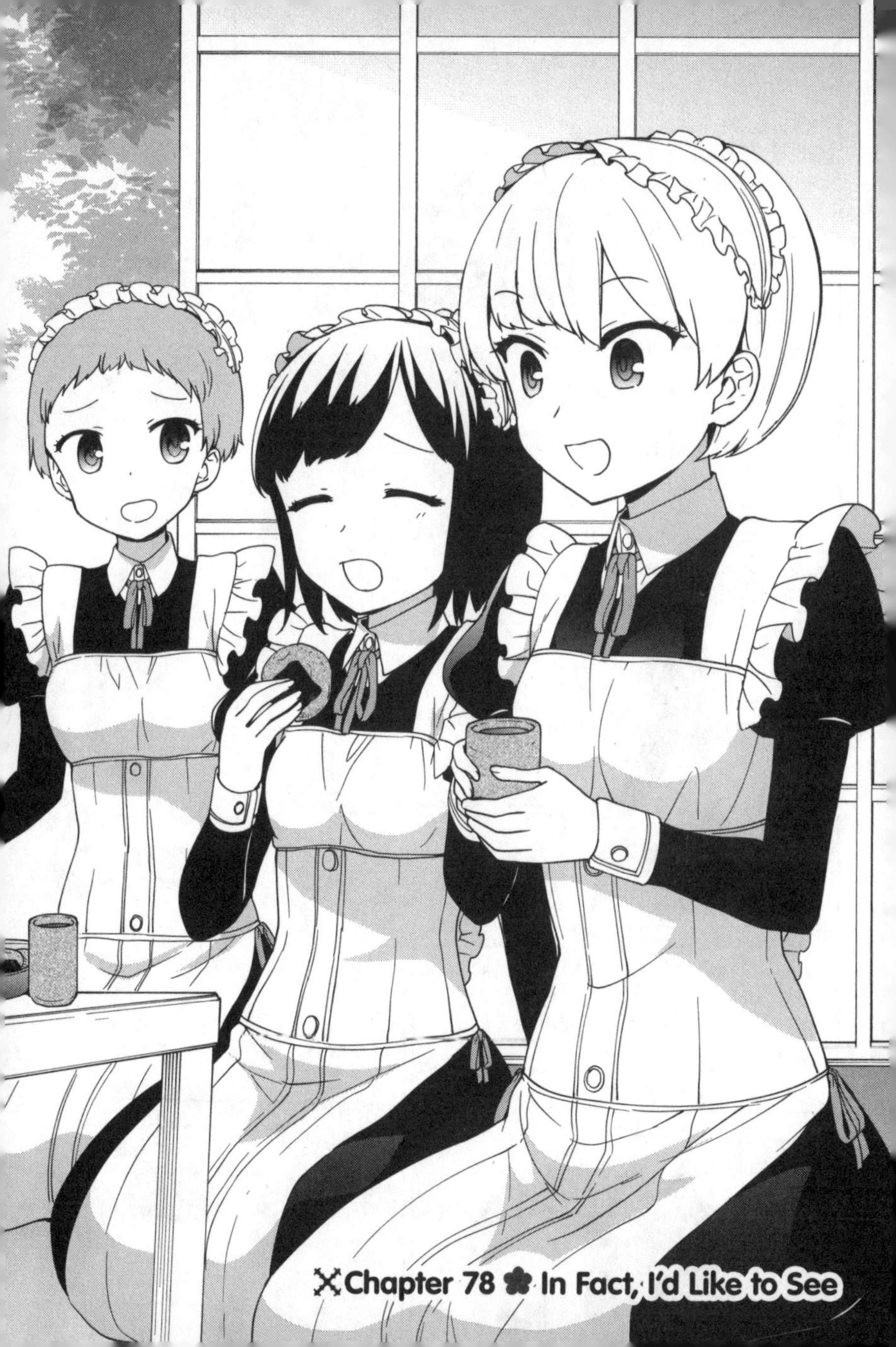
Chapter 78 In Fact, I'd Like to See

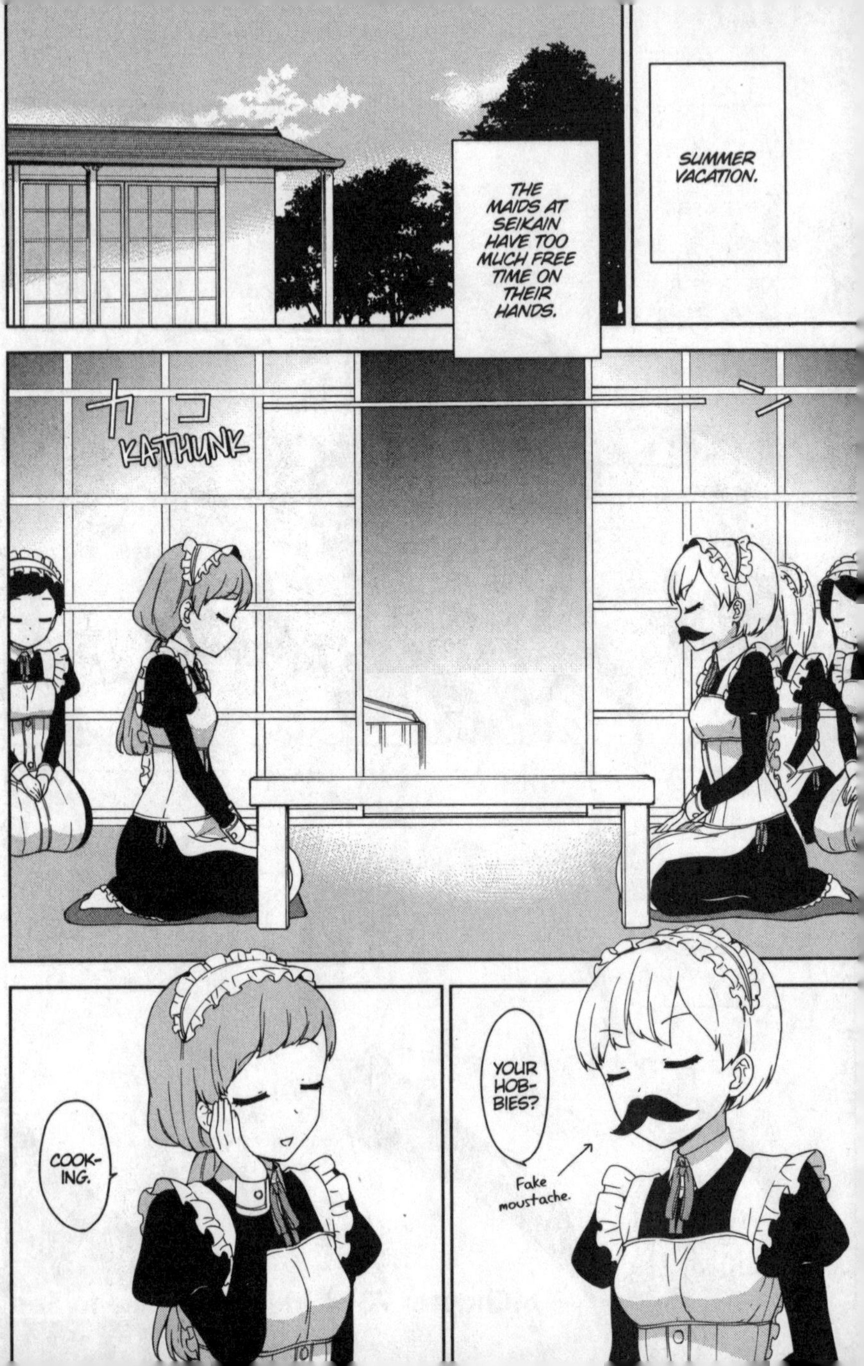
SUMMER VACATION.
THE MAIDS AT SEIKAIN HAVE TOO MUCH FREE TIME ON THEIR HANDS.
KATHUNK
YOUR HOB-BIES?
Fake moustache.
COOK-ING.

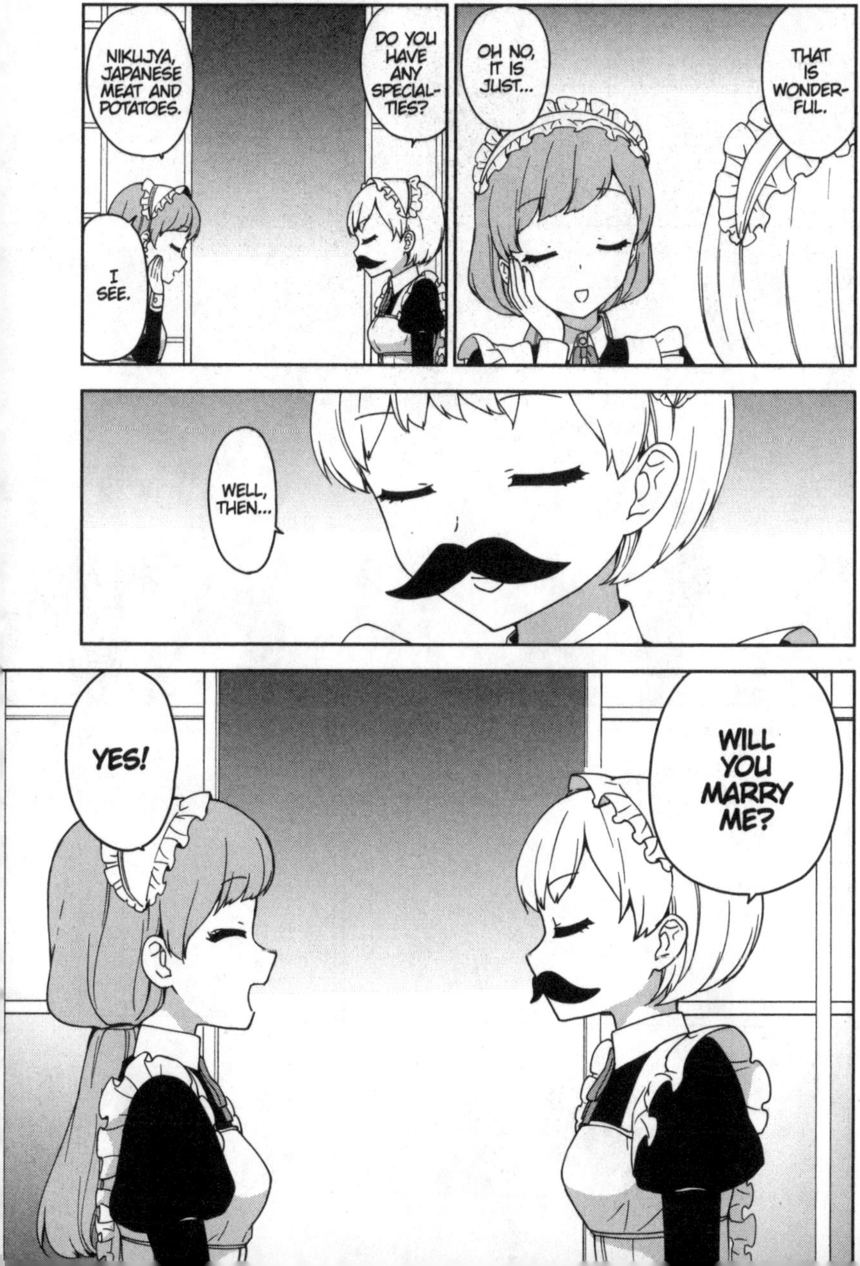
THAT IS WONDER-FUL.
OH NO, IT IS JUST...
DO YOU HAVE ANY SPECIAL-TIES?
NIKUJYA, JAPANESE MEAT AND POTATOES.
I SEE.
WELL, THEN...
WILL YOU MARRY ME?
YES!

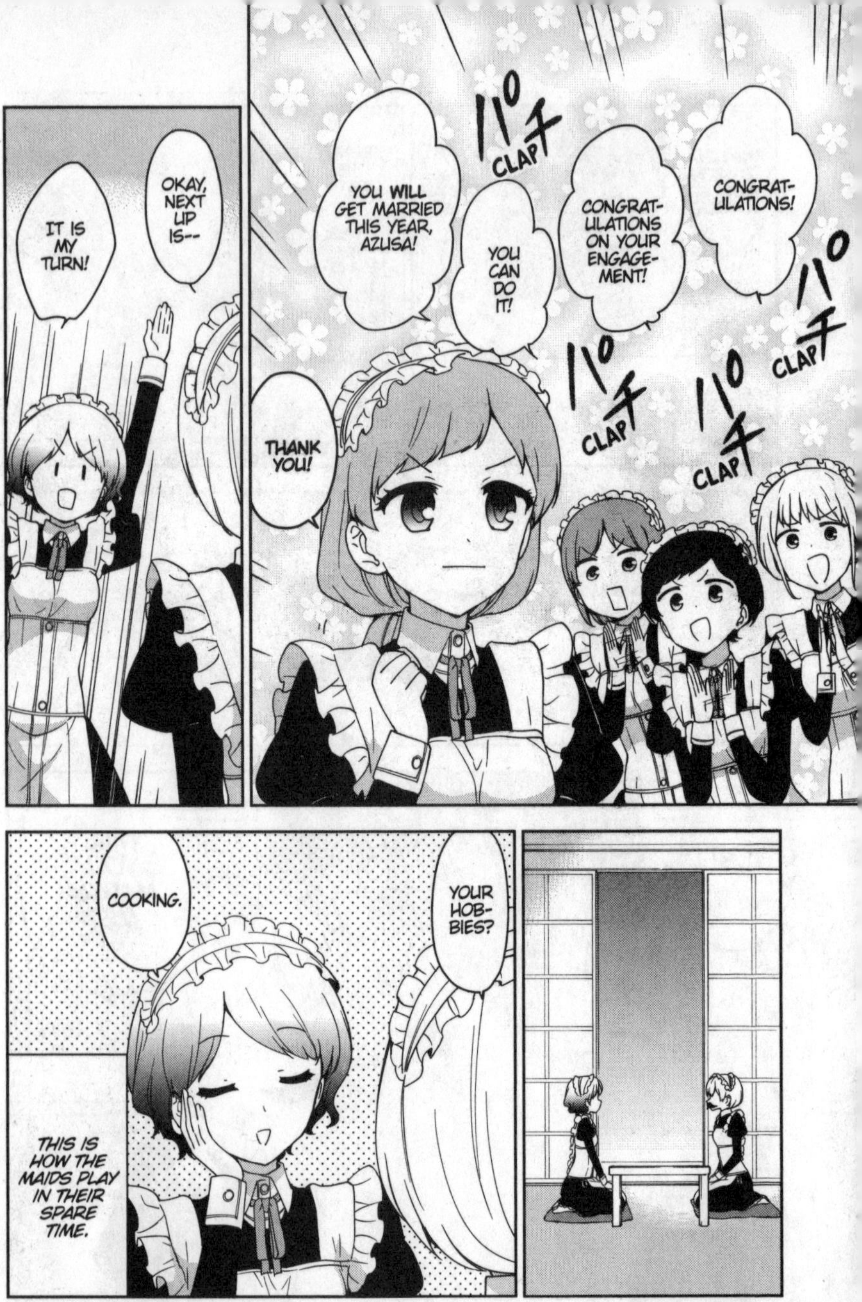
CONGRAT-ULATIONS!
パチ CLAP
CONGRAT-ULATIONS ON YOUR ENGAGE-MENT!
パチ CLAP
パチ CLAP
パチ CLAP
パチ CLAP
YOU CAN DO IT!
YOU WILL GET MARRIED THIS YEAR, AZUSA!
THANK YOU!
OKAY, NEXT UP IS--
IT IS MY TURN!
YOUR HOB-BIES?
COOKING.
THIS IS HOW THE MAIDS PLAY IN THEIR SPARE TIME.

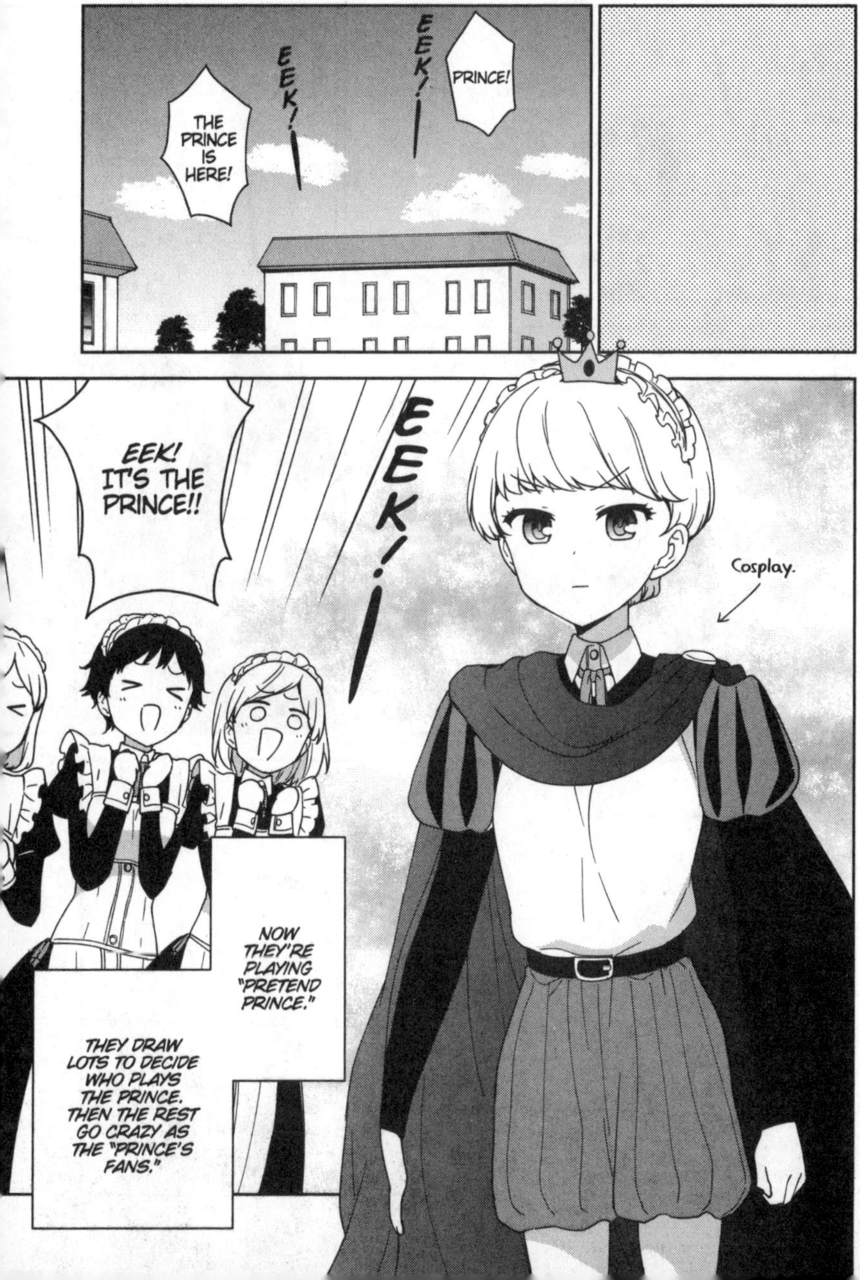
PRINCE!
EEK!
EEK!
THE PRINCE IS HERE!
Cosplay.
EEK!
EEK! IT'S THE PRINCE!!
NOW THEY'RE PLAYING "PRETEND PRINCE."
THEY DRAW LOTS TO DECIDE WHO PLAYS THE PRINCE. THEN THE REST GO CRAZY AS THE "PRINCE'S FANS."

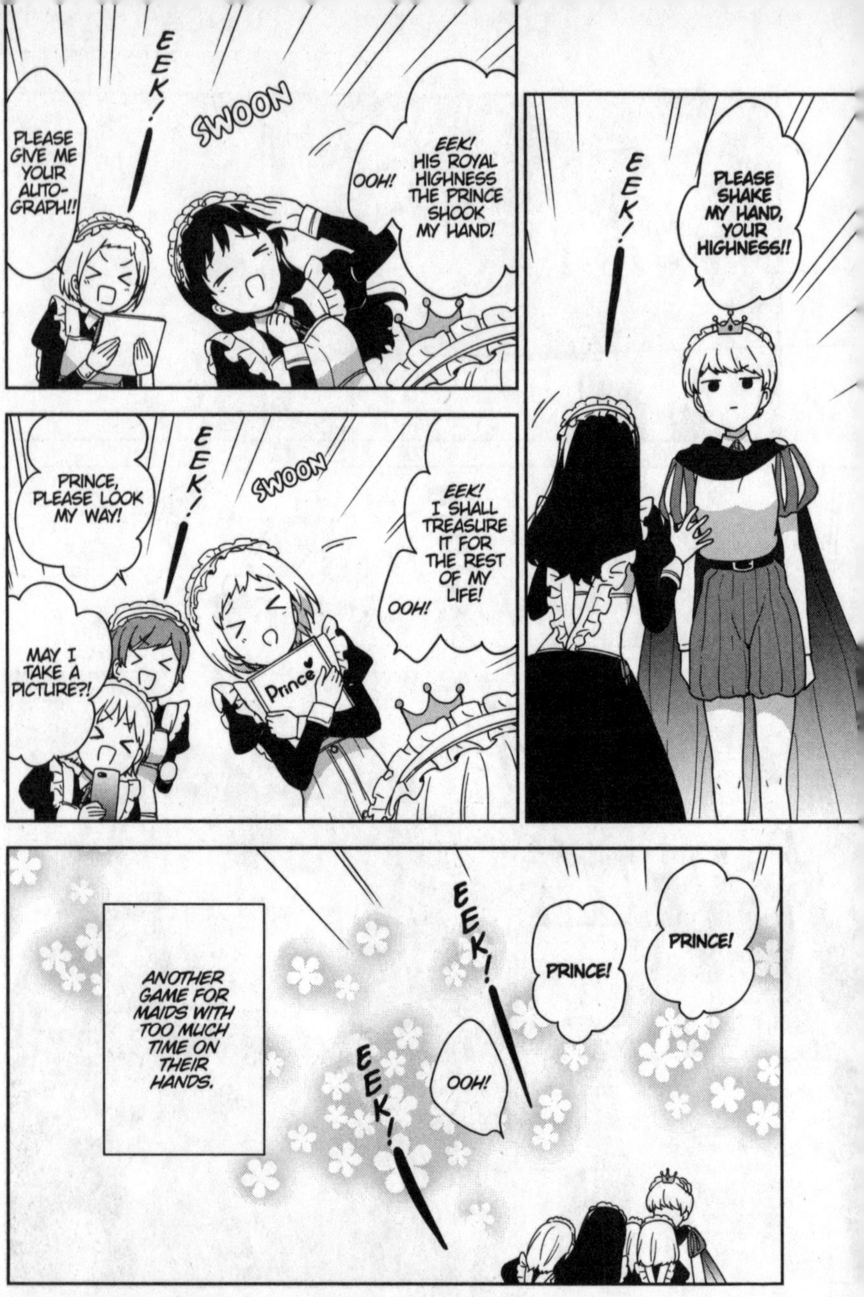
PLEASE SHAKE MY HAND, YOUR HIGHNESS!!
EEK!
EEK! HIS ROYAL HIGHNESS THE PRINCE SHOOK MY HAND!
OOH!
SWOON
EEK!
PLEASE GIVE ME YOUR AUTO-GRAPH!!
EEK! I SHALL TREASURE IT FOR THE REST OF MY LIFE!
OOH!
SWOON
EEK!
PRINCE, PLEASE LOOK MY WAY!
Prince
MAY I TAKE A PICTURE?!
PRINCE!
PRINCE!
EEK!
OOH!
EEK!
ANOTHER GAME FOR MAIDS WITH TOO MUCH TIME ON THEIR HANDS.

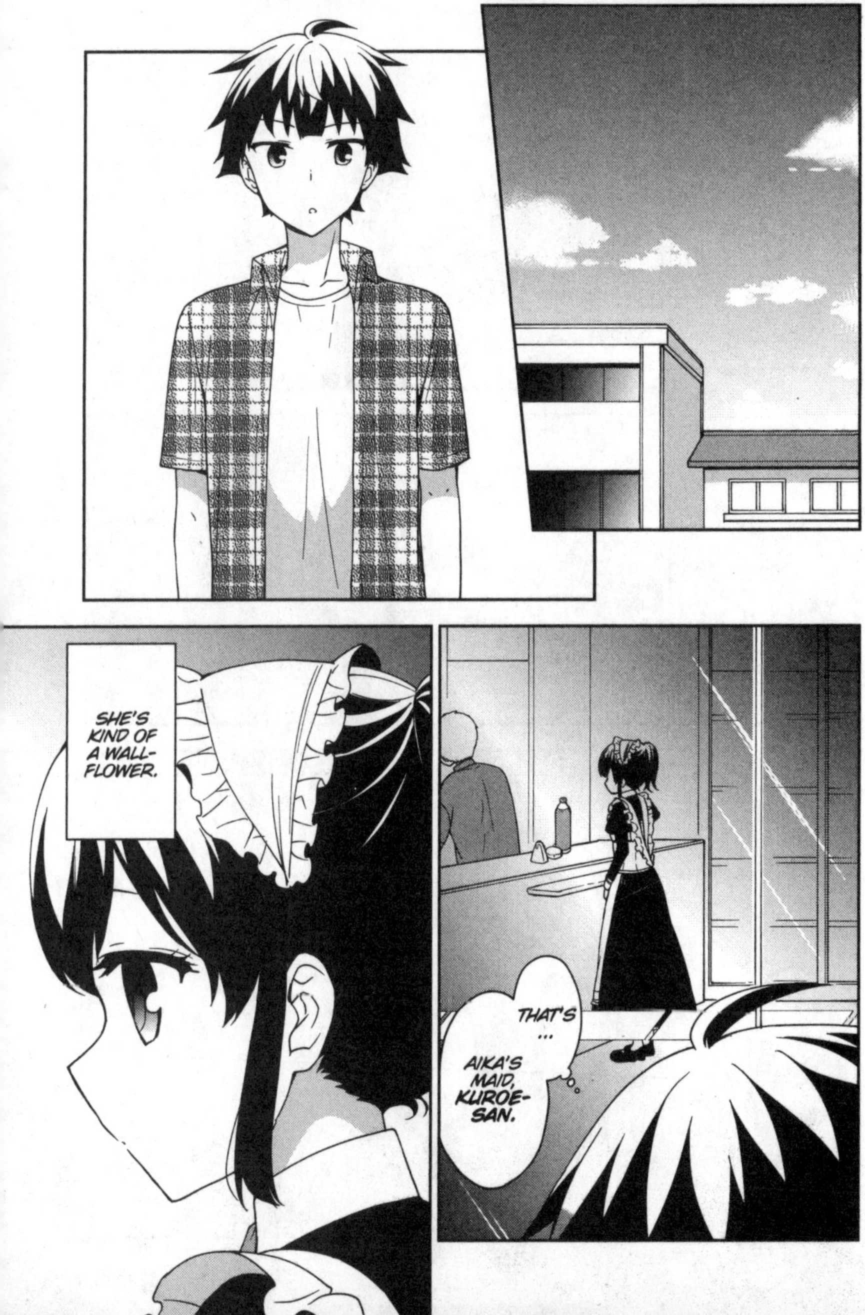
THAT'S ... AIKA'S MAID, KUROE-SAN.
SHE'S KIND OF A WALL-FLOWER.

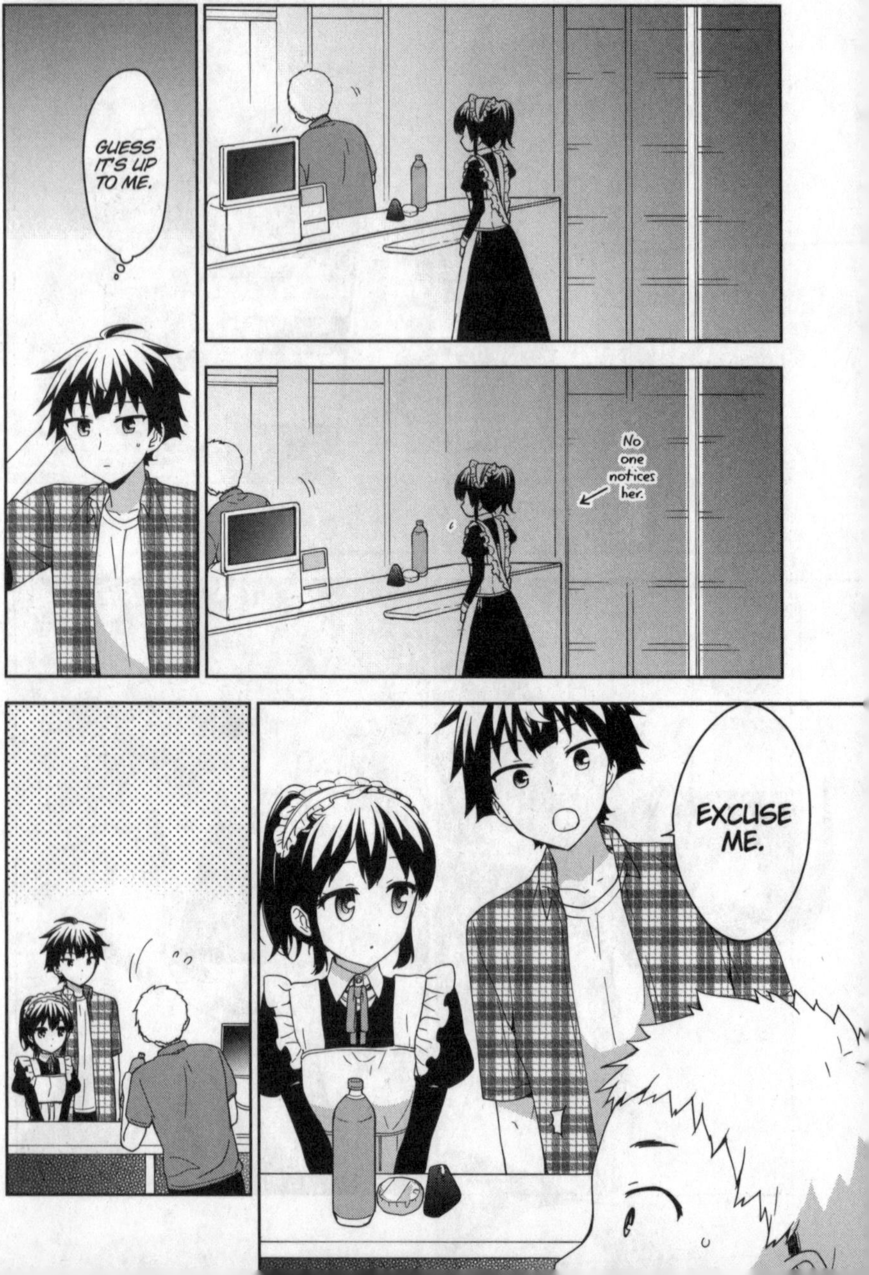
No one notices her.
GUESS IT'S UP TO ME.
EXCUSE ME.

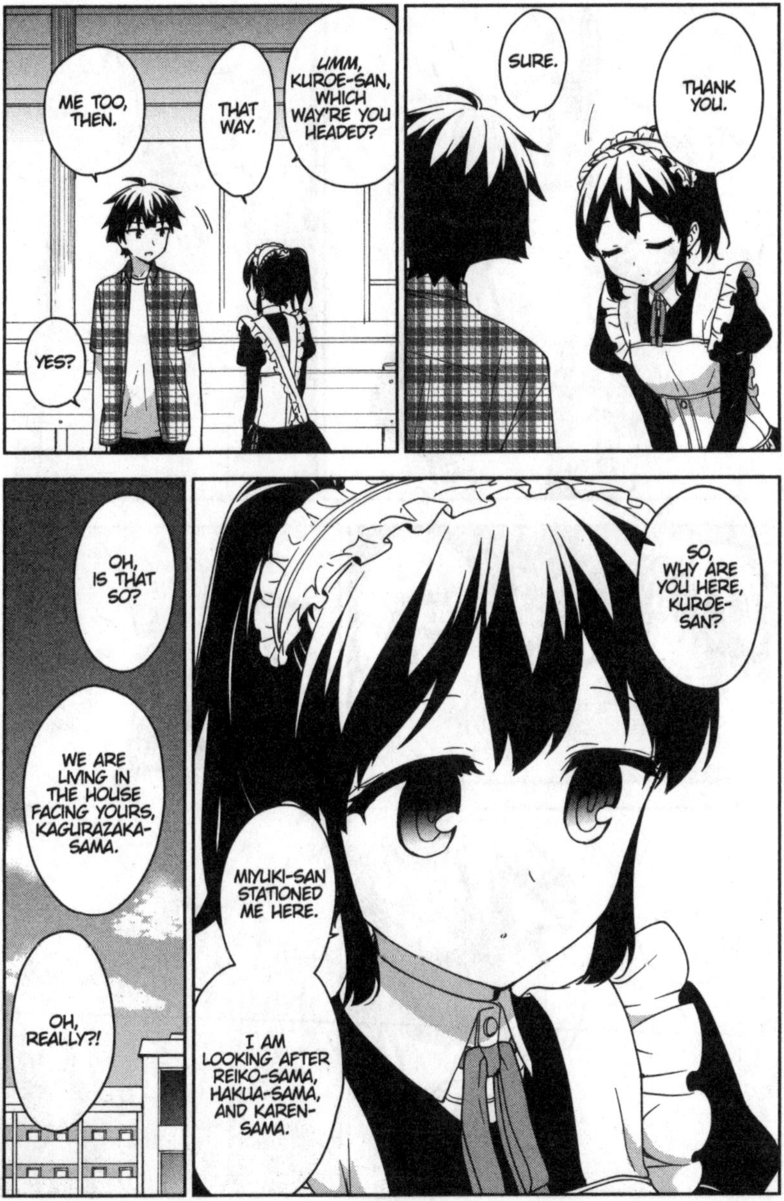
THANK YOU.
SURE.
UMM, KUROE-SAN, WHICH WAY'RE YOU HEADED?
THAT WAY.
ME TOO, THEN.
YES?
SO, WHY ARE YOU HERE, KUROE-SAN?
MIYUKI-SAN STATIONED ME HERE.
I AM LOOKING AFTER REIKO-SAMA, HAKUA-SAMA, AND KAREN-SAMA.
OH, IS THAT SO?
WE ARE LIVING IN THE HOUSE FACING YOURS, KAGURAZAKA-SAMA.
OH, REALLY?!

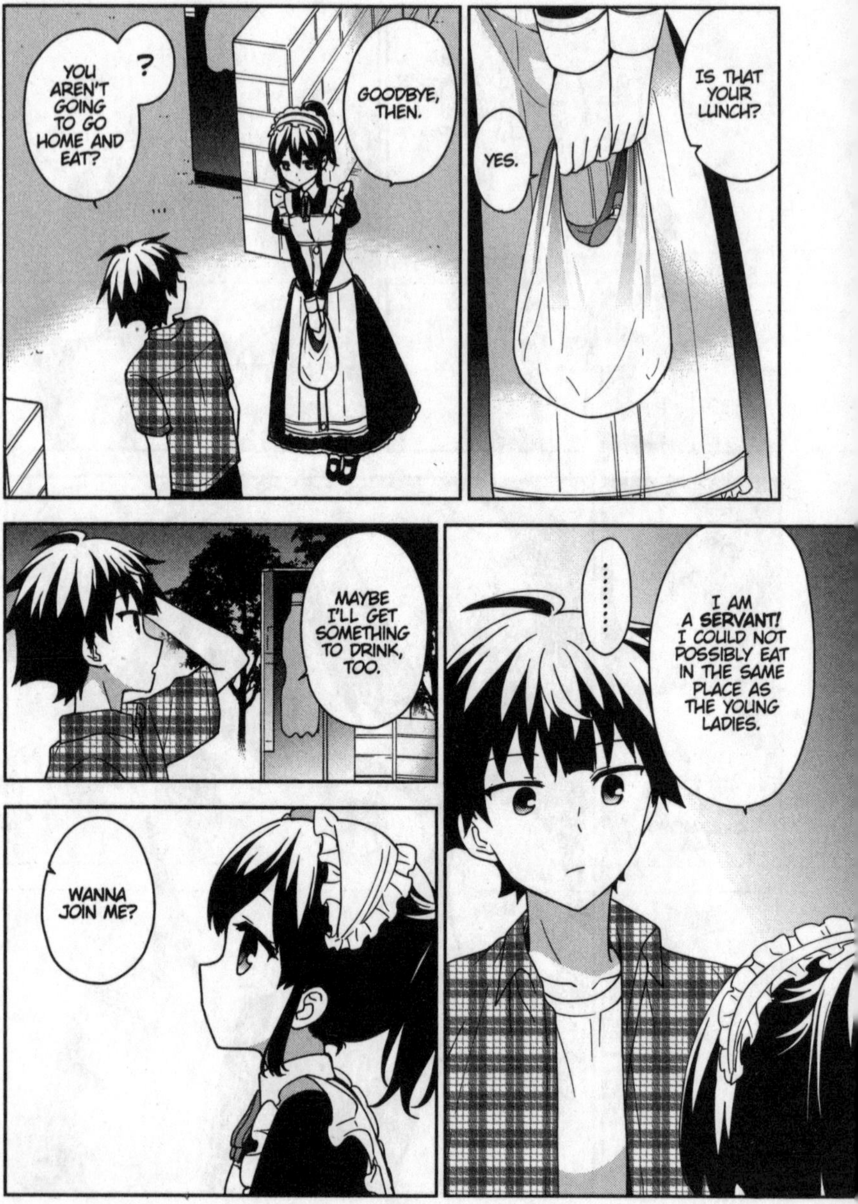
IS THAT YOUR LUNCH?
YES.
GOODBYE, THEN.
?
YOU AREN'T GOING TO GO HOME AND EAT?
...
I AM A **SERVANT!** I COULD NOT POSSIBLY EAT IN THE SAME PLACE AS THE YOUNG LADIES.
......
MAYBE I'LL GET SOMETHING TO DRINK, TOO.
WANNA JOIN ME?

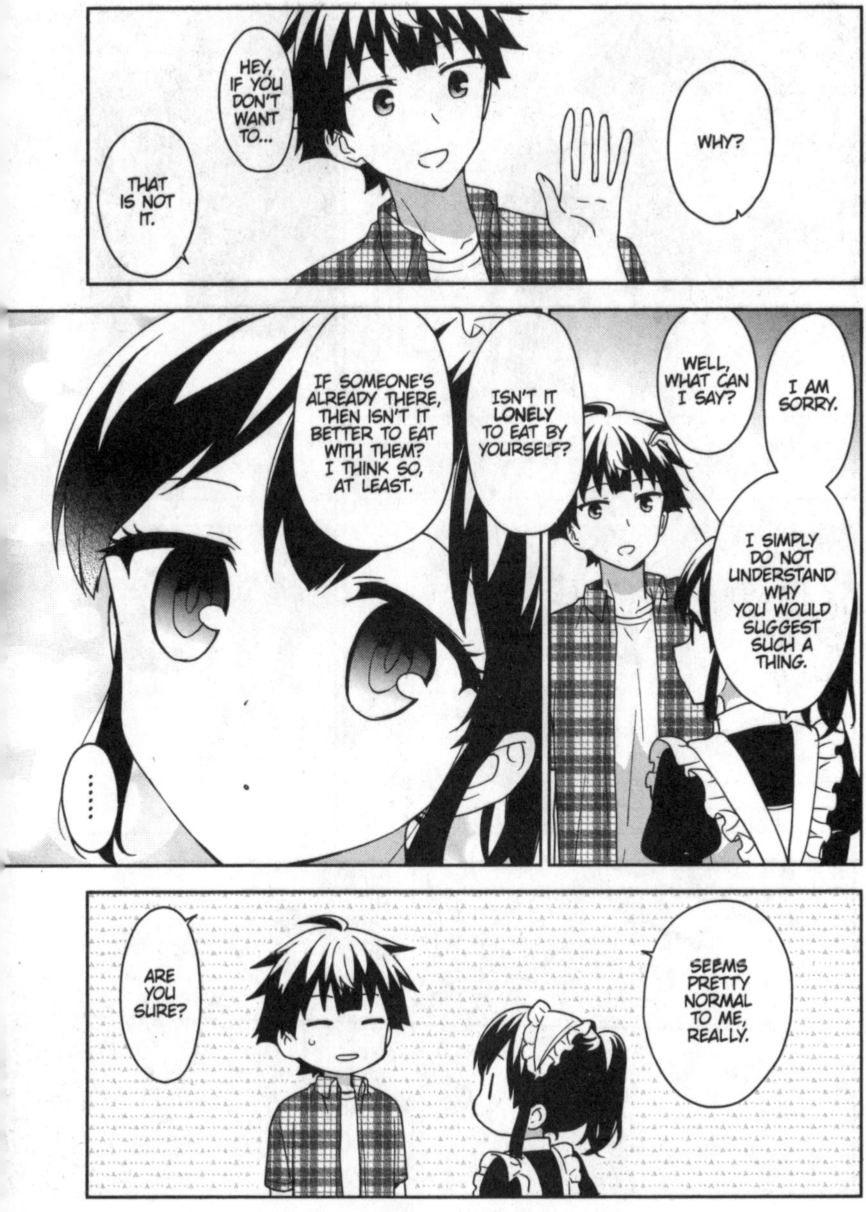
WHY?
HEY, IF YOU DON'T WANT TO...
THAT IS NOT IT.
I AM SORRY.
I SIMPLY DO NOT UNDERSTAND WHY YOU WOULD SUGGEST SUCH A THING.
WELL, WHAT CAN I SAY?
ISN'T IT LONELY TO EAT BY YOURSELF?
IF SOMEONE'S ALREADY THERE, THEN ISN'T IT BETTER TO EAT WITH THEM? I THINK SO, AT LEAST.
......
SEEMS PRETTY NORMAL TO ME, REALLY.
ARE YOU SURE?

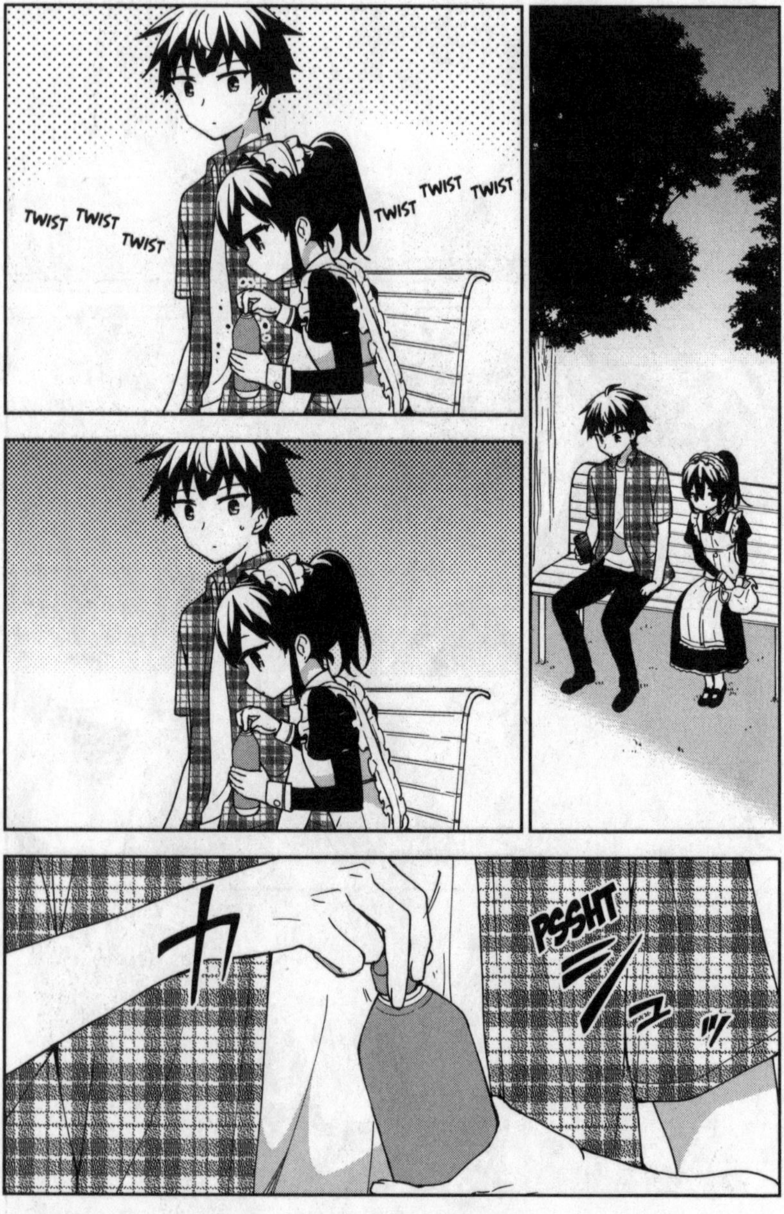
TWIST TWIST TWIST
TWIST TWIST TWIST
PSSHT
シュッ
カ

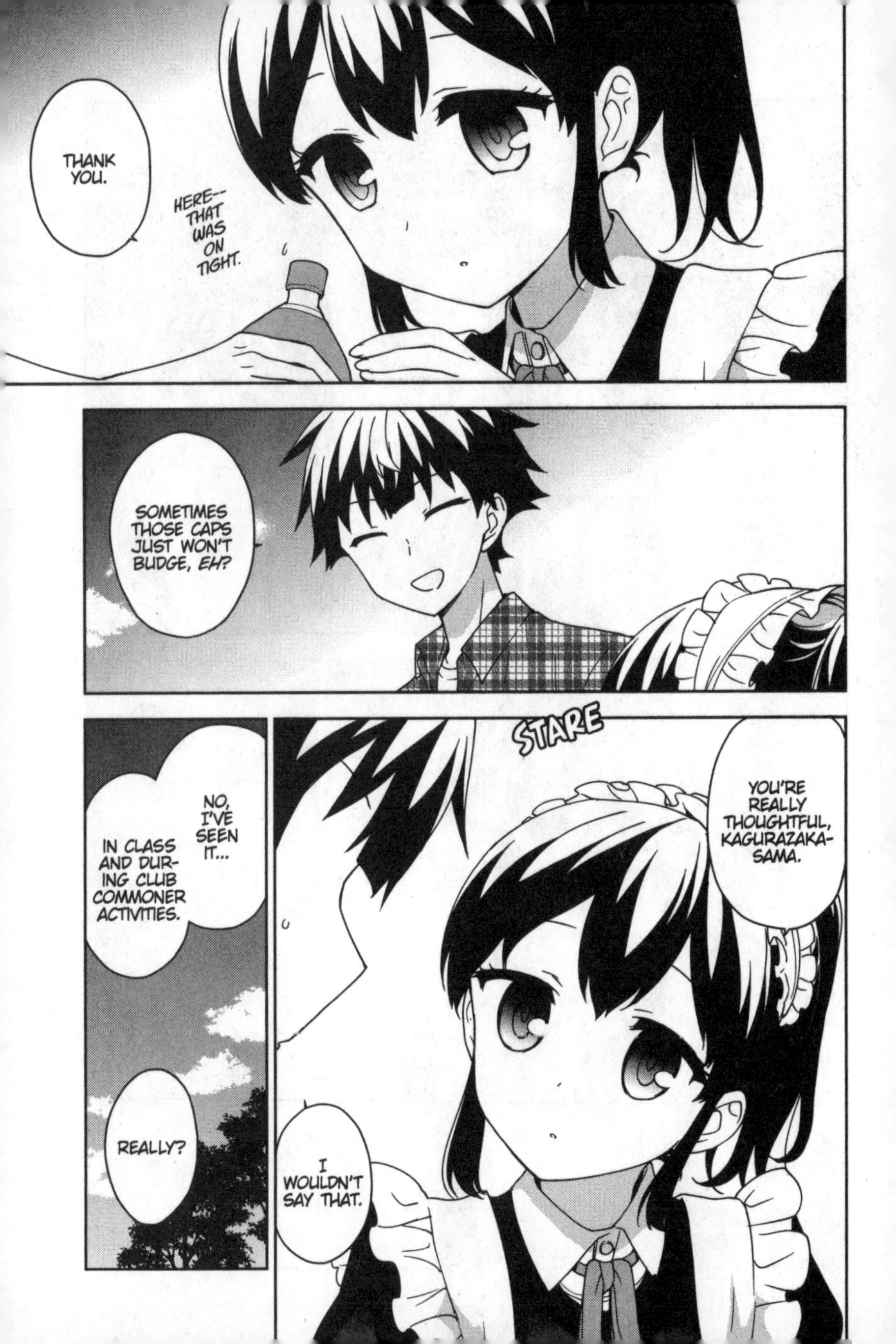
HERE-- THAT WAS ON TIGHT.
THANK YOU.
SOMETIMES THOSE CAPS JUST WON'T BUDGE, *EH?*
STARE
YOU'RE REALLY THOUGHTFUL, KAGURAZAKA-SAMA.
I WOULDN'T SAY THAT.
NO, I'VE SEEN IT...
IN CLASS AND DUR-ING CLUB COMMONER ACTIVITIES.
REALLY?

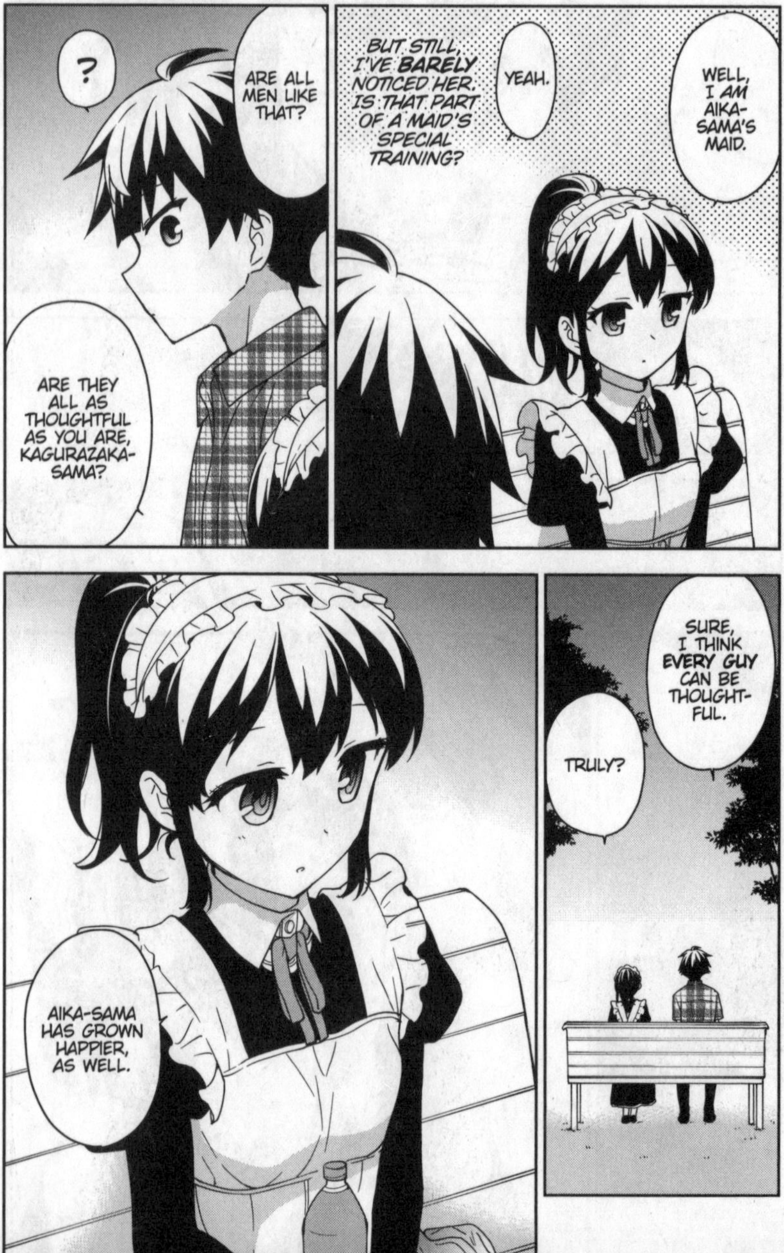
WELL, I AM AIKA-SAMA'S MAID.
YEAH.
BUT STILL, I'VE BARELY NOTICED HER. IS THAT PART OF A MAID'S SPECIAL TRAINING?
ARE ALL MEN LIKE THAT?
?
ARE THEY ALL AS THOUGHTFUL AS YOU ARE, KAGURAZAKA-SAMA?
SURE, I THINK EVERY GUY CAN BE THOUGHTFUL.
TRULY?
AIKA-SAMA HAS GROWN HAPPIER, AS WELL.

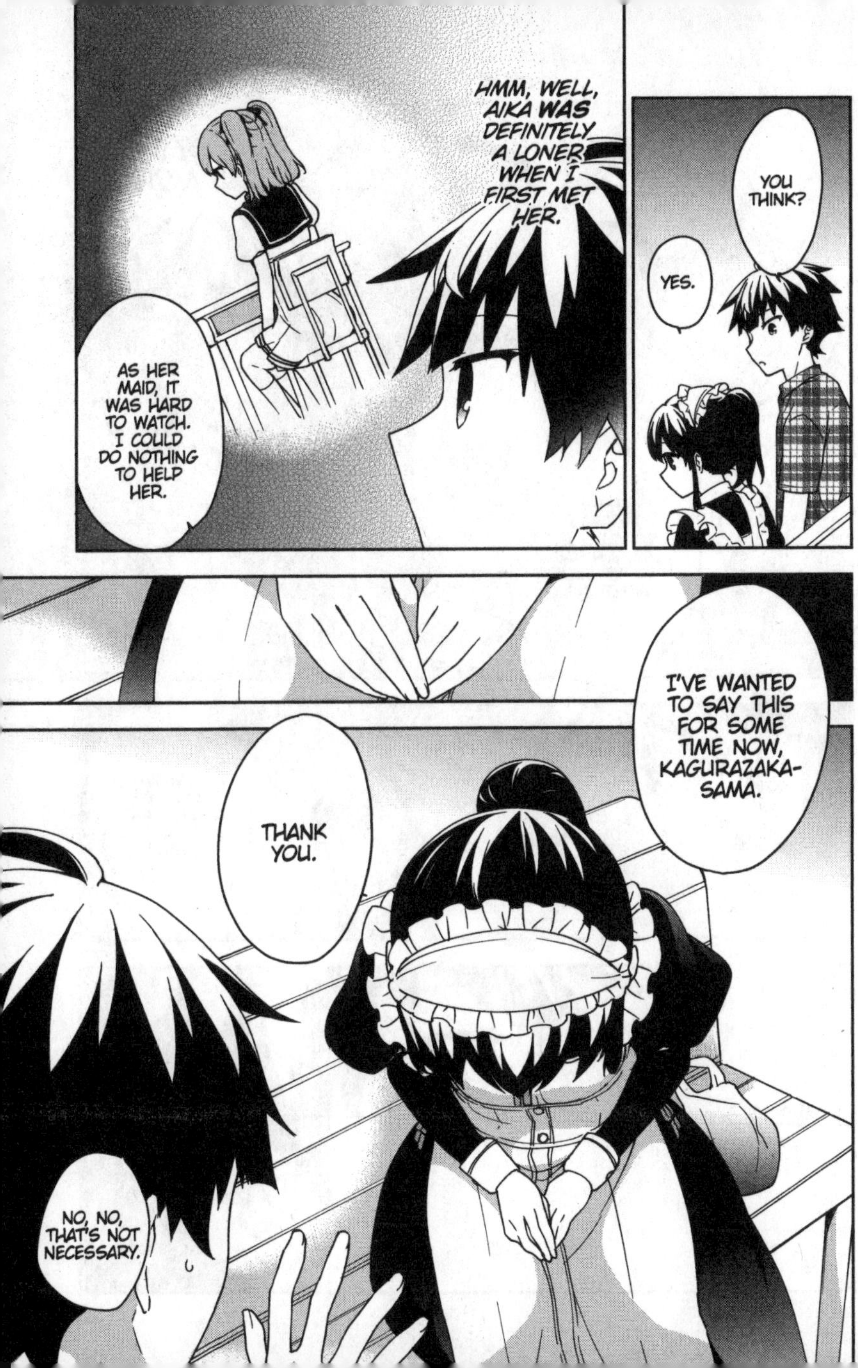
YOU THINK?
YES.
HMM, WELL, AIKA WAS DEFINITELY A LONER WHEN I FIRST MET HER.
AS HER MAID, IT WAS HARD TO WATCH. I COULD DO NOTHING TO HELP HER.
I'VE WANTED TO SAY THIS FOR SOME TIME NOW, KAGURAZAKA-SAMA.
THANK YOU.
NO, NO, THAT'S NOT NECESSARY.

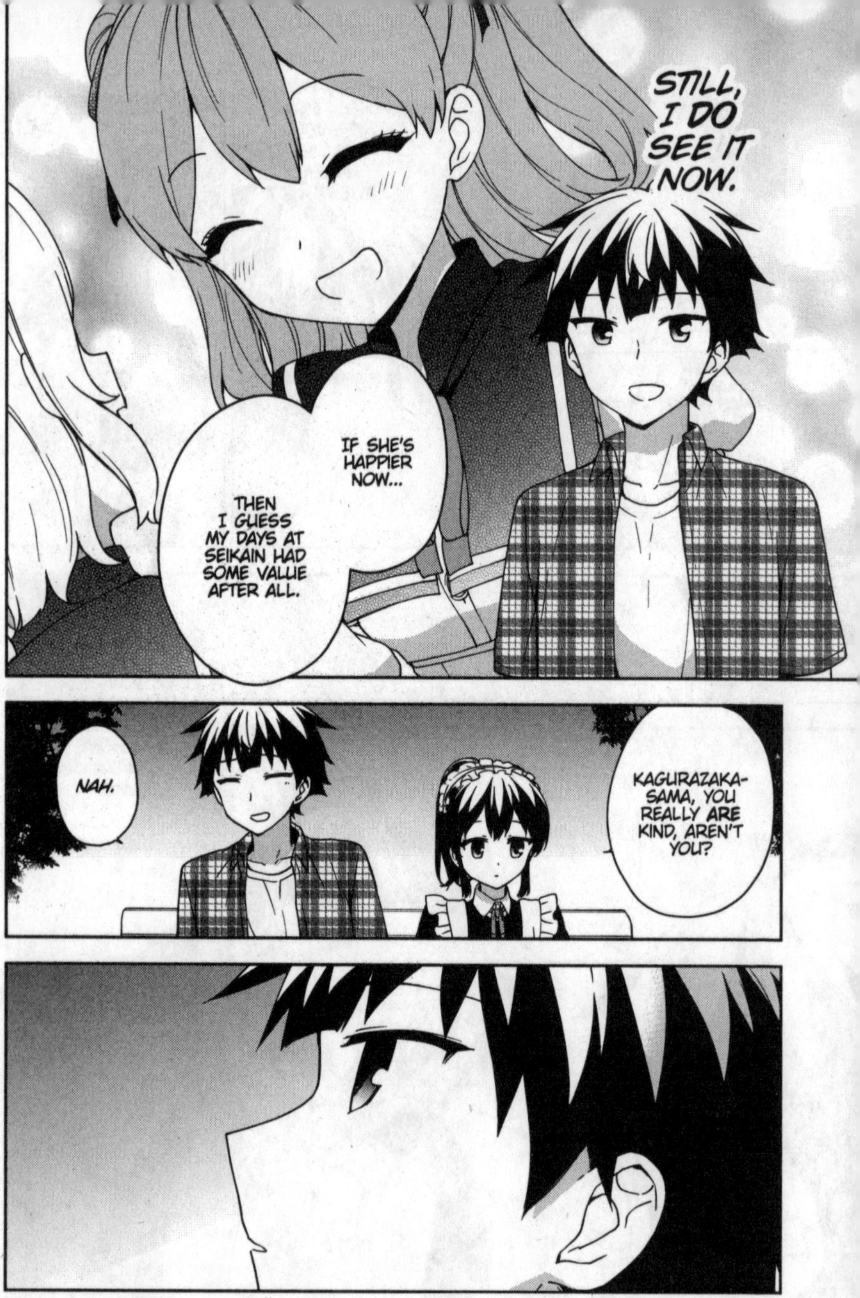
STILL, I DO SEE IT NOW.
IF SHE'S HAPPIER NOW...
THEN I GUESS MY DAYS AT SEIKAIN HAD SOME VALUE AFTER ALL.
KAGURAZAKA-SAMA, YOU REALLY ARE KIND, AREN'T YOU?
NAH.

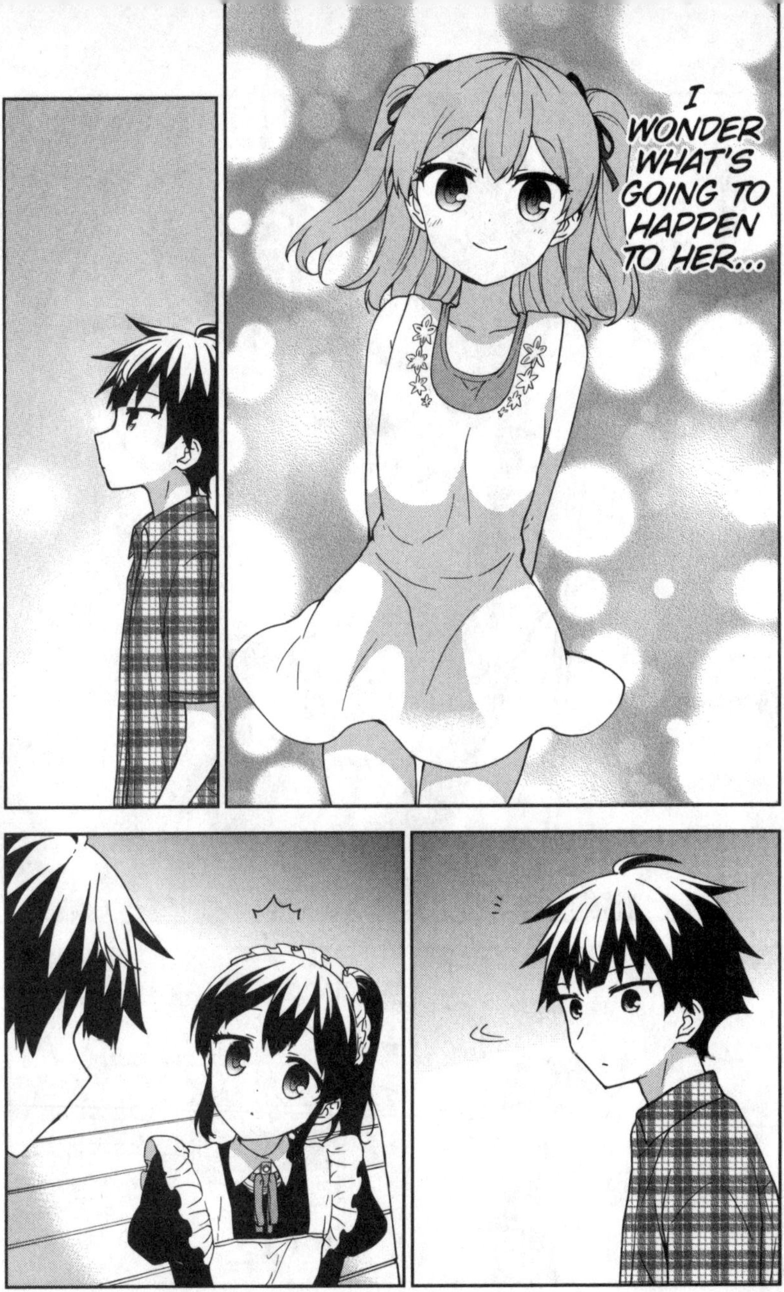
I WONDER WHAT'S GOING TO HAPPEN TO HER...

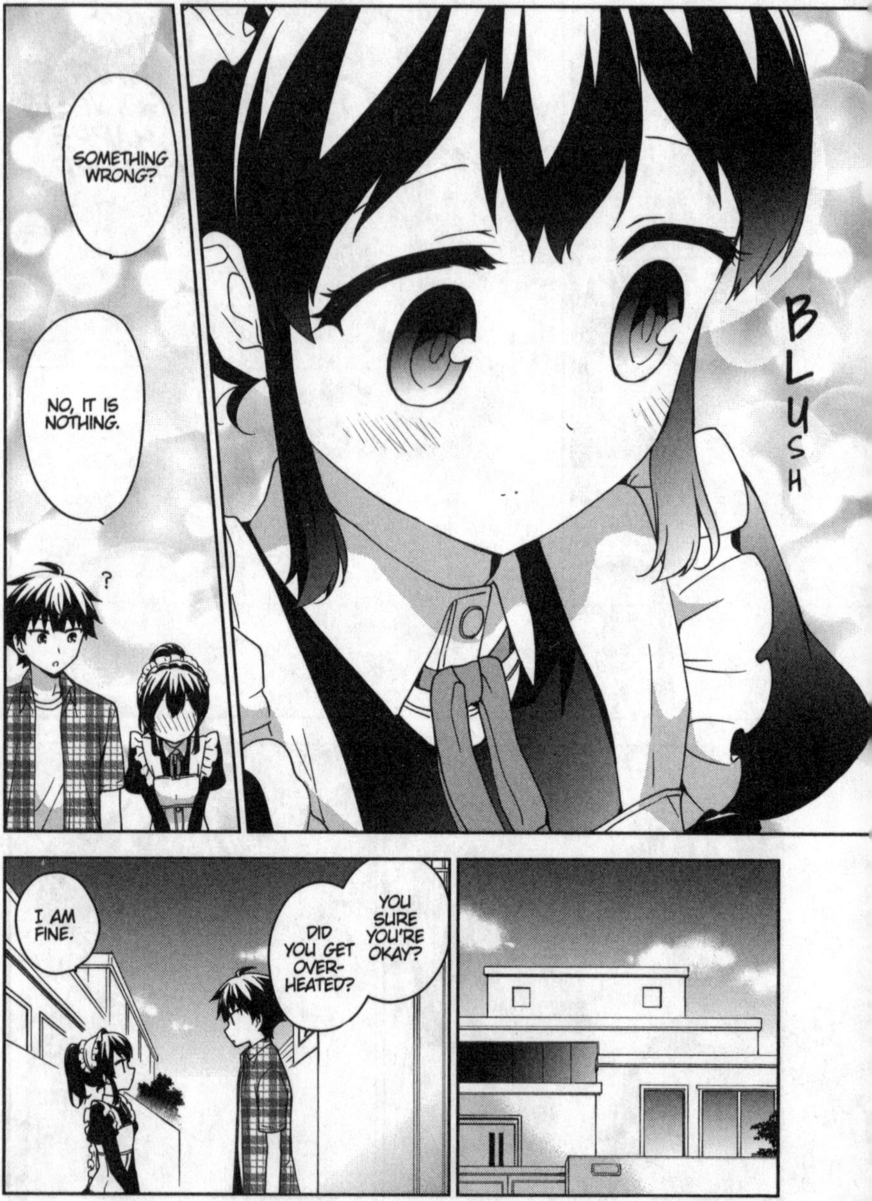
BLUSH
SOMETHING WRONG?
NO, IT IS NOTHING.
?
YOU SURE YOU'RE OKAY?
DID YOU GET OVER-HEATED?
I AM FINE.

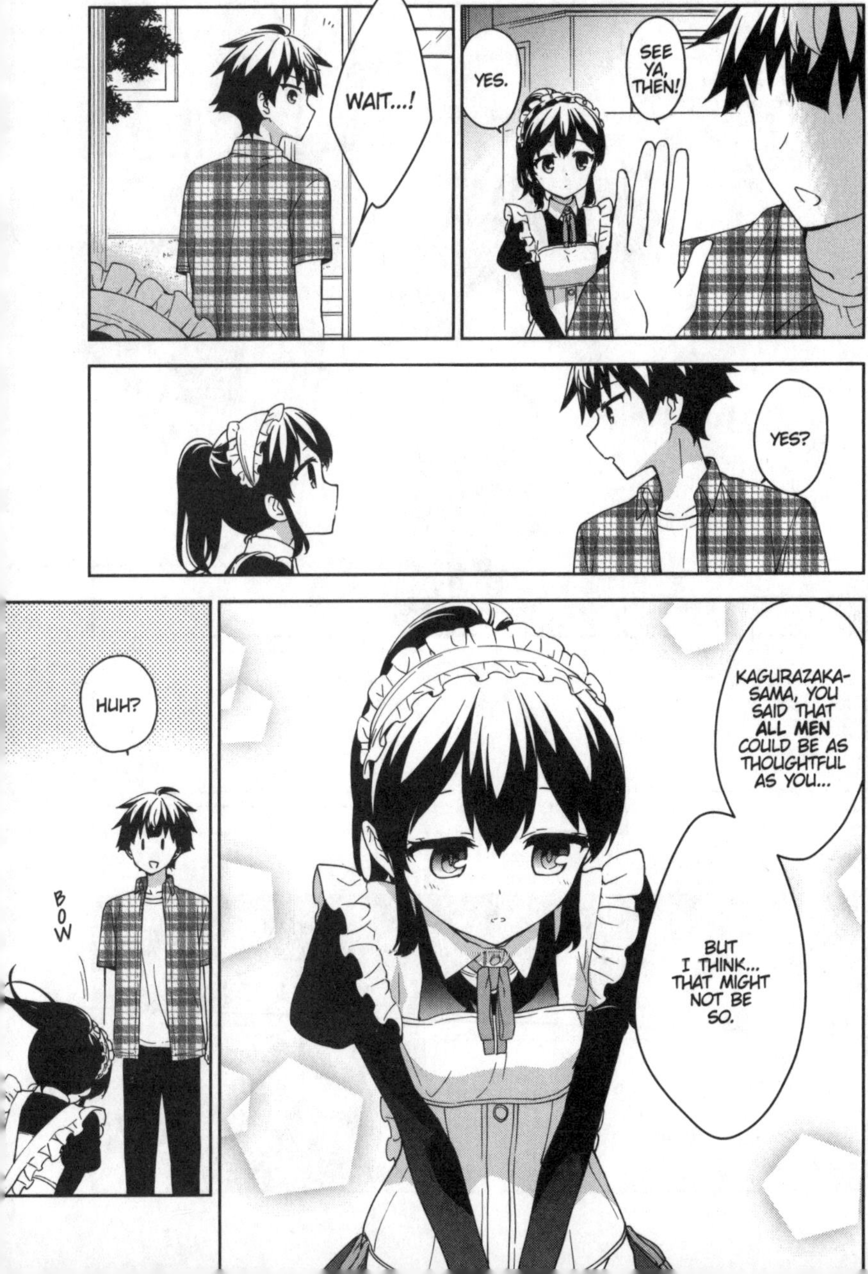
SEE YA, THEN!
YES.
WAIT...!
YES?
KAGURAZAKA-SAMA, YOU SAID THAT ALL MEN COULD BE AS THOUGHTFUL AS YOU...
BUT I THINK... THAT MIGHT NOT BE SO.
HUH?
BOW

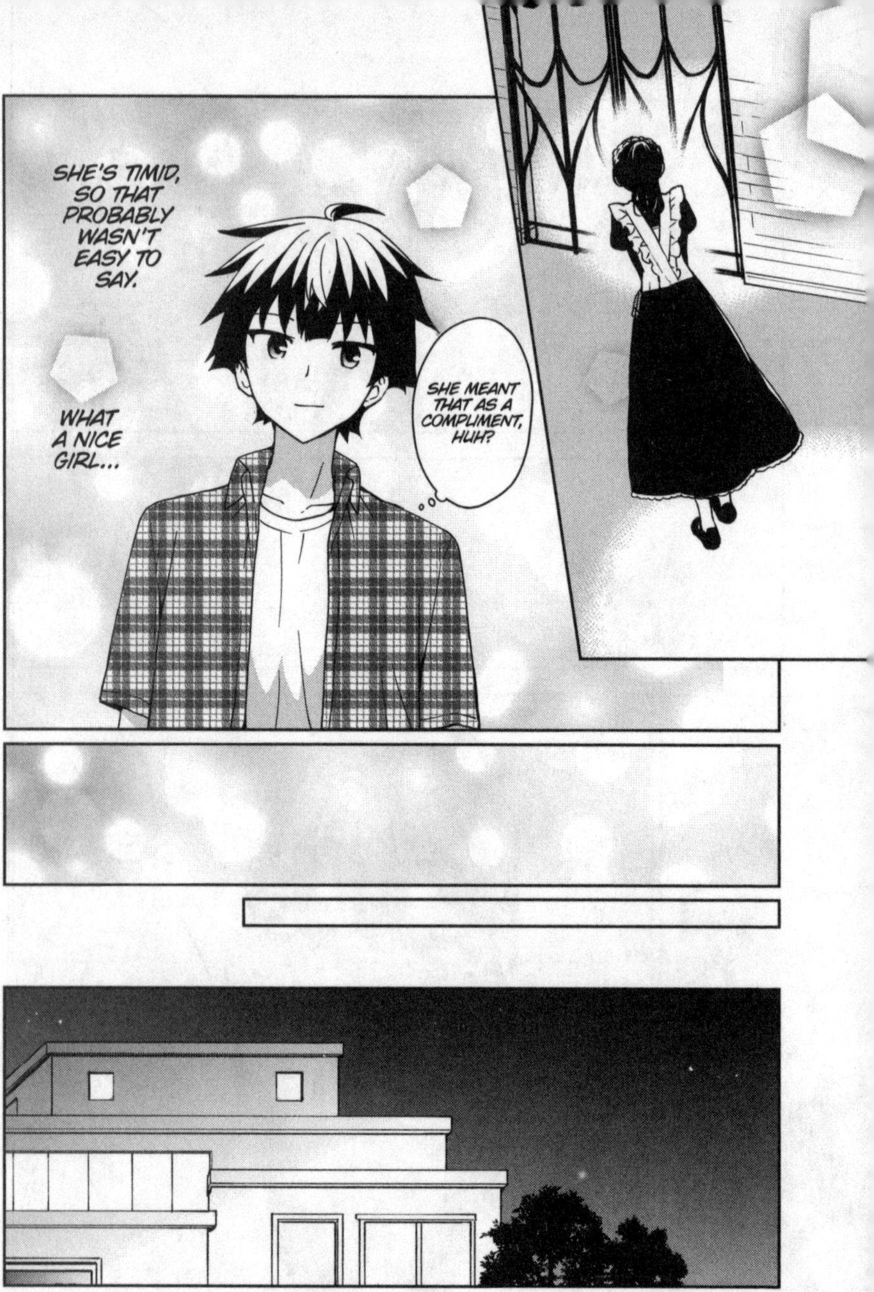
SHE MEANT THAT AS A COMPLIMENT, HUH?
SHE'S TIMID, SO THAT PROBABLY WASN'T EASY TO SAY.
WHAT A NICE GIRL...

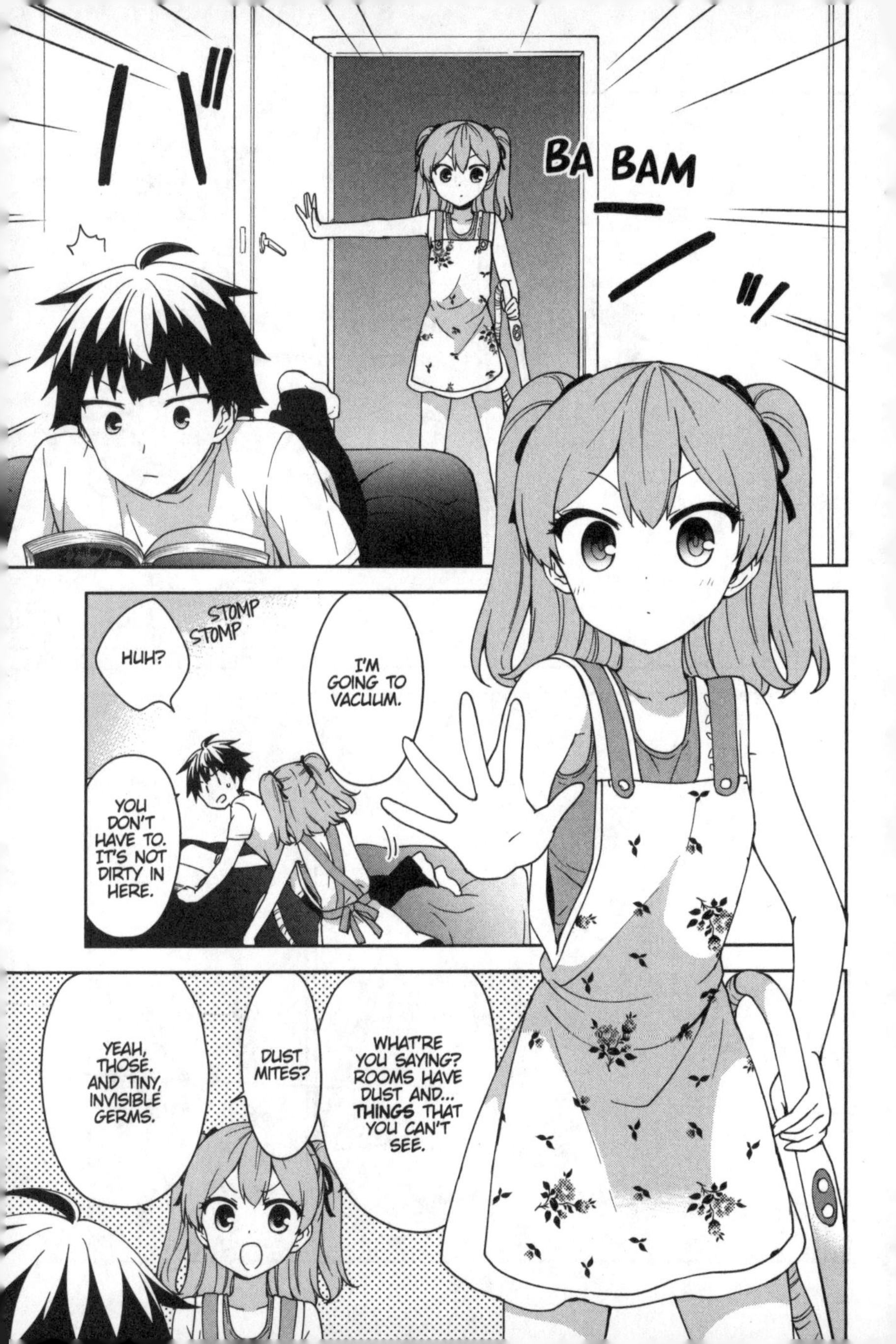
BA BAM
I'M GOING TO VACUUM.
STOMP STOMP
HUH?
YOU DON'T HAVE TO. IT'S NOT DIRTY IN HERE.
WHAT'RE YOU SAYING? ROOMS HAVE DUST AND... **THINGS** THAT YOU CAN'T SEE.
DUST MITES?
YEAH, THOSE. AND TINY, INVISIBLE GERMS.

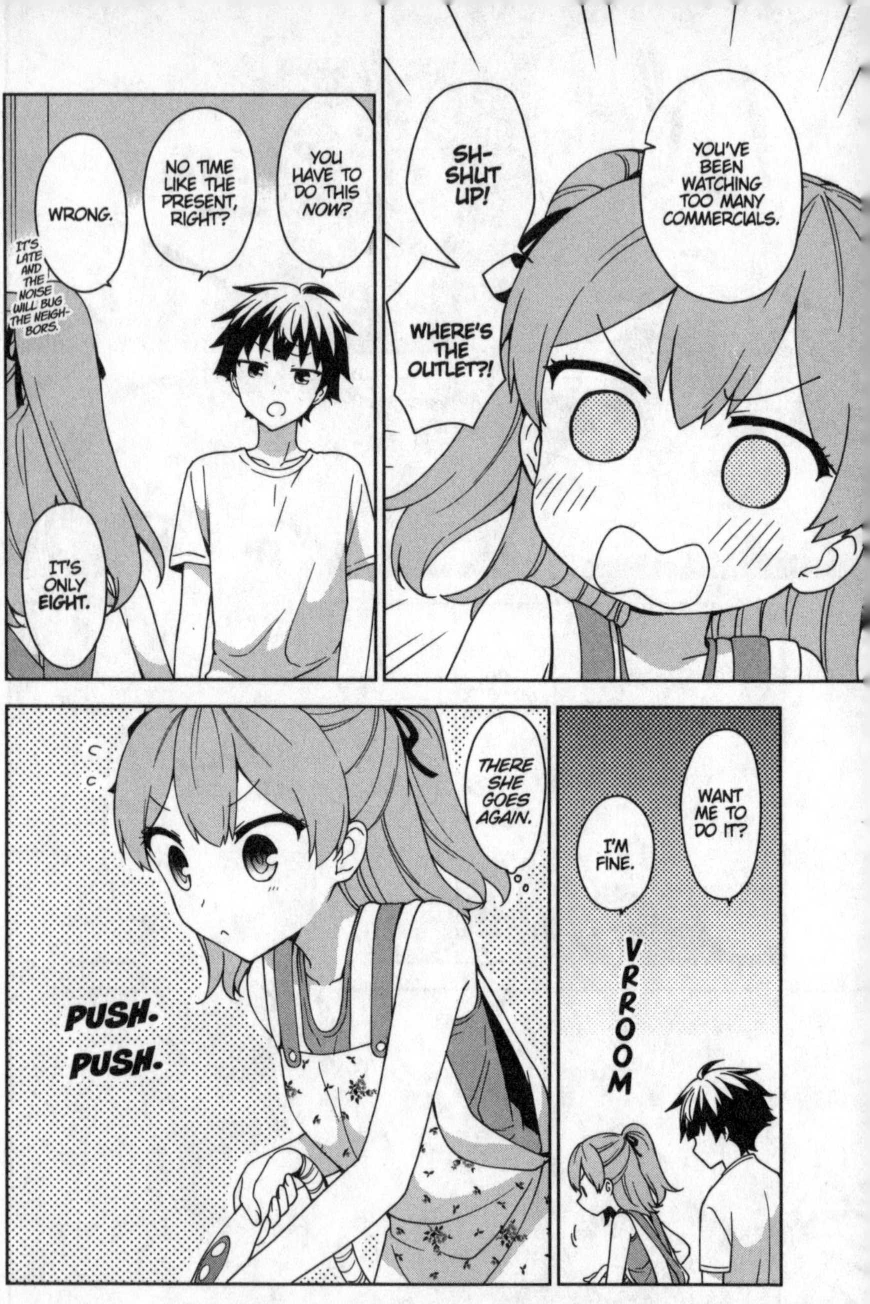
YOU'VE BEEN WATCHING TOO MANY COMMERCIALS.
SH-SHUT UP!
WHERE'S THE OUTLET?!
YOU HAVE TO DO THIS NOW?
NO TIME LIKE THE PRESENT, RIGHT?
WRONG.
IT'S LATE AND THE NOISE WILL BUG THE NEIGH-BORS.
IT'S ONLY EIGHT.
WANT ME TO DO IT?
I'M FINE.
VRROOM
THERE SHE GOES AGAIN.
PUSH.
PUSH.

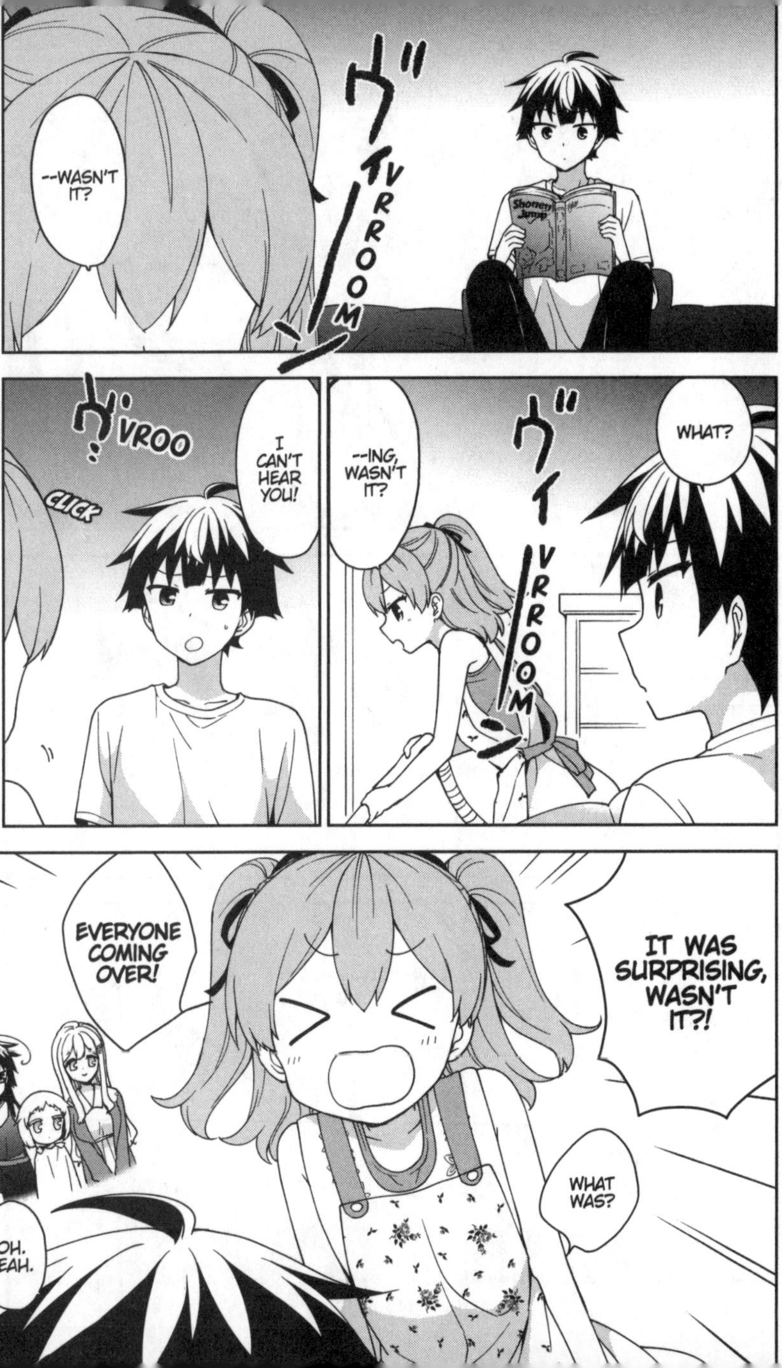

--WASN'T IT?
VRROOM
Shonen Jump
WHAT?
--ING, WASN'T IT?
VRROOM
I CAN'T HEAR YOU!
VROO
CLICK
IT WAS SURPRISING, WASN'T IT?!
WHAT WAS?
EVERYONE COMING OVER!
OH. YEAH.

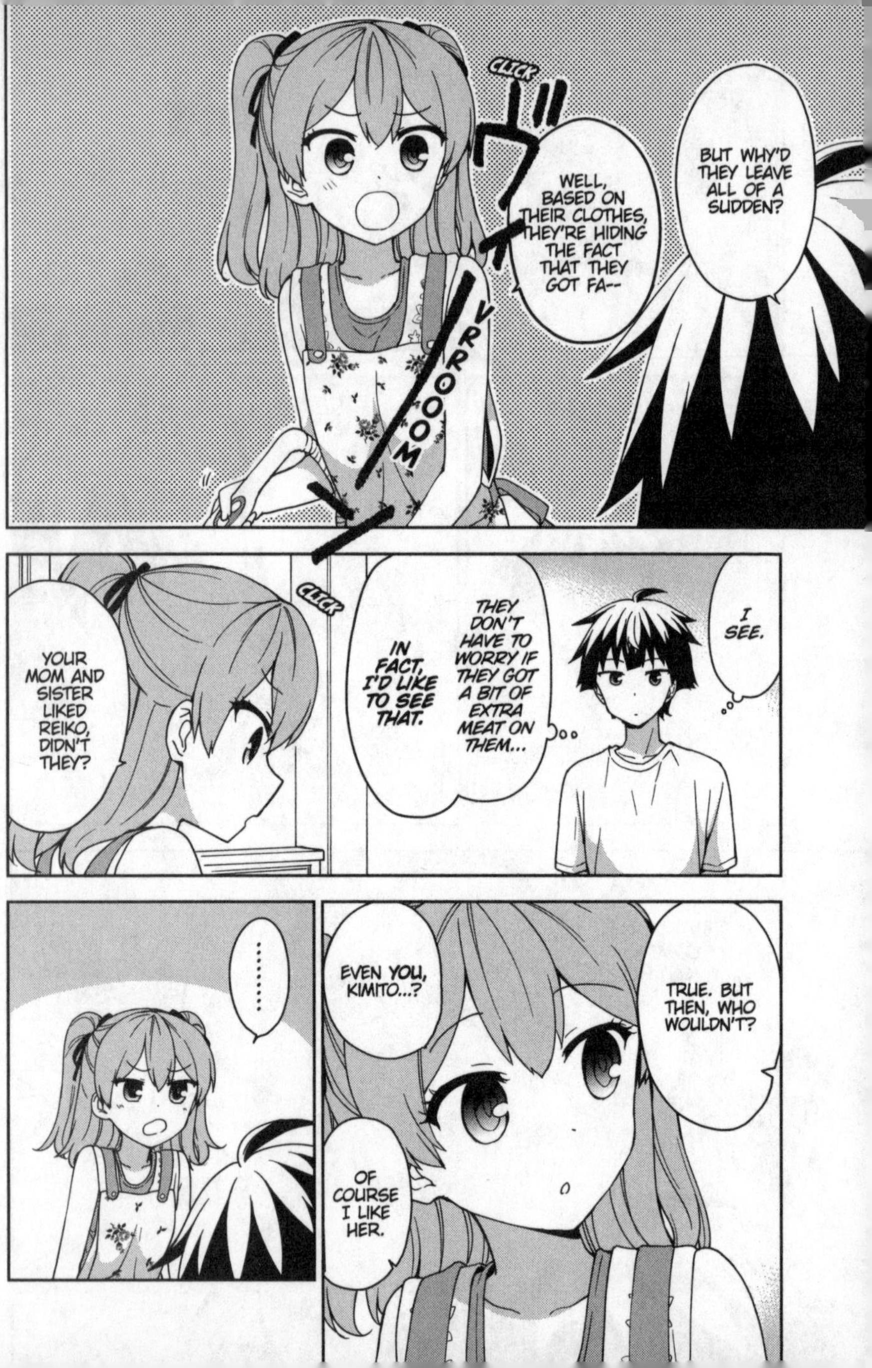
BUT WHY'D THEY LEAVE ALL OF A SUDDEN?
CLICK
WELL, BASED ON THEIR CLOTHES, THEY'RE HIDING THE FACT THAT THEY GOT FA--
VRROOOOM
I SEE.
THEY DON'T HAVE TO WORRY IF THEY GOT A BIT OF EXTRA MEAT ON THEM...
IN FACT, I'D LIKE TO SEE THAT.
CLICK
YOUR MOM AND SISTER LIKED REIKO, DIDN'T THEY?
TRUE. BUT THEN, WHO WOULDN'T?
EVEN YOU, KIMITO...?
OF COURSE I LIKE HER.
......

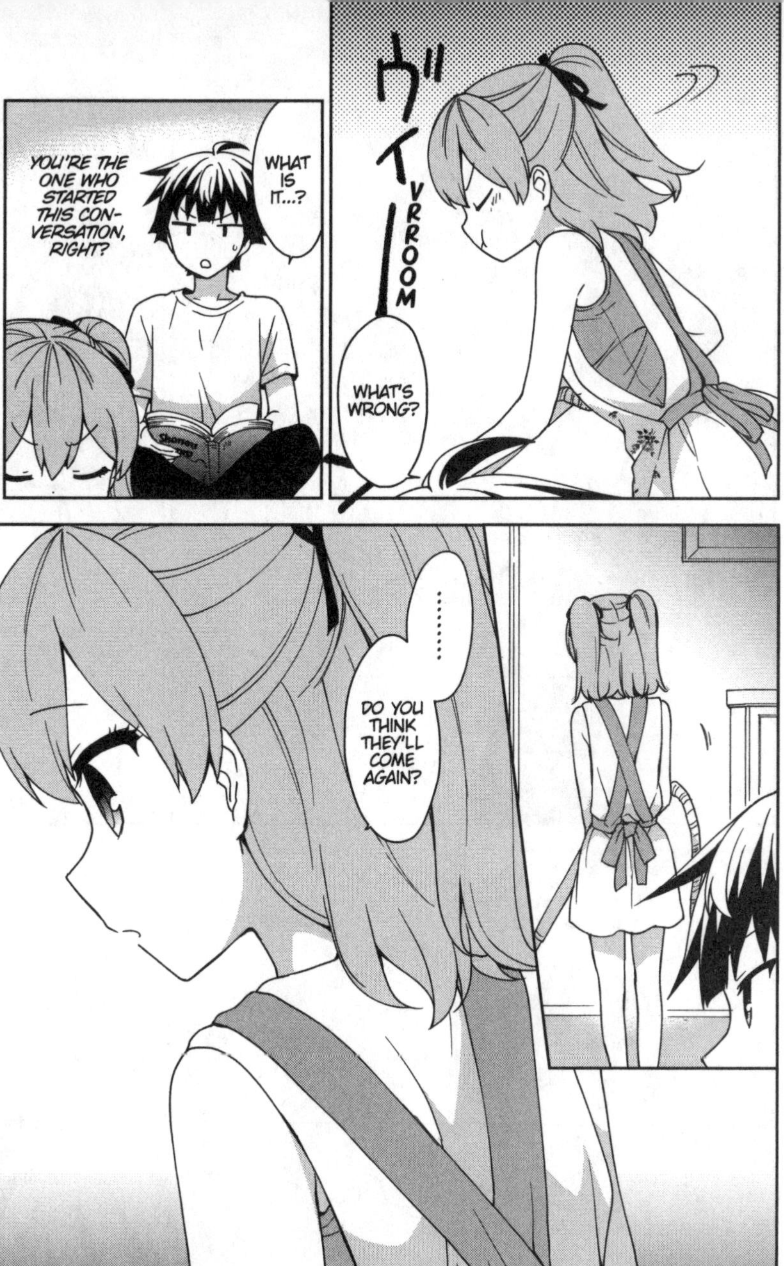
ヴィー
VRROOM
WHAT'S WRONG?
WHAT IS IT...?
YOU'RE THE ONE WHO STARTED THIS CONVERSATION, RIGHT?
......
DO YOU THINK THEY'LL COME AGAIN?

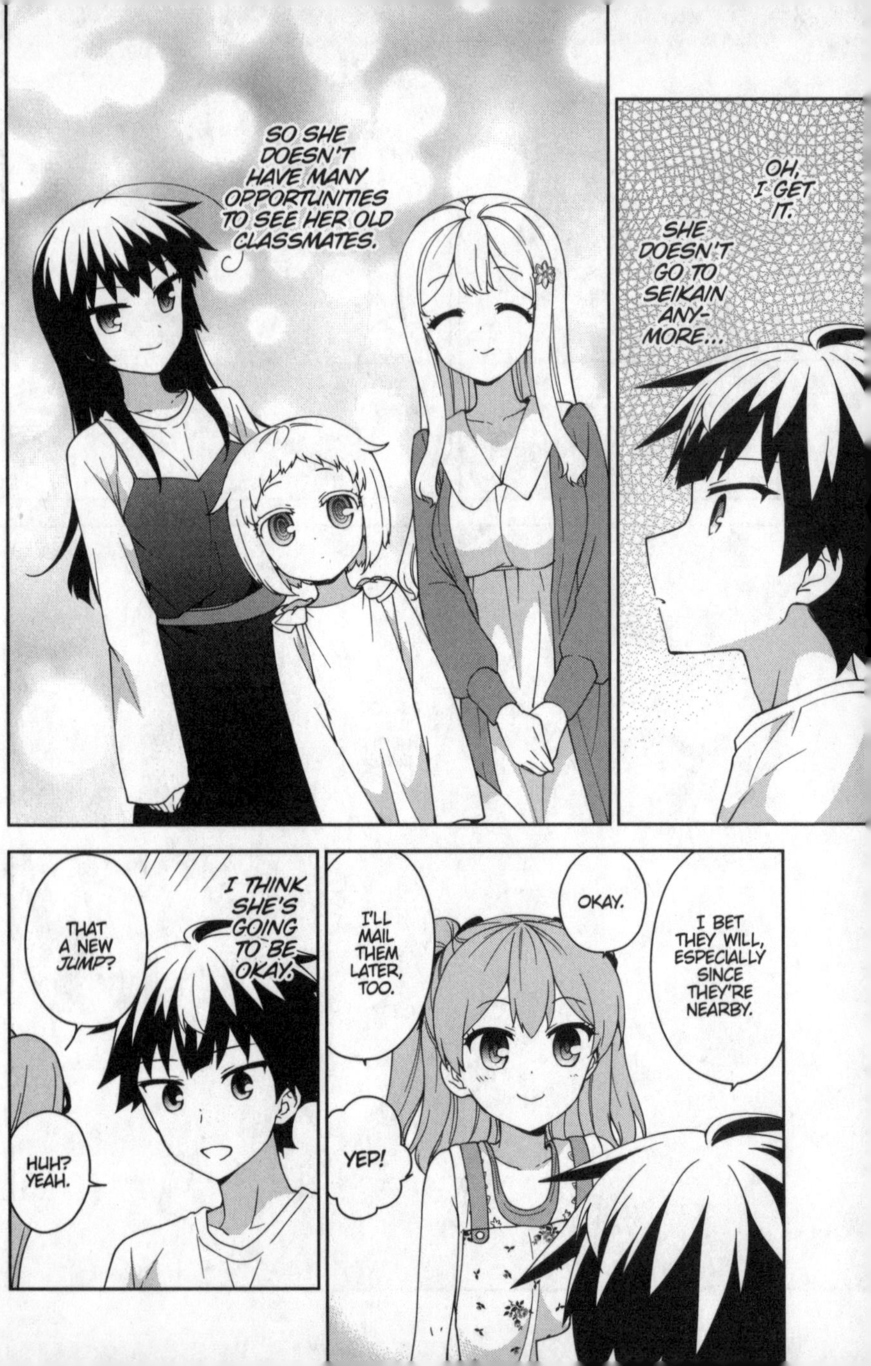
OH, I GET IT.
SHE DOESN'T GO TO SEIKAIN ANY-MORE...
SO SHE DOESN'T HAVE MANY OPPORTUNITIES TO SEE HER OLD CLASSMATES.
I BET THEY WILL, ESPECIALLY SINCE THEY'RE NEARBY.
OKAY.
I'LL MAIL THEM LATER, TOO.
YEP!
I THINK SHE'S GOING TO BE OKAY.
THAT A NEW JUMP?
HUH? YEAH.

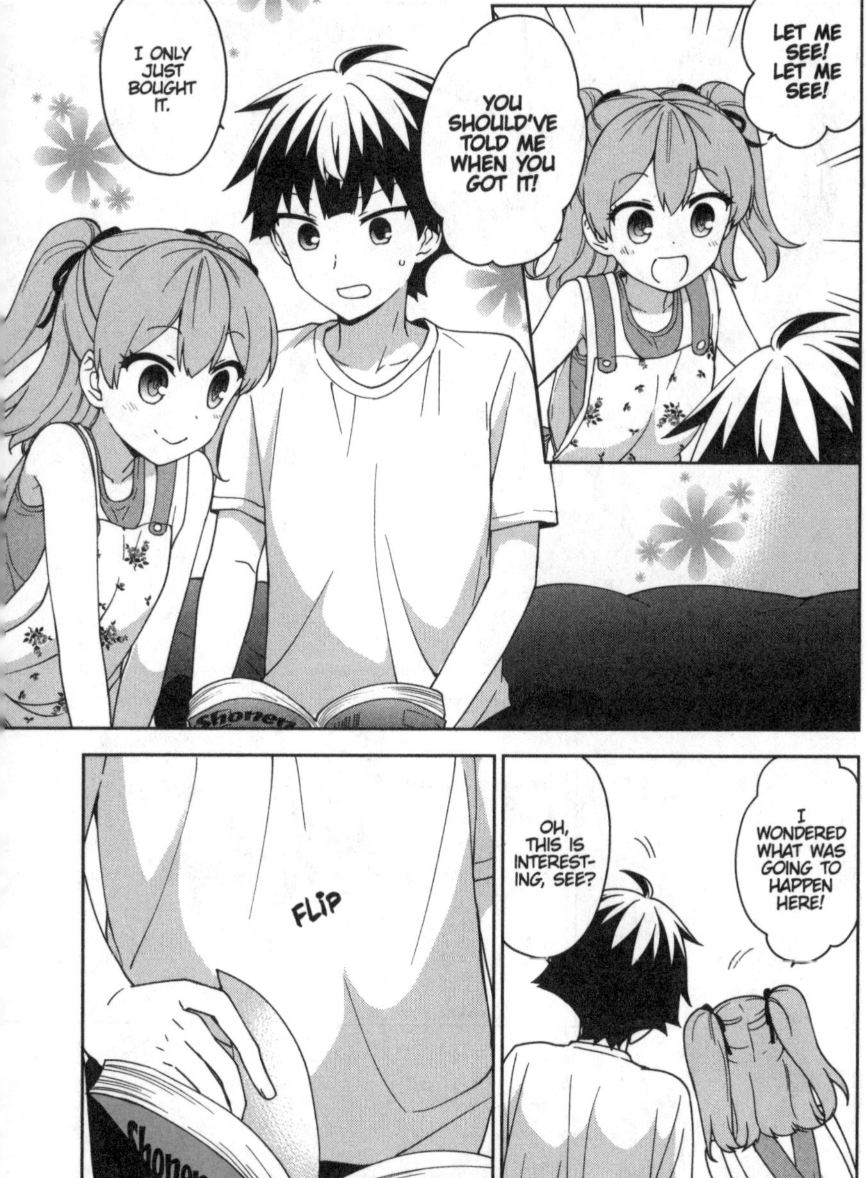
LET ME SEE! LET ME SEE!
YOU SHOULD'VE TOLD ME WHEN YOU GOT IT!
I ONLY JUST BOUGHT IT.
I WONDERED WHAT WAS GOING TO HAPPEN HERE!
OH, THIS IS INTEREST-ING, SEE?
FLIP

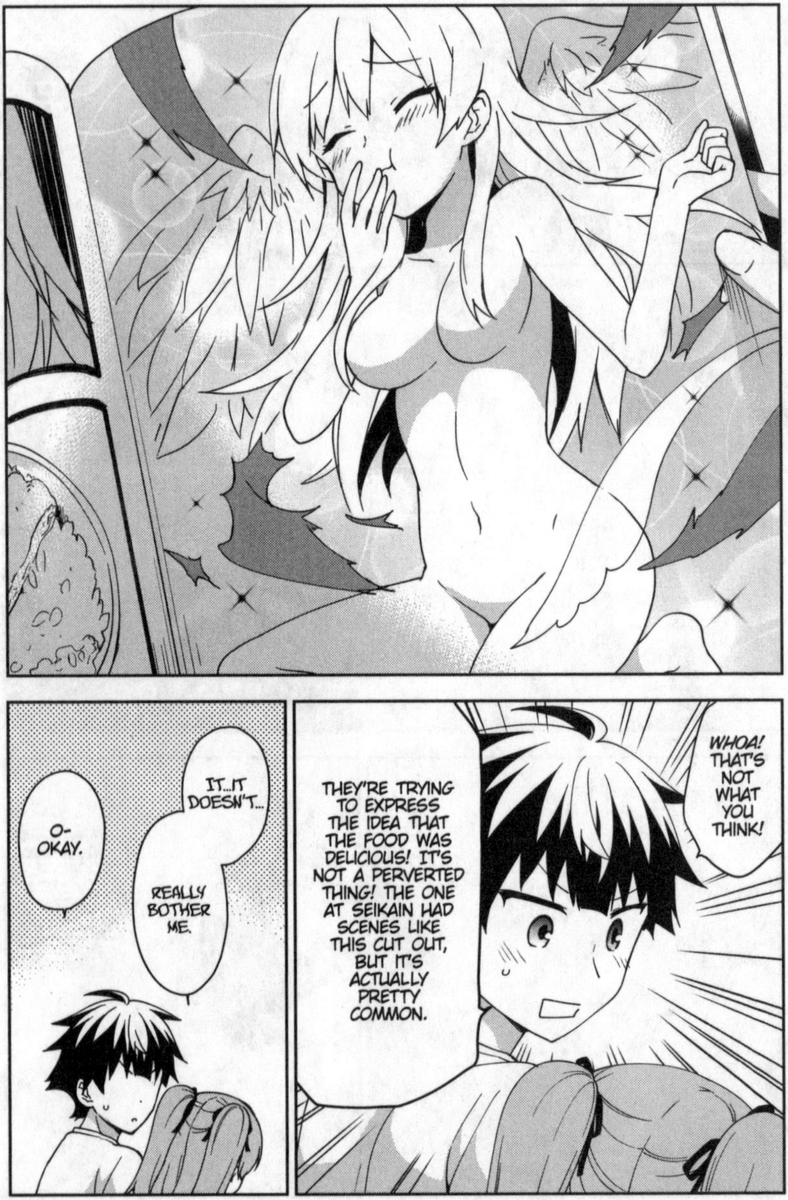
WHOA! THAT'S NOT WHAT YOU THINK!
THEY'RE TRYING TO EXPRESS THE IDEA THAT THE FOOD WAS DELICIOUS! IT'S NOT A PERVERTED THING! THE ONE AT SEIKAIN HAD SCENES LIKE THIS CUT OUT, BUT IT'S ACTUALLY PRETTY COMMON.
IT...IT DOESN'T...
REALLY BOTHER ME.
O-OKAY.

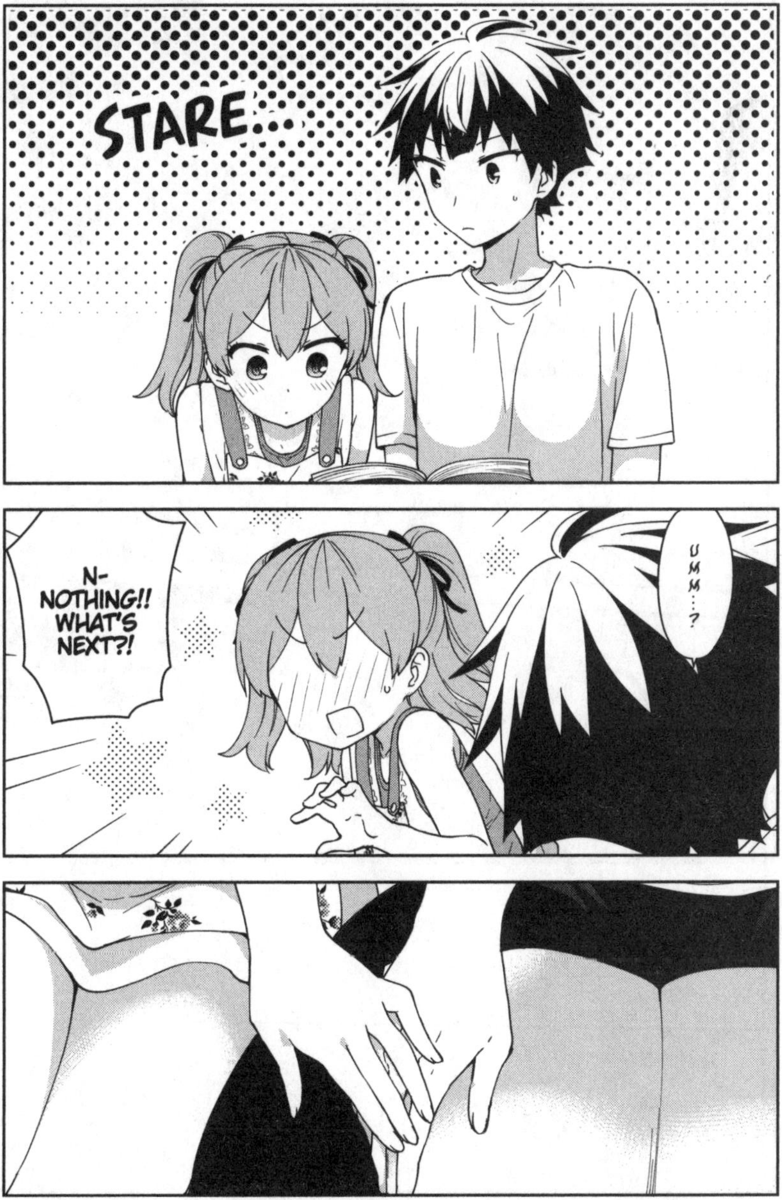
STARE...
UMM...?
N-NOTHING!! WHAT'S NEXT?!

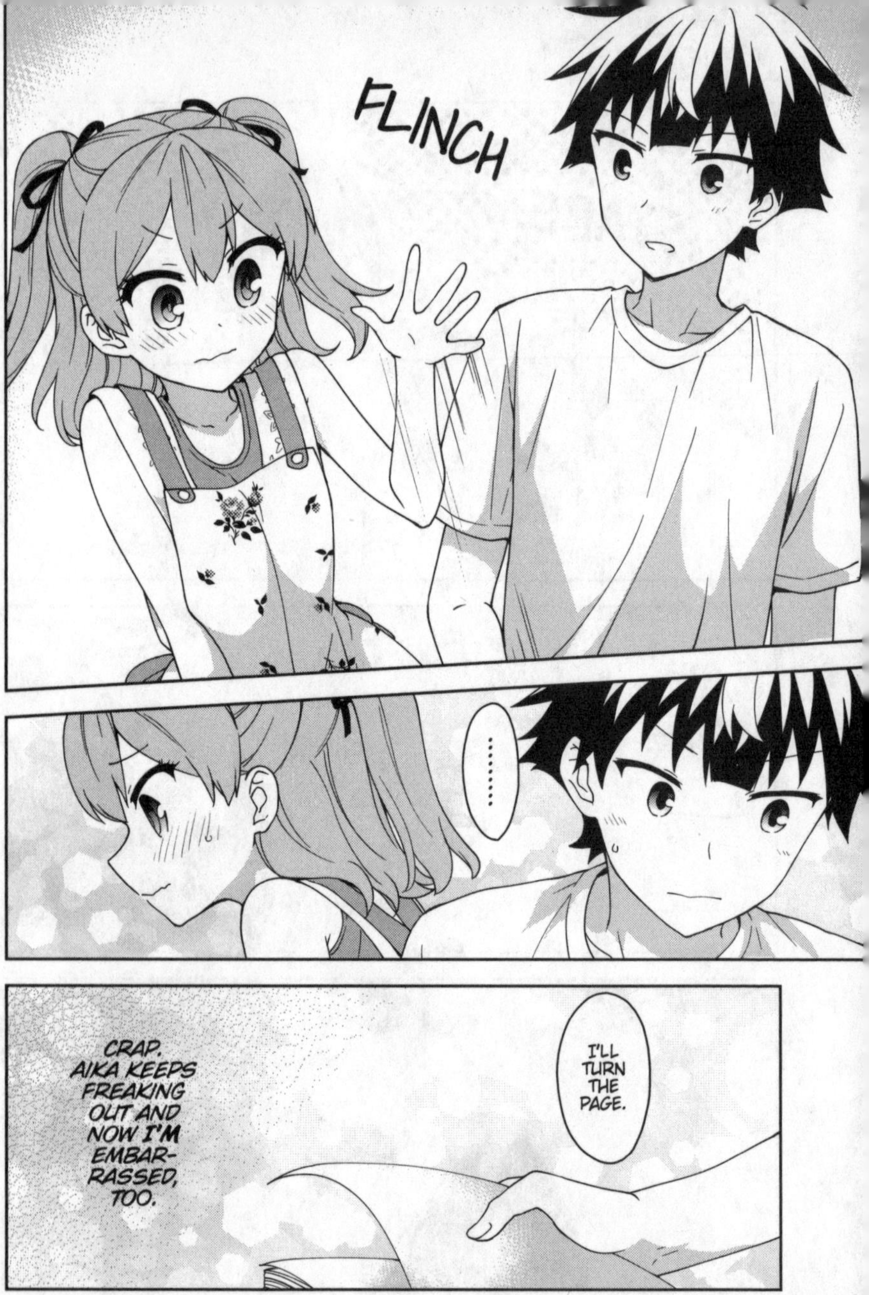
FLINCH
……
I'LL TURN THE PAGE.
CRAP. AIKA KEEPS FREAKING OUT AND NOW I'M EMBAR-RASSED, TOO.

SHOMIN SAMPLE 15

I Was Abducted by an Elite All-Girls
School as a Sample Commoner

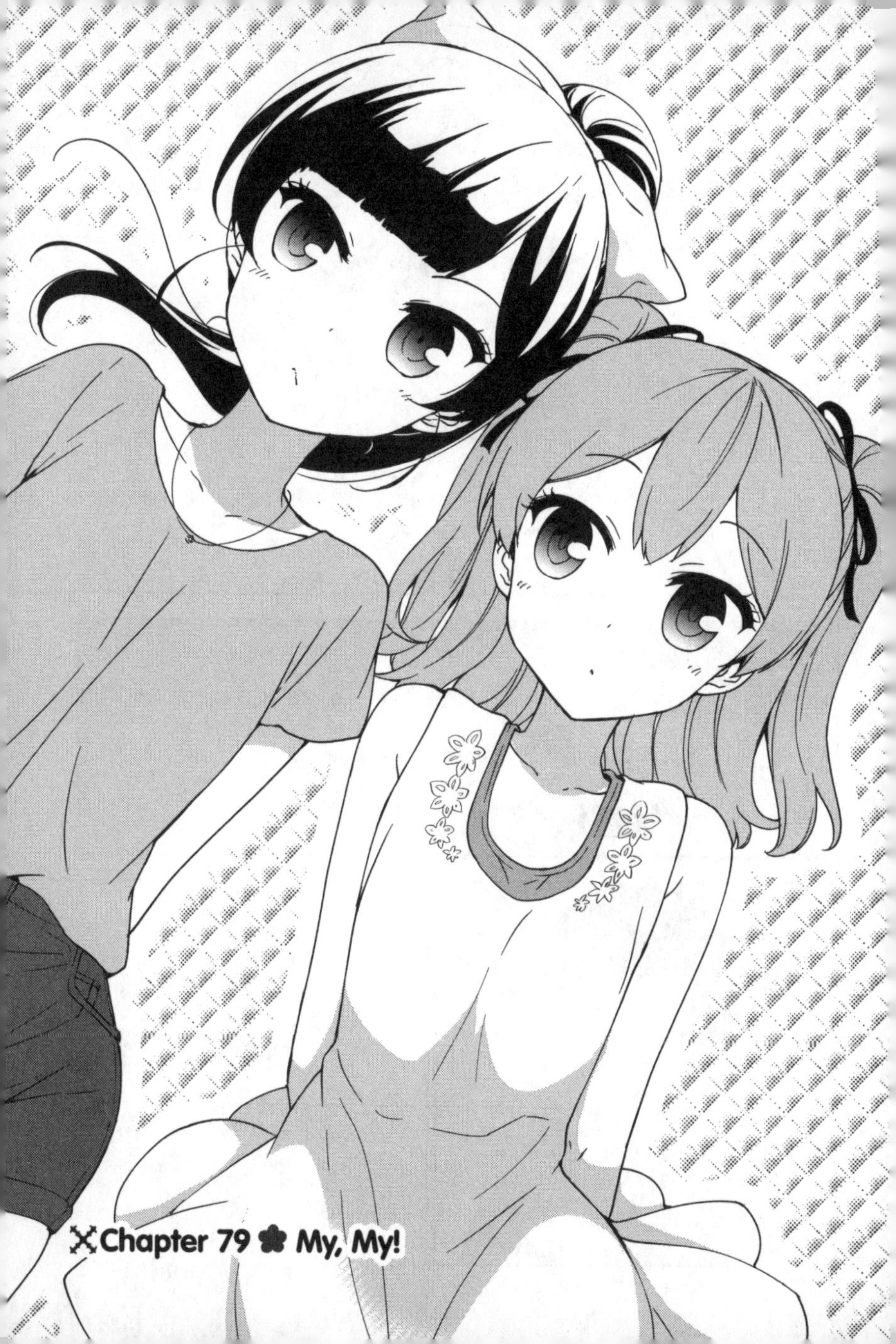

Chapter 79 ✿ My, My!

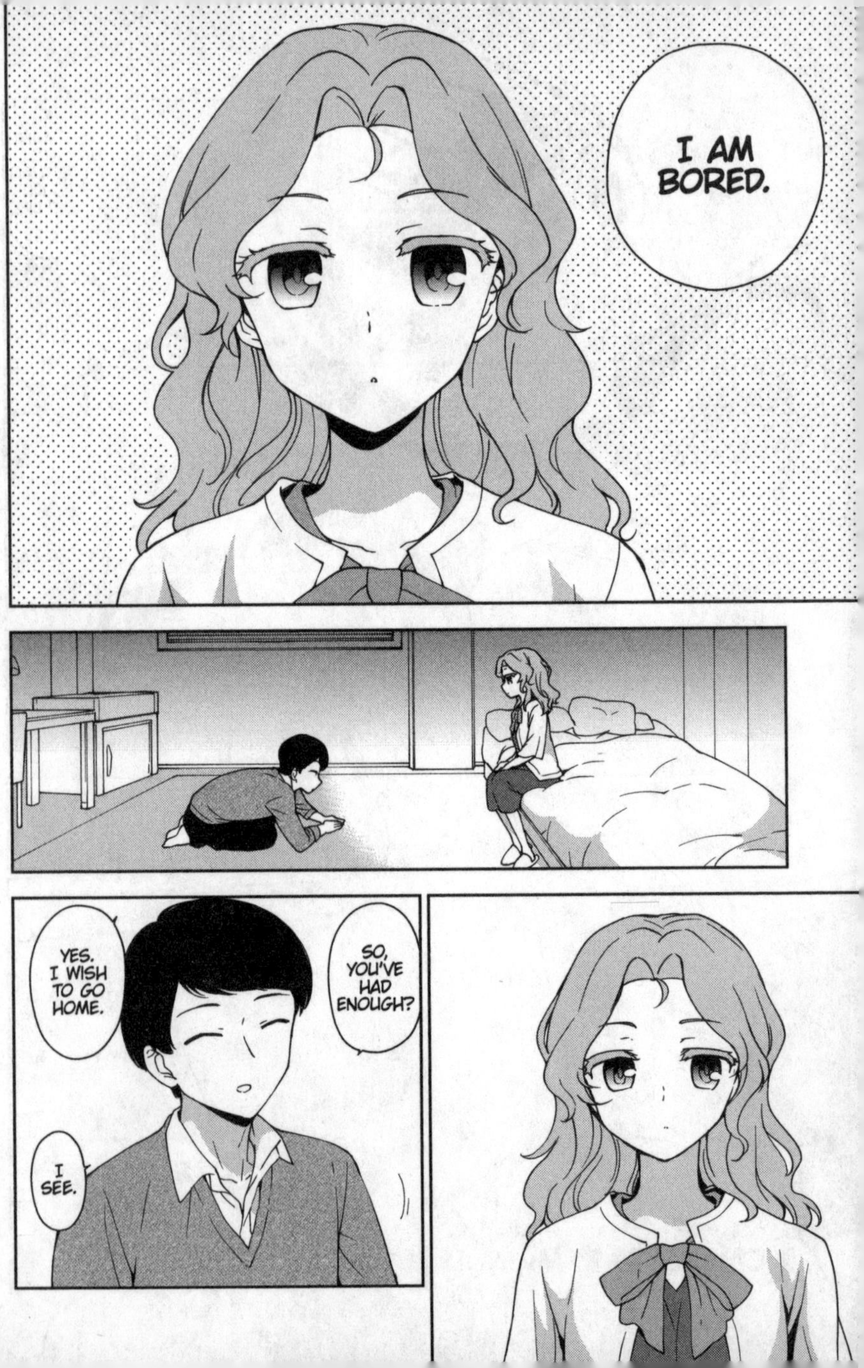
I AM BORED.
SO, YOU'VE HAD ENOUGH?
YES. I WISH TO GO HOME.
I SEE.

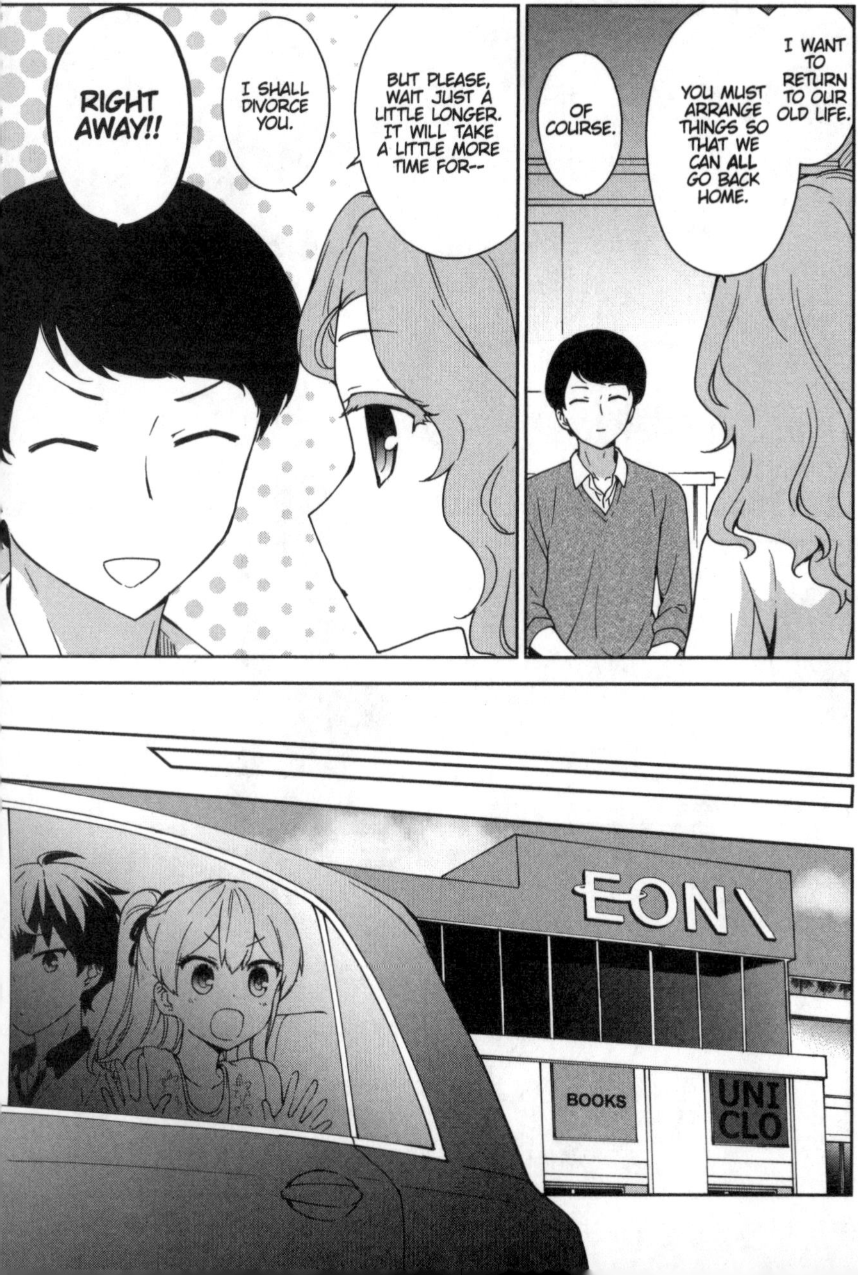
I WANT TO RETURN TO OUR OLD LIFE.
YOU MUST ARRANGE THINGS SO THAT WE CAN ALL GO BACK HOME.
OF COURSE.
BUT PLEASE, WAIT JUST A LITTLE LONGER. IT WILL TAKE A LITTLE MORE TIME FOR--
I SHALL DIVORCE YOU.
RIGHT AWAY!!
EON
BOOKS
UNI CLO

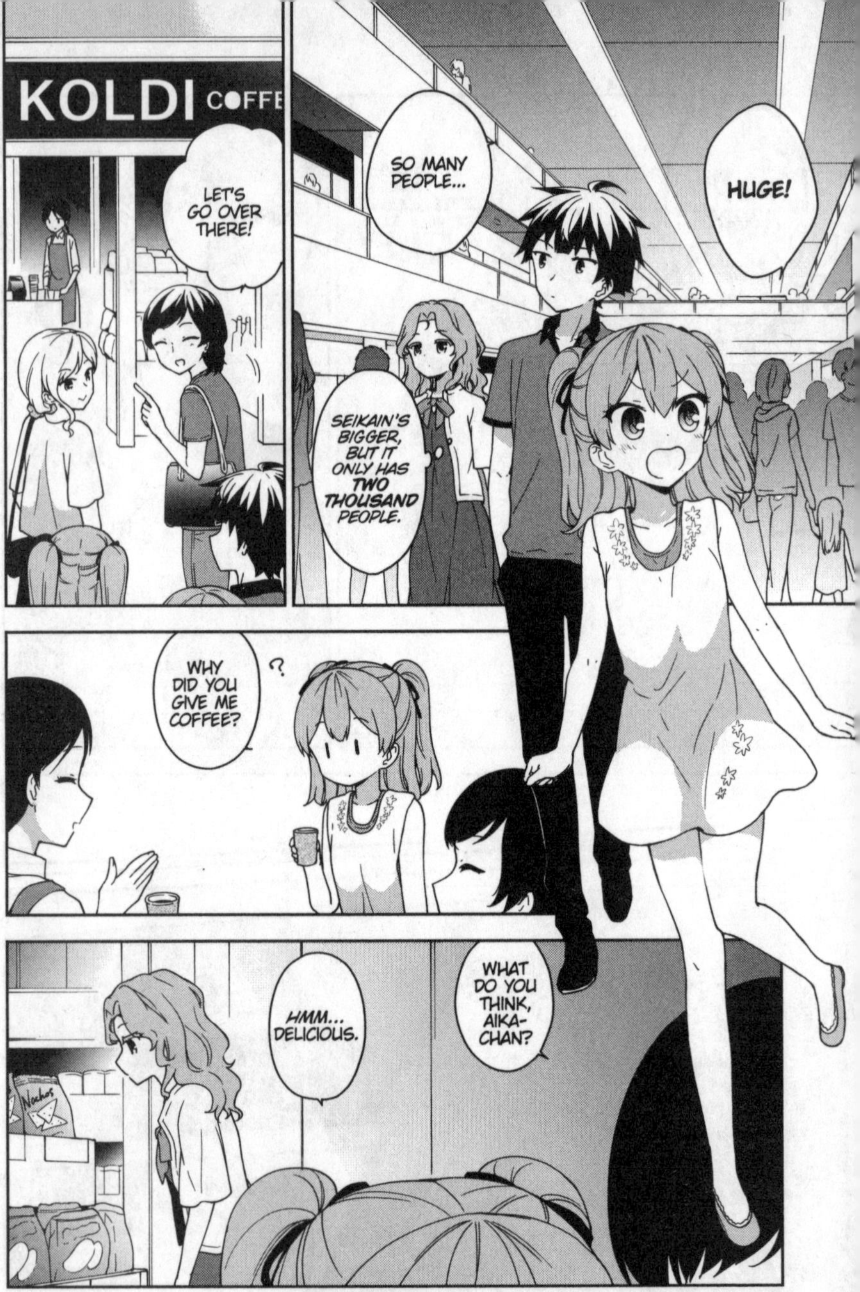
HUGE!
SO MANY PEOPLE...
SEIKAIN'S BIGGER, BUT IT ONLY HAS TWO THOUSAND PEOPLE.
KOLDI COFFE
LET'S GO OVER THERE!
WHY DID YOU GIVE ME COFFEE?
?
WHAT DO YOU THINK, AIKA-CHAN?
HMM... DELICIOUS.
Nachos

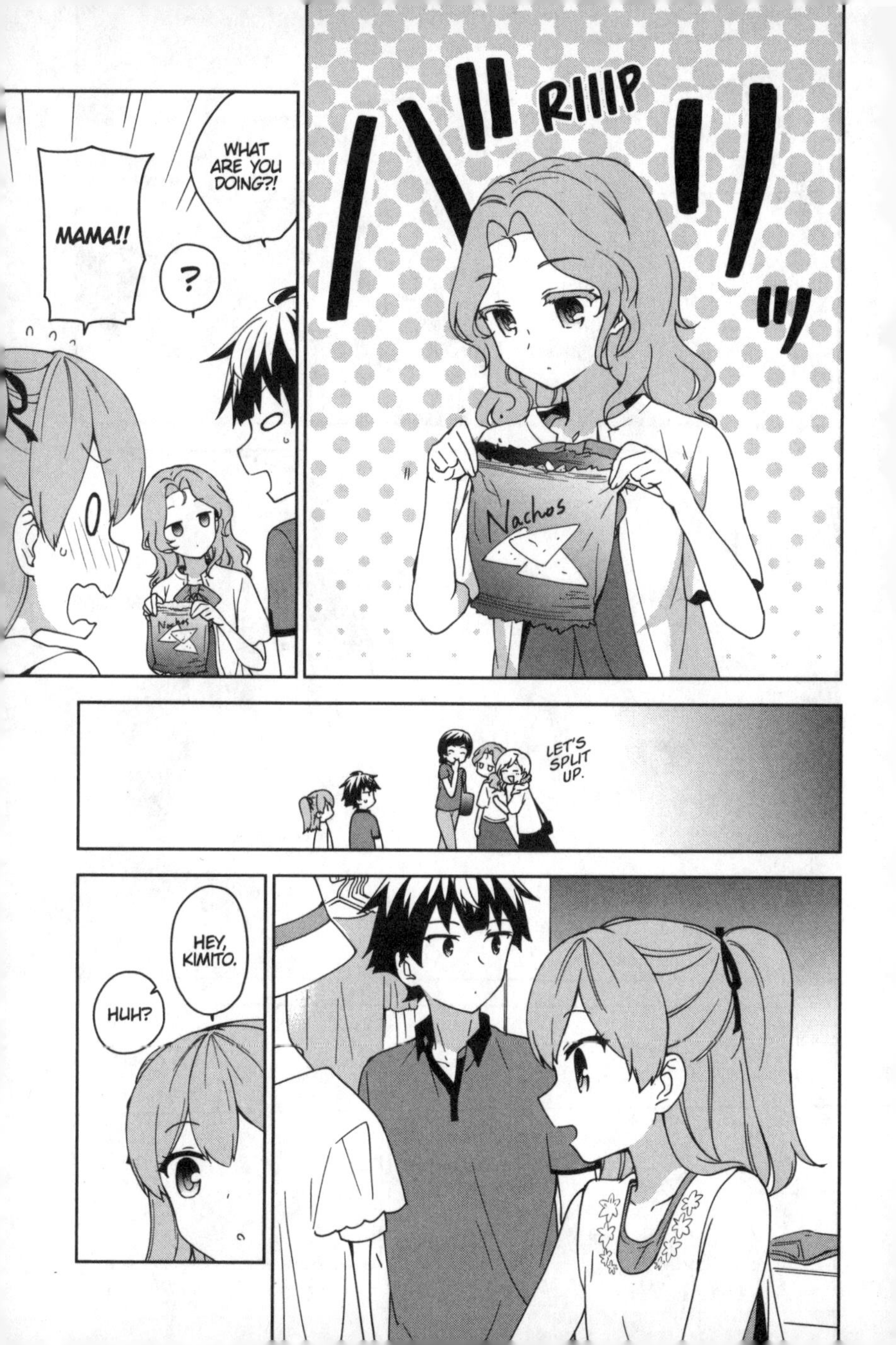
RIIIP
WHAT ARE YOU DOING?!
MAMA!!
?
LET'S SPLIT UP.
HEY, KIMITO.
HUH?

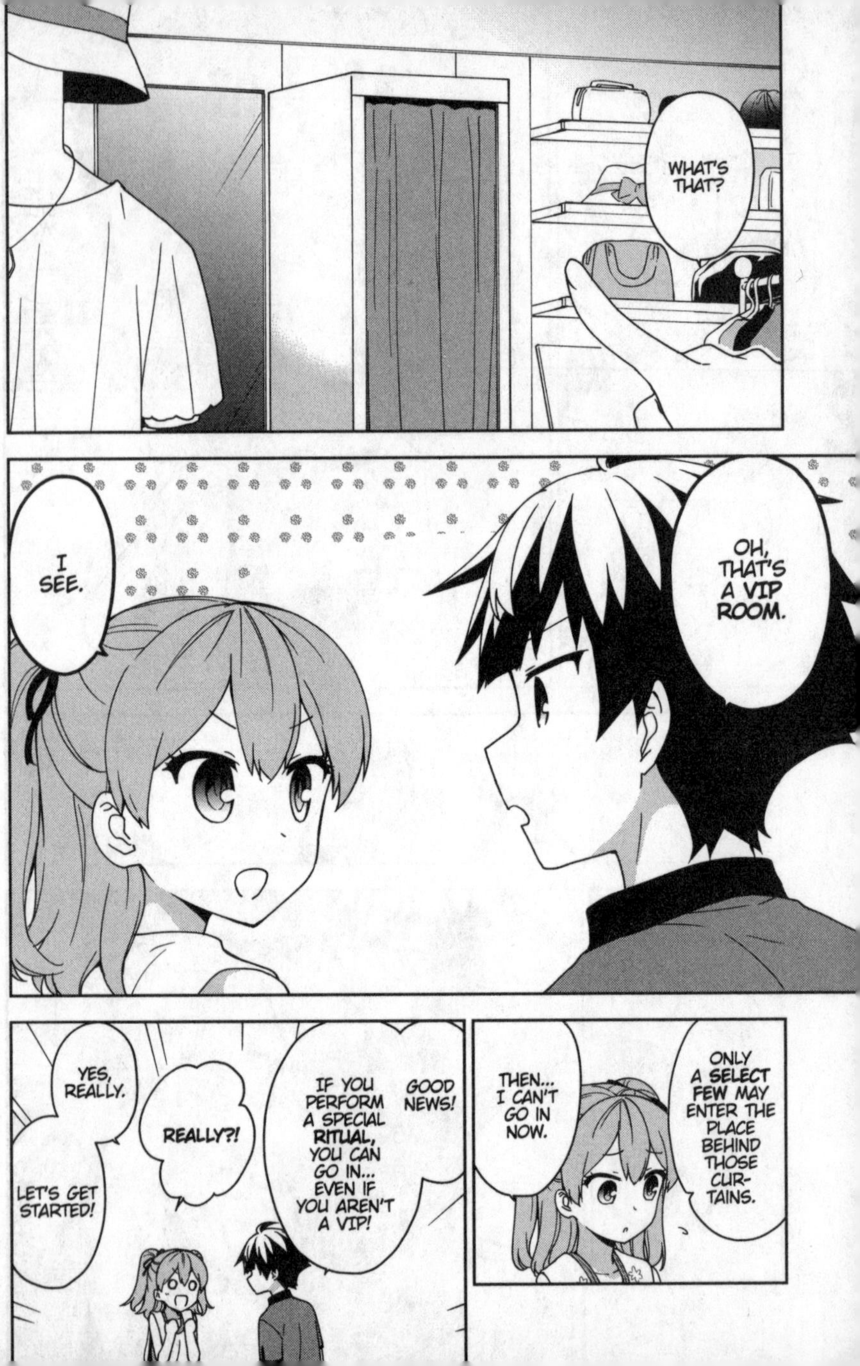
WHAT'S THAT?
OH, THAT'S A VIP ROOM.
I SEE.
ONLY A SELECT FEW MAY ENTER THE PLACE BEHIND THOSE CUR-TAINS.
THEN... I CAN'T GO IN NOW.
GOOD NEWS!
IF YOU PERFORM A SPECIAL RITUAL, YOU CAN GO IN... EVEN IF YOU AREN'T A VIP!
REALLY?!
YES, REALLY.
LET'S GET STARTED!

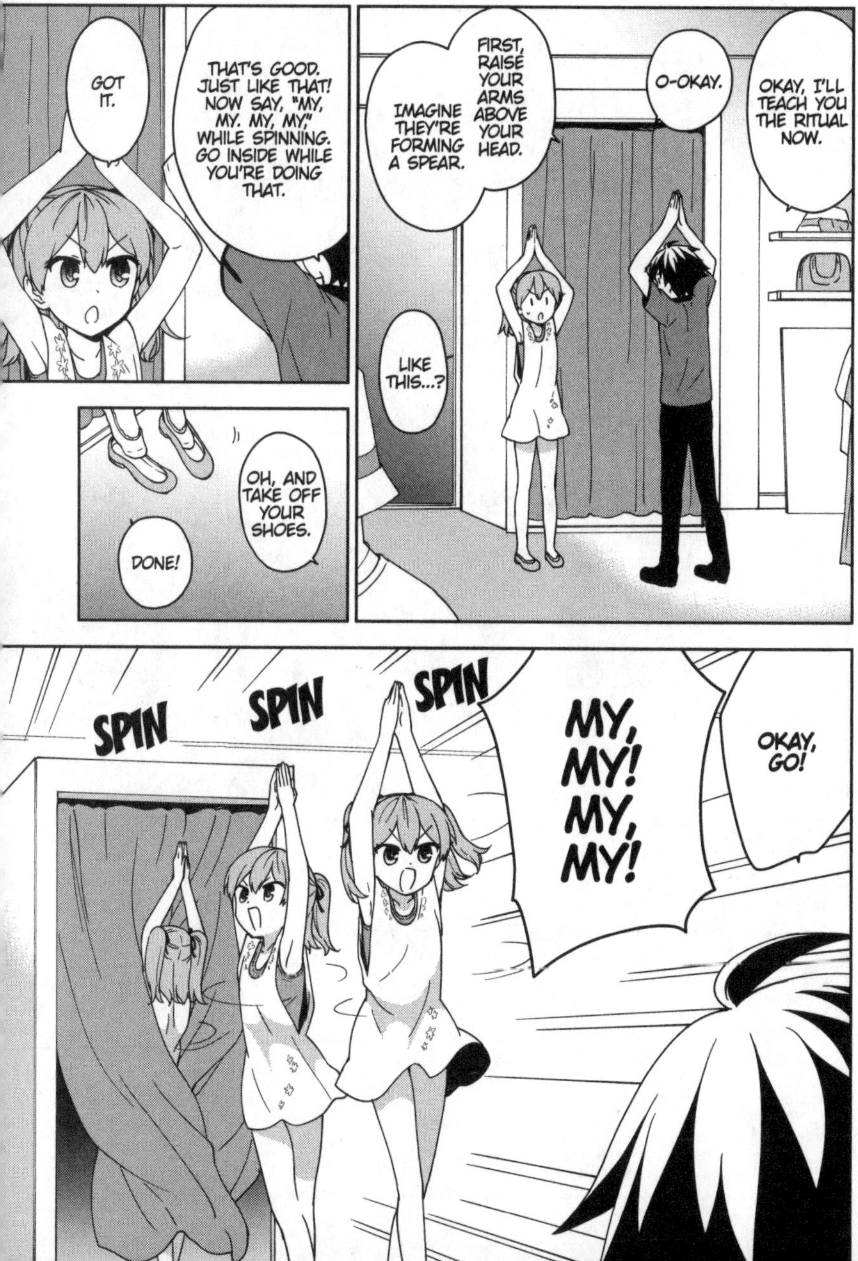
OKAY, I'LL TEACH YOU THE RITUAL NOW.
O-OKAY.
FIRST, RAISE YOUR ARMS ABOVE YOUR HEAD.
IMAGINE THEY'RE FORMING A SPEAR.
LIKE THIS...?
THAT'S GOOD. JUST LIKE THAT! NOW SAY, "MY, MY. MY, MY," WHILE SPINNING. GO INSIDE WHILE YOU'RE DOING THAT.
GOT IT.
OH, AND TAKE OFF YOUR SHOES.
DONE!
OKAY, GO!
MY, MY! MY, MY!
SPIN
SPIN
SPIN

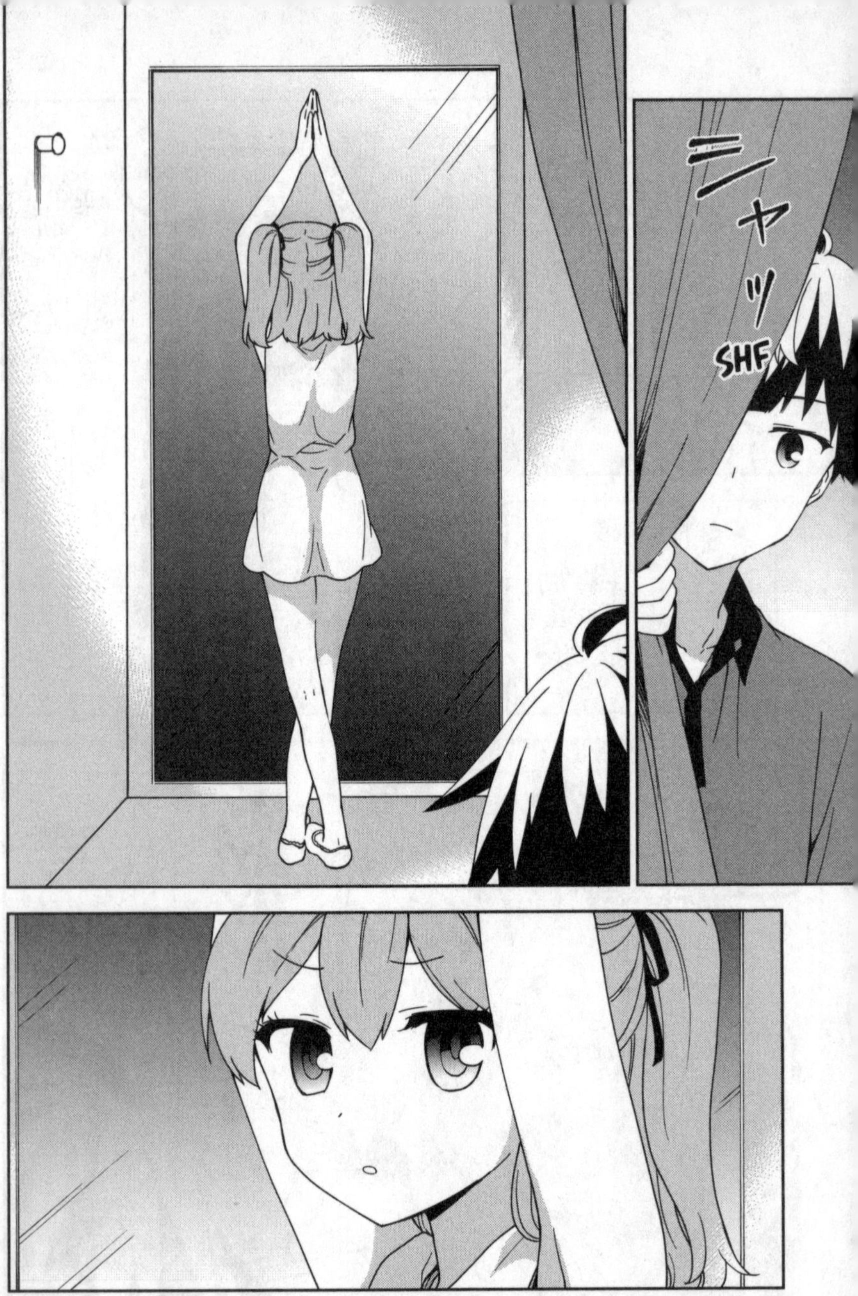
シャッ
SHF

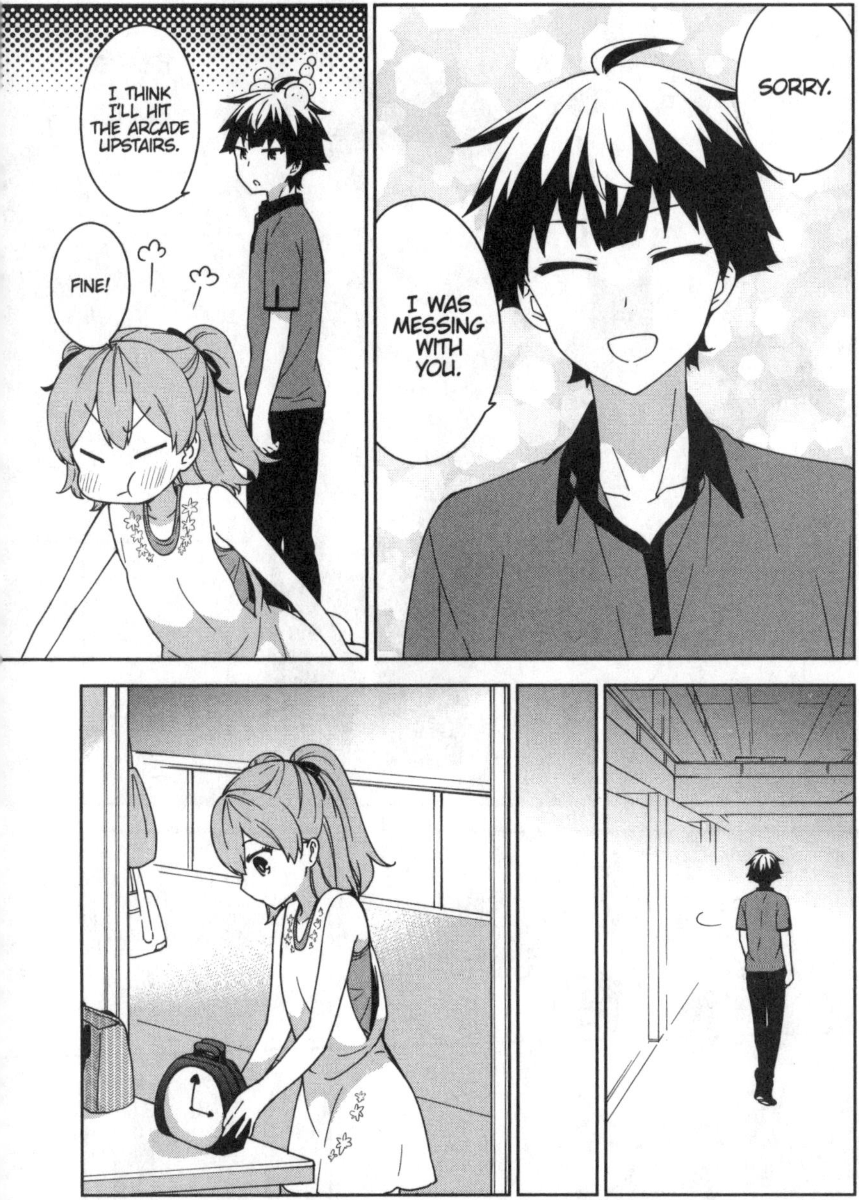
SORRY.
I WAS MESSING WITH YOU.
I THINK I'LL HIT THE ARCADE UPSTAIRS.
FINE!

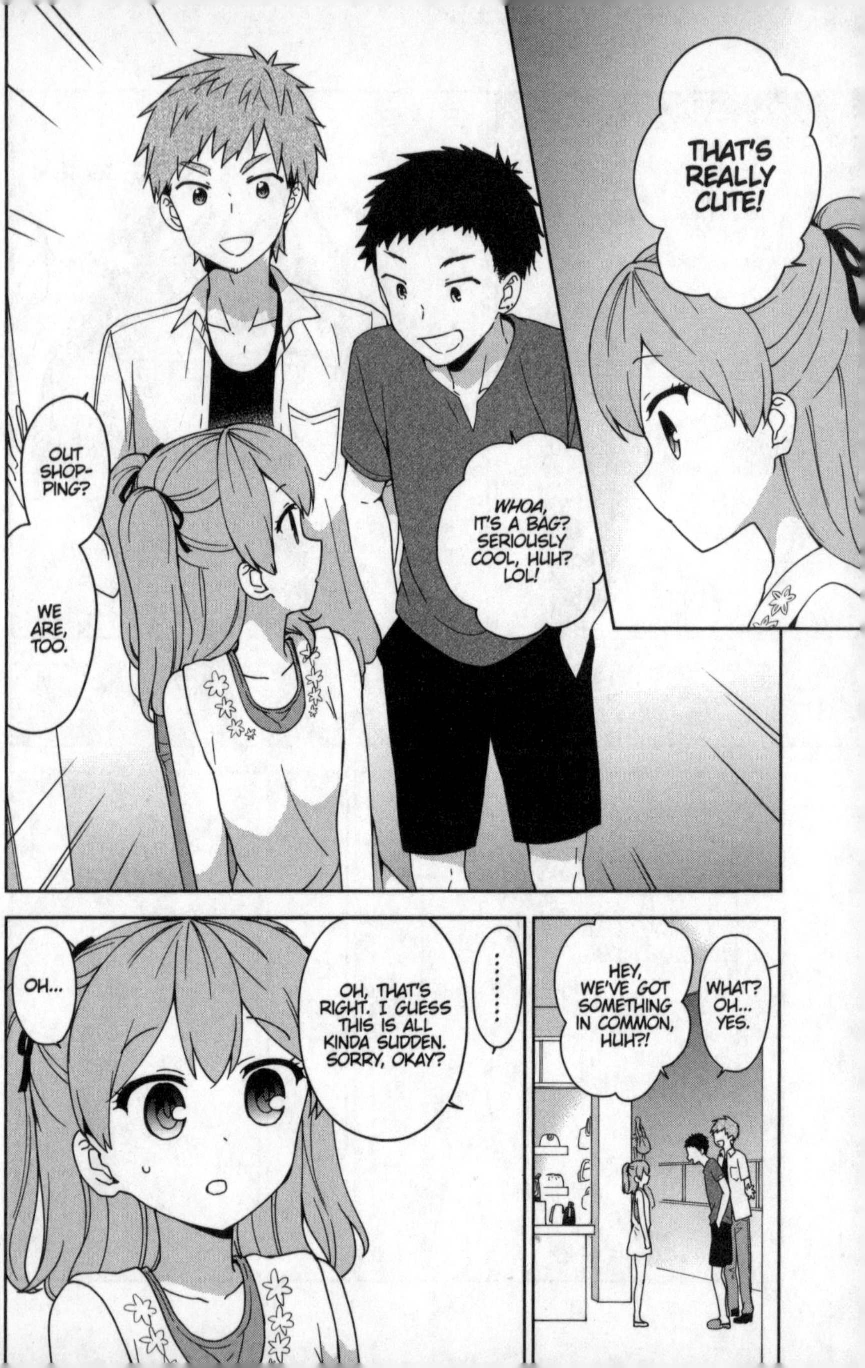
THAT'S REALLY CUTE!
OUT SHOP-PING?
WHOA, IT'S A BAG? SERIOUSLY COOL, HUH? LOL!
WE ARE, TOO.
HEY, WE'VE GOT SOMETHING IN COMMON, HUH?!
WHAT? OH... YES.
......
OH, THAT'S RIGHT. I GUESS THIS IS ALL KINDA SUDDEN. SORRY, OKAY?
OH...

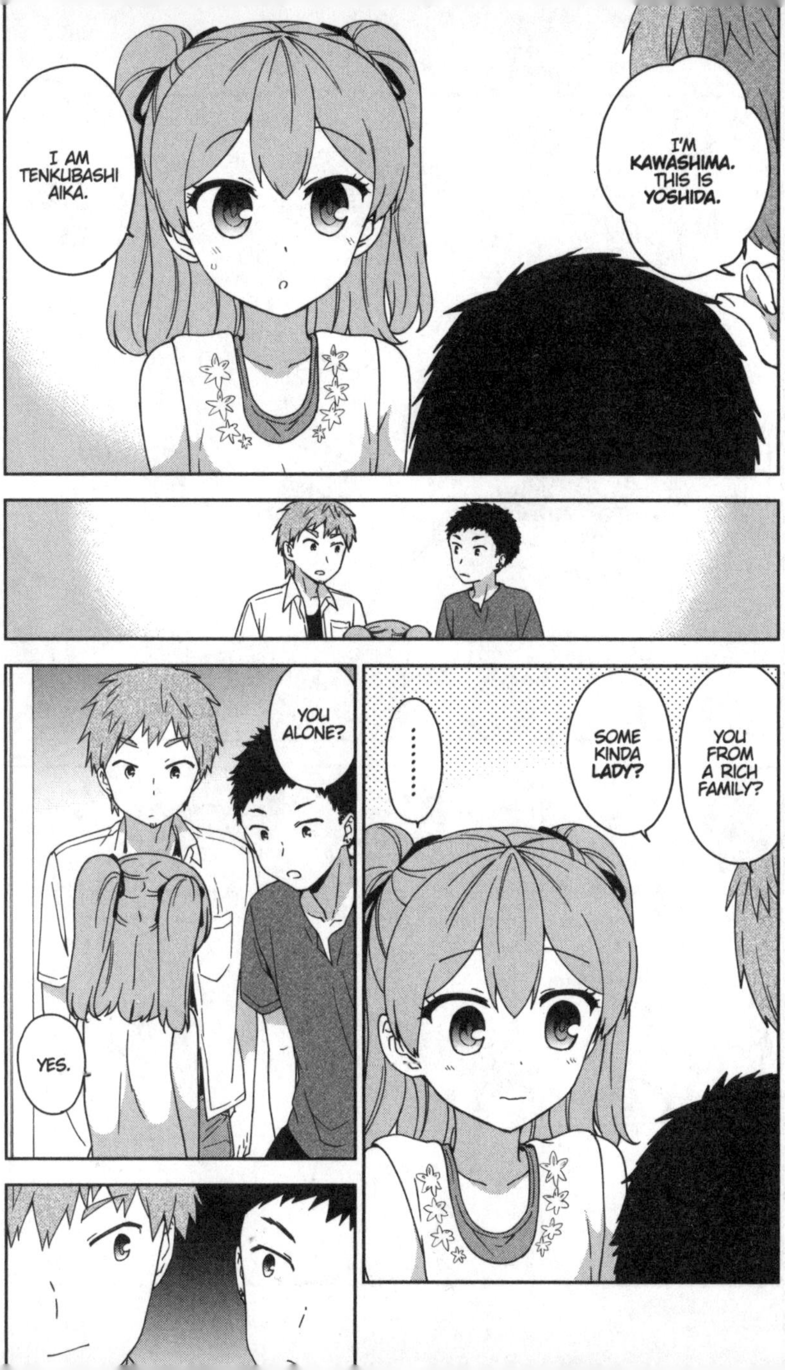
I'M KAWASHIMA. THIS IS YOSHIDA.
I AM TENKUBASHI AIKA.
YOU FROM A RICH FAMILY?
SOME KINDA LADY?
....
YOU ALONE?
YES.

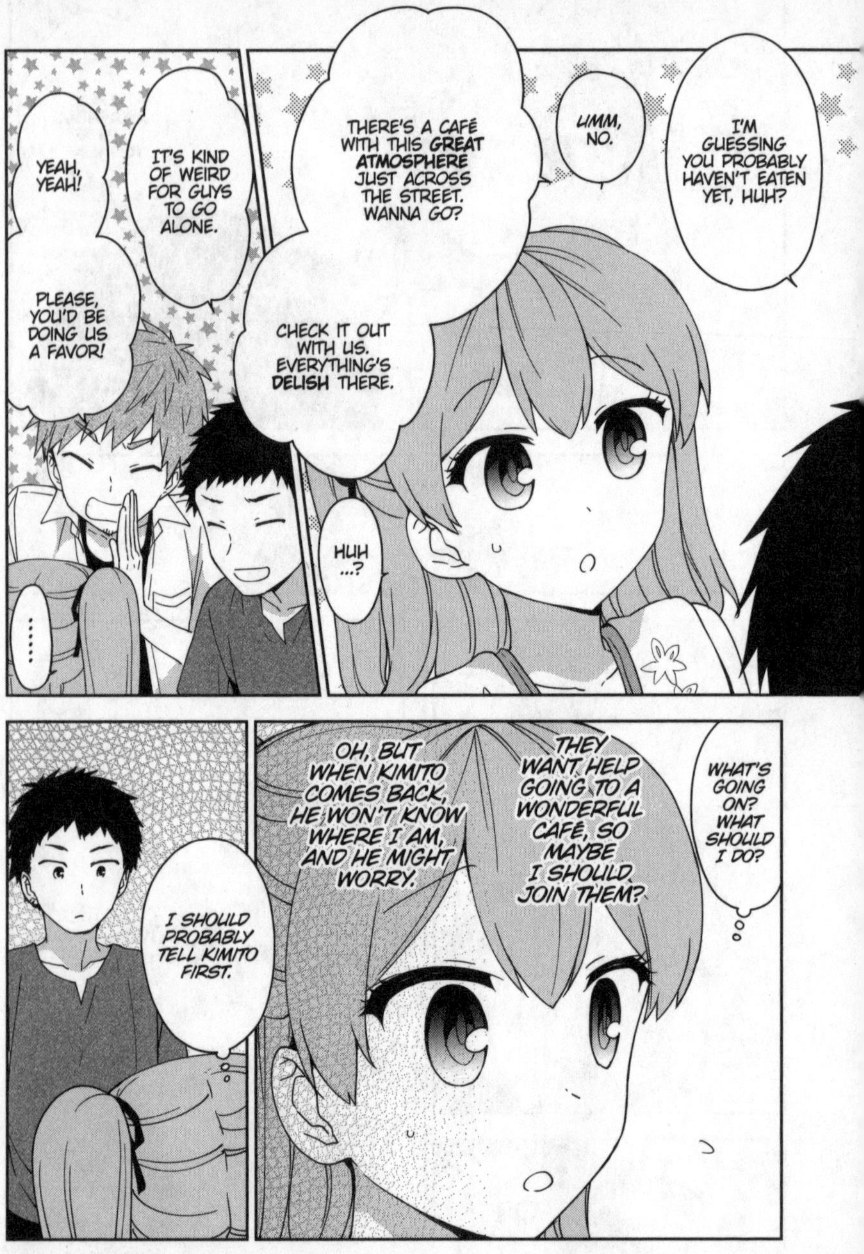

I'M GUESSING YOU PROBABLY HAVEN'T EATEN YET, HUH?
UMM, NO.
THERE'S A CAFÉ WITH THIS **GREAT ATMOSPHERE** JUST ACROSS THE STREET. WANNA GO?
CHECK IT OUT WITH US. EVERYTHING'S **DELISH** THERE.
HUH ...?
IT'S KIND OF WEIRD FOR GUYS TO GO ALONE.
YEAH, YEAH!
PLEASE, YOU'D BE DOING US A FAVOR!
......
WHAT'S GOING ON? WHAT SHOULD I DO?
THEY WANT HELP GOING TO A WONDERFUL CAFÉ, SO MAYBE I SHOULD JOIN THEM?
OH, BUT WHEN KIMITO COMES BACK, HE WON'T KNOW WHERE I AM, AND HE MIGHT WORRY.
I SHOULD PROBABLY TELL KIMITO FIRST.

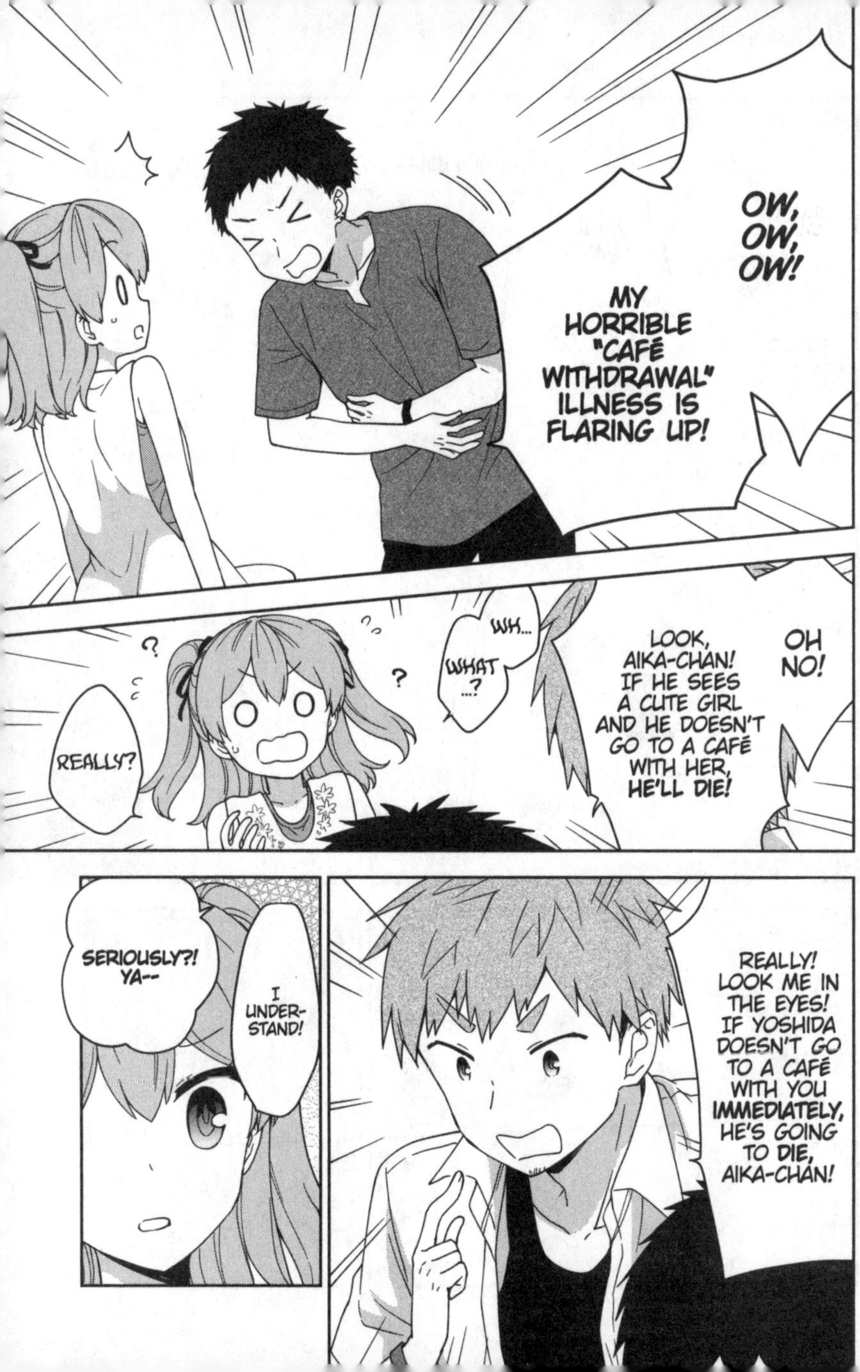
OW, OW, OW!
MY HORRIBLE "CAFÉ WITHDRAWAL" ILLNESS IS FLARING UP!
OH NO!
LOOK, AIKA-CHAN! IF HE SEES A CUTE GIRL AND HE DOESN'T GO TO A CAFÉ WITH HER, HE'LL DIE!
WH...
WHAT ...?
REALLY?
REALLY! LOOK ME IN THE EYES! IF YOSHIDA DOESN'T GO TO A CAFÉ WITH YOU IMMEDIATELY, HE'S GOING TO DIE, AIKA-CHAN!
I UNDER-STAND!
SERIOUSLY?! YA--

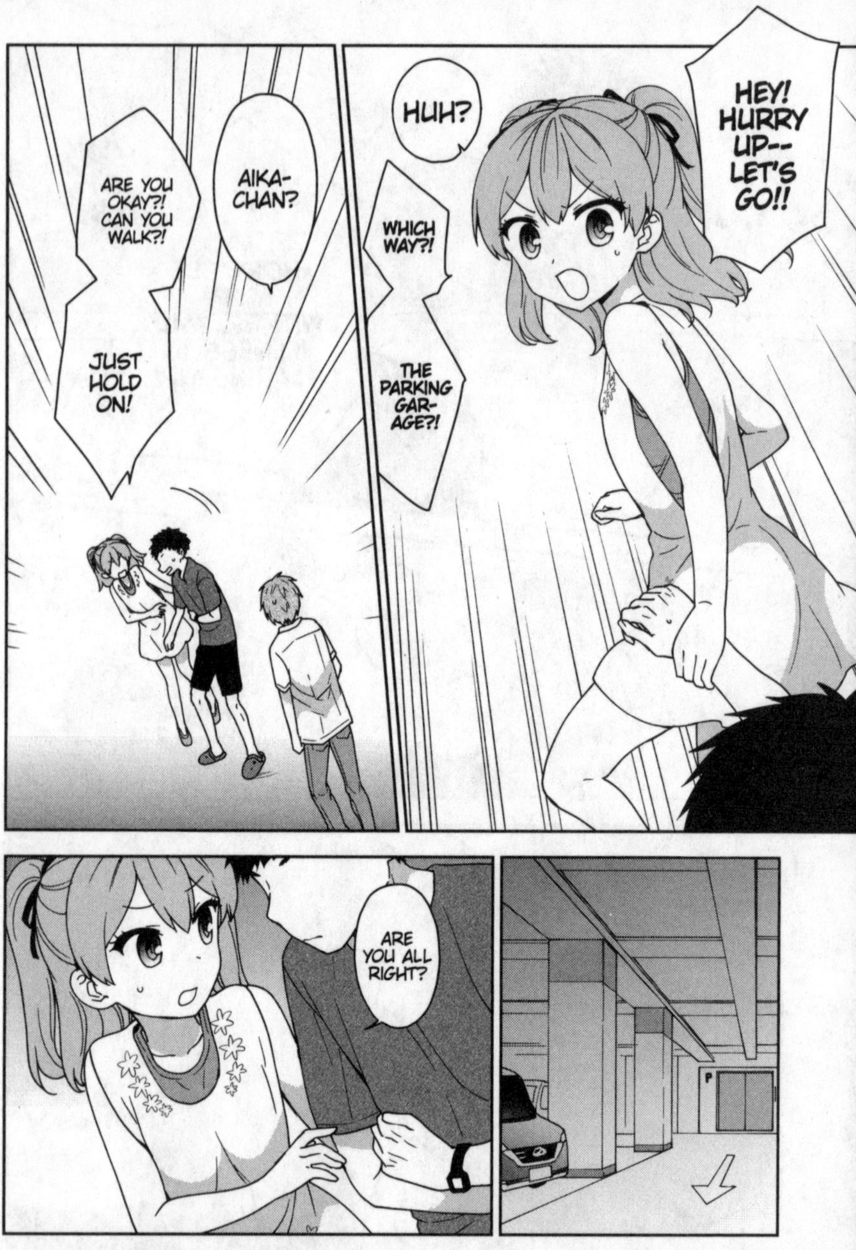
HEY! HURRY UP-- LET'S GO!!
HUH?
WHICH WAY?!
THE PARKING GAR-AGE?!
AIKA-CHAN?
ARE YOU OKAY?! CAN YOU WALK?!
JUST HOLD ON!
ARE YOU ALL RIGHT?

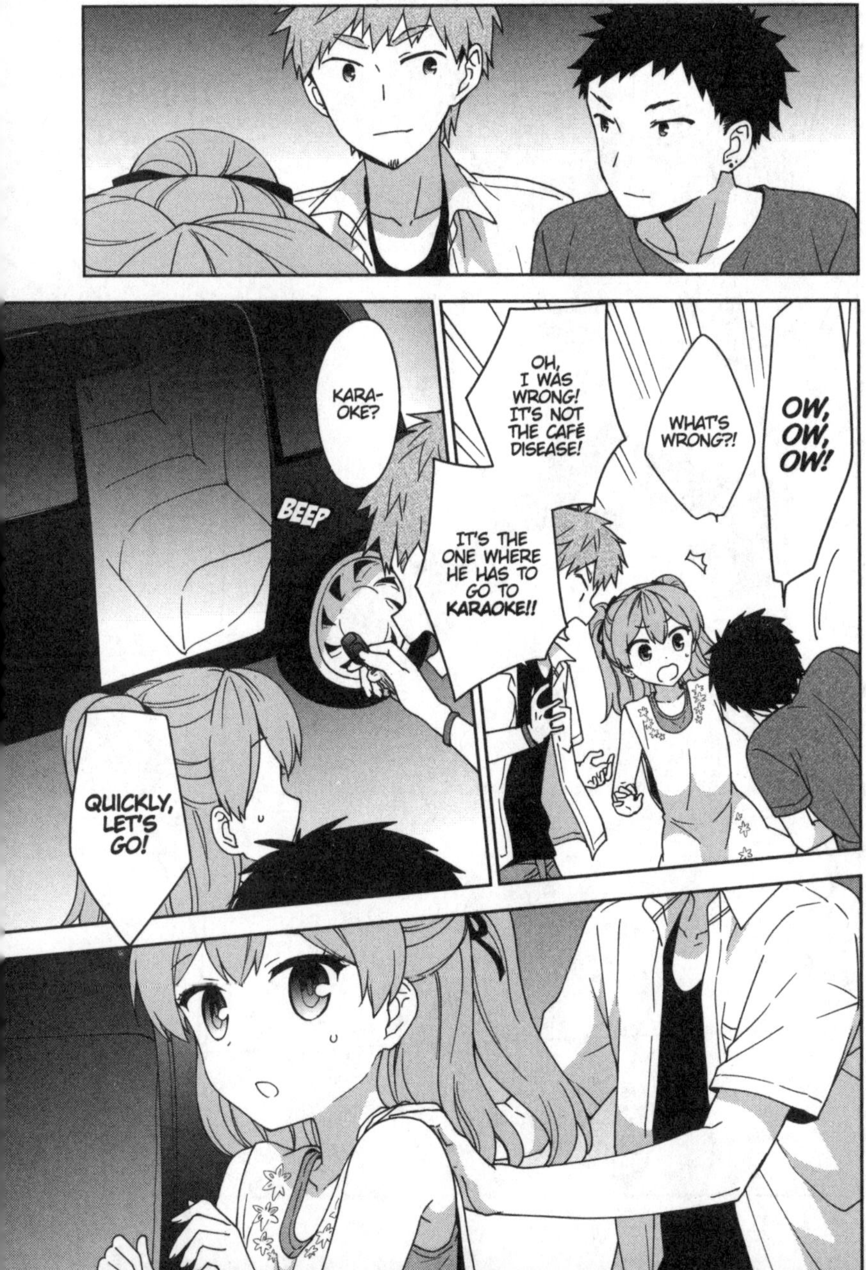
OW, OW, OW!
WHAT'S WRONG?!
OH, I WAS WRONG! IT'S NOT THE CAFÉ DISEASE!
IT'S THE ONE WHERE HE HAS TO GO TO KARAOKE!!
KARA-OKE?
BEEP
QUICKLY, LET'S GO!

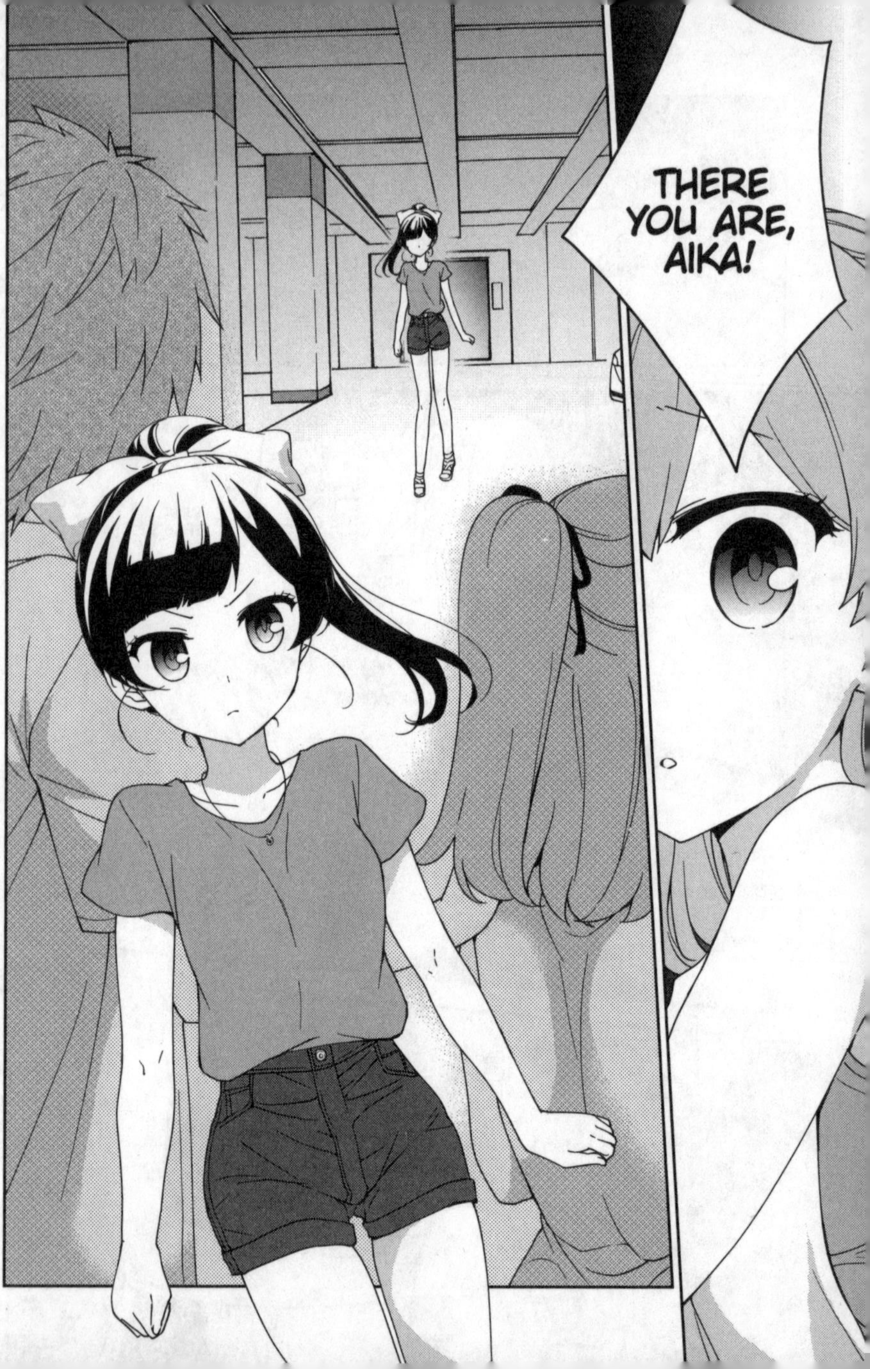
THERE YOU ARE, AIKA!

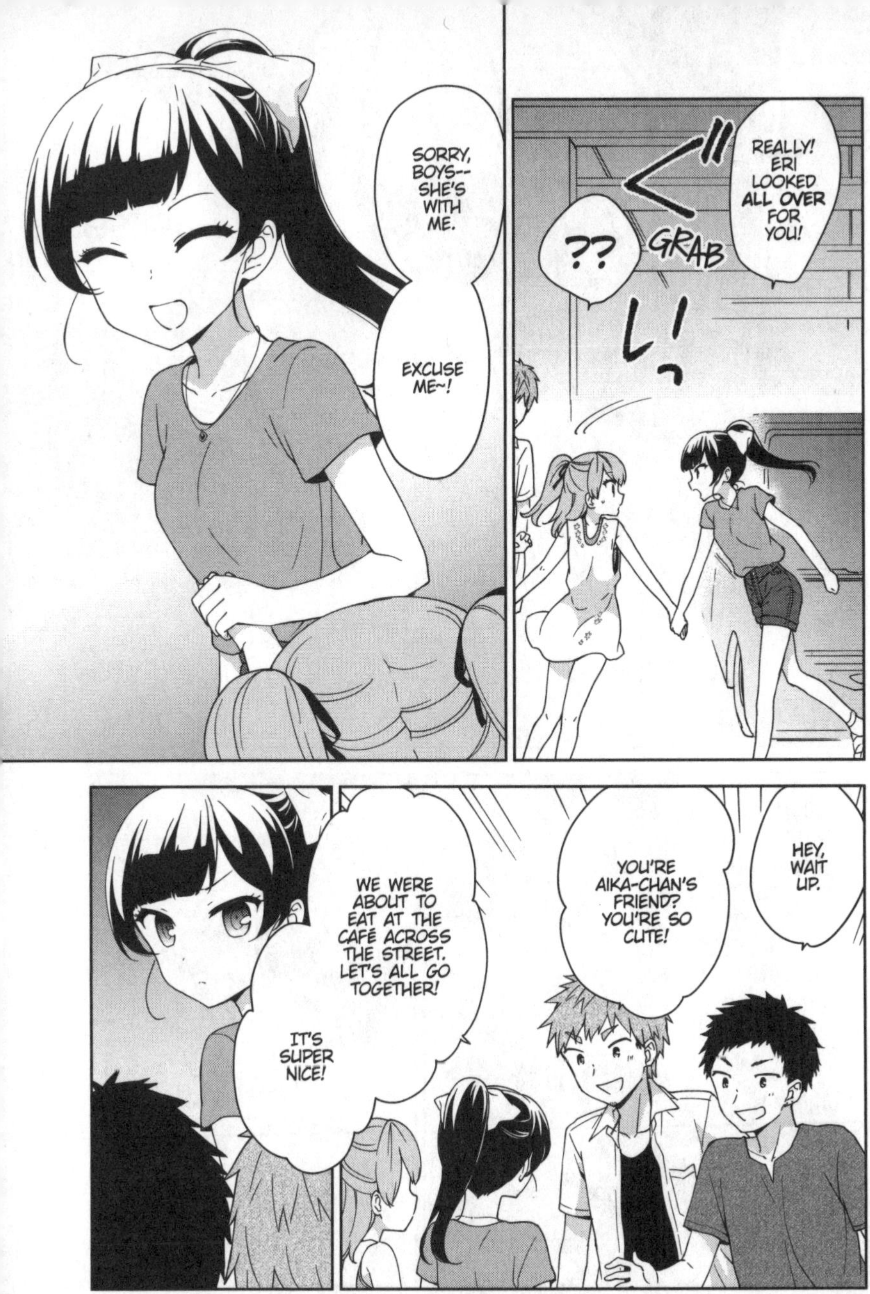
REALLY! ERI LOOKED ALL OVER FOR YOU!
??
GRAB
SORRY, BOYS-- SHE'S WITH ME.
EXCUSE ME~!
HEY, WAIT UP.
YOU'RE AIKA-CHAN'S FRIEND? YOU'RE SO CUTE!
WE WERE ABOUT TO EAT AT THE CAFÉ ACROSS THE STREET. LET'S ALL GO TOGETHER!
IT'S SUPER NICE!

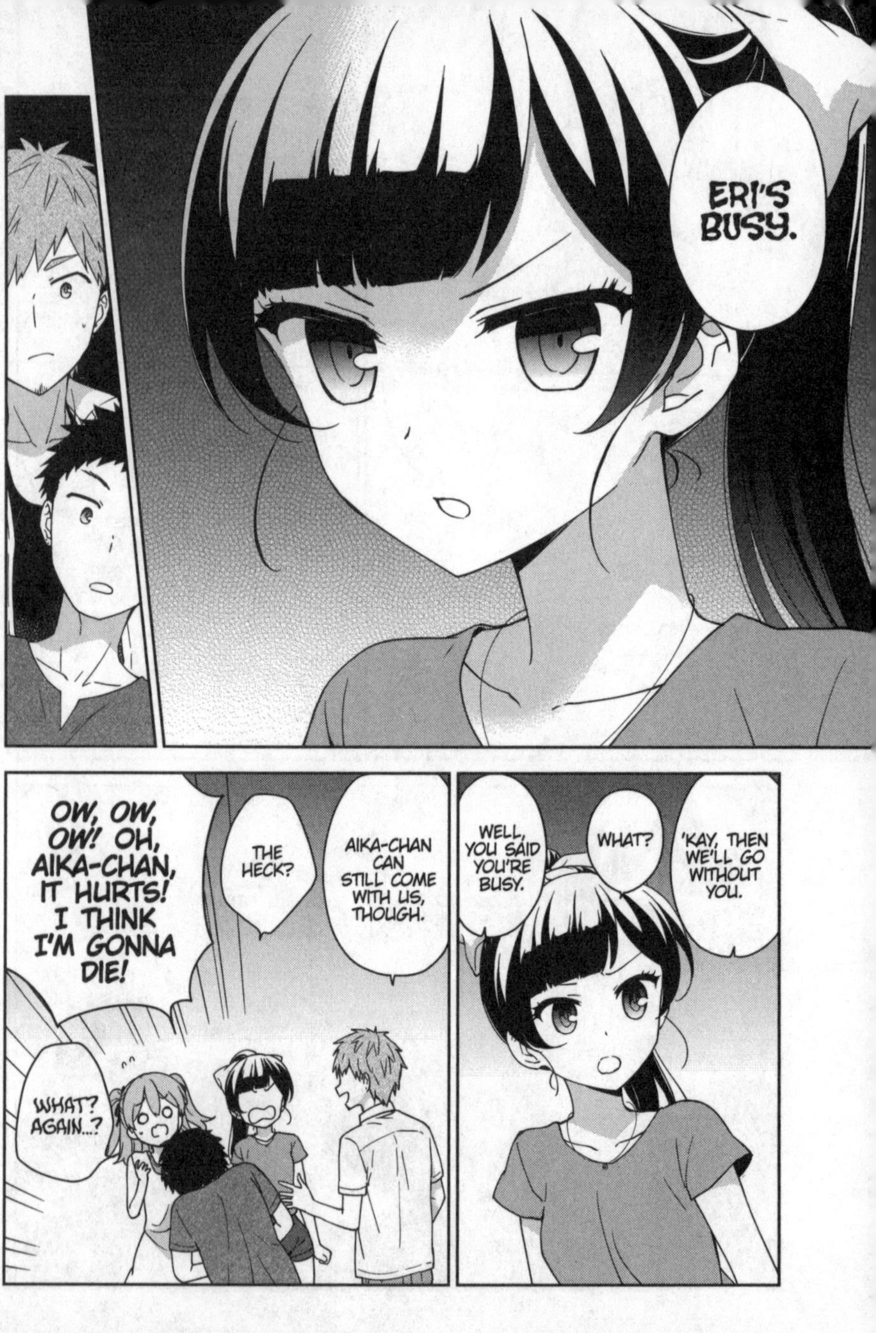
ERI'S BUSY.
'KAY, THEN WE'LL GO WITHOUT YOU.
WHAT?
WELL, YOU SAID YOU'RE BUSY.
AIKA-CHAN CAN STILL COME WITH US, THOUGH.
THE HECK?
OW, OW, OW! OH, AIKA-CHAN, IT HURTS! I THINK I'M GONNA DIE!
WHAT? AGAIN...?

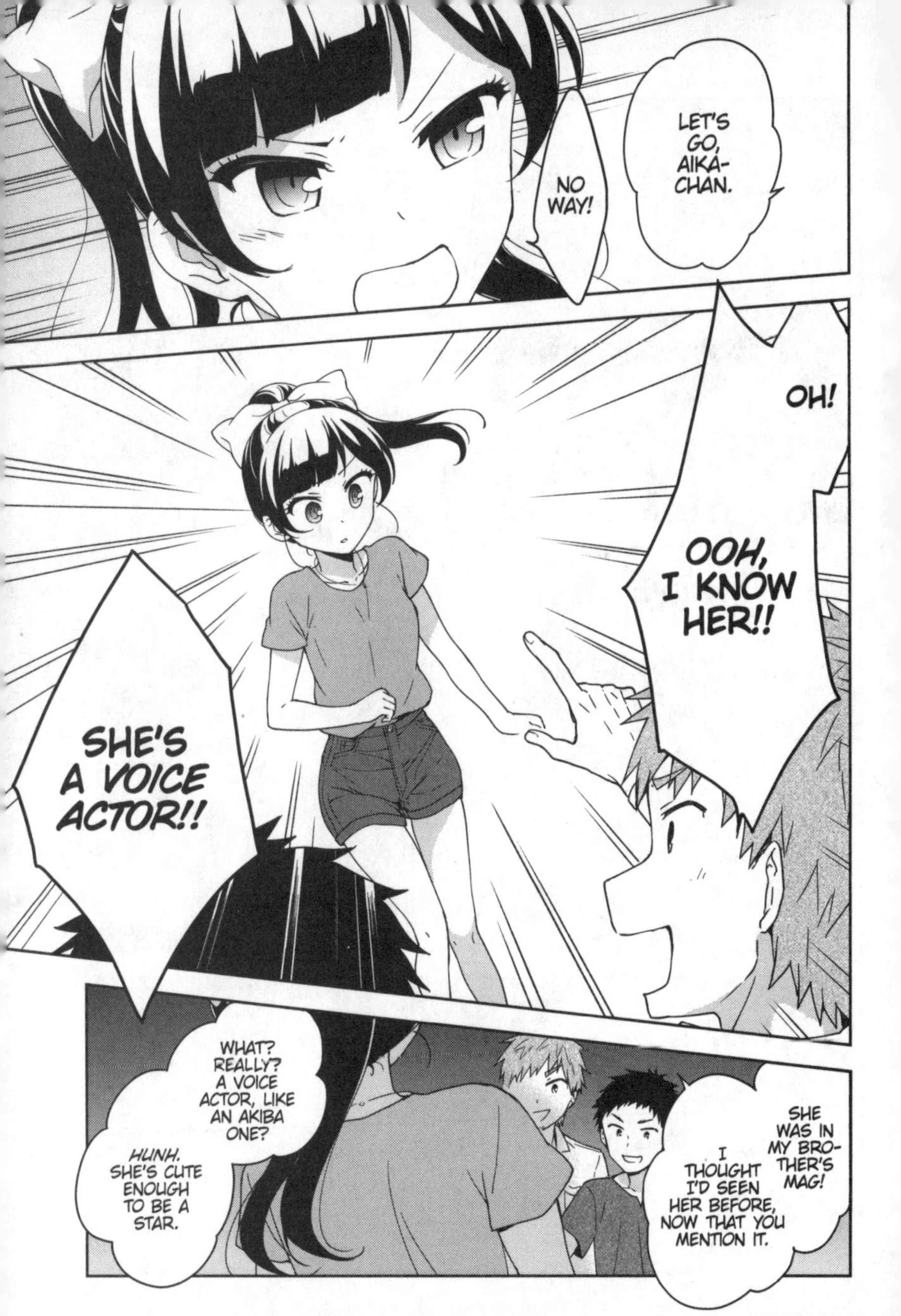
LET'S GO, AIKA-CHAN.
NO WAY!
OH!
OOH, I KNOW HER!!
SHE'S A *VOICE ACTOR*!!
SHE WAS IN MY BROTHER'S MAG!
I THOUGHT I'D SEEN HER BEFORE, NOW THAT YOU MENTION IT.
WHAT? REALLY? A VOICE ACTOR, LIKE AN AKIBA ONE?
HUNH. SHE'S CUTE ENOUGH TO BE A STAR.

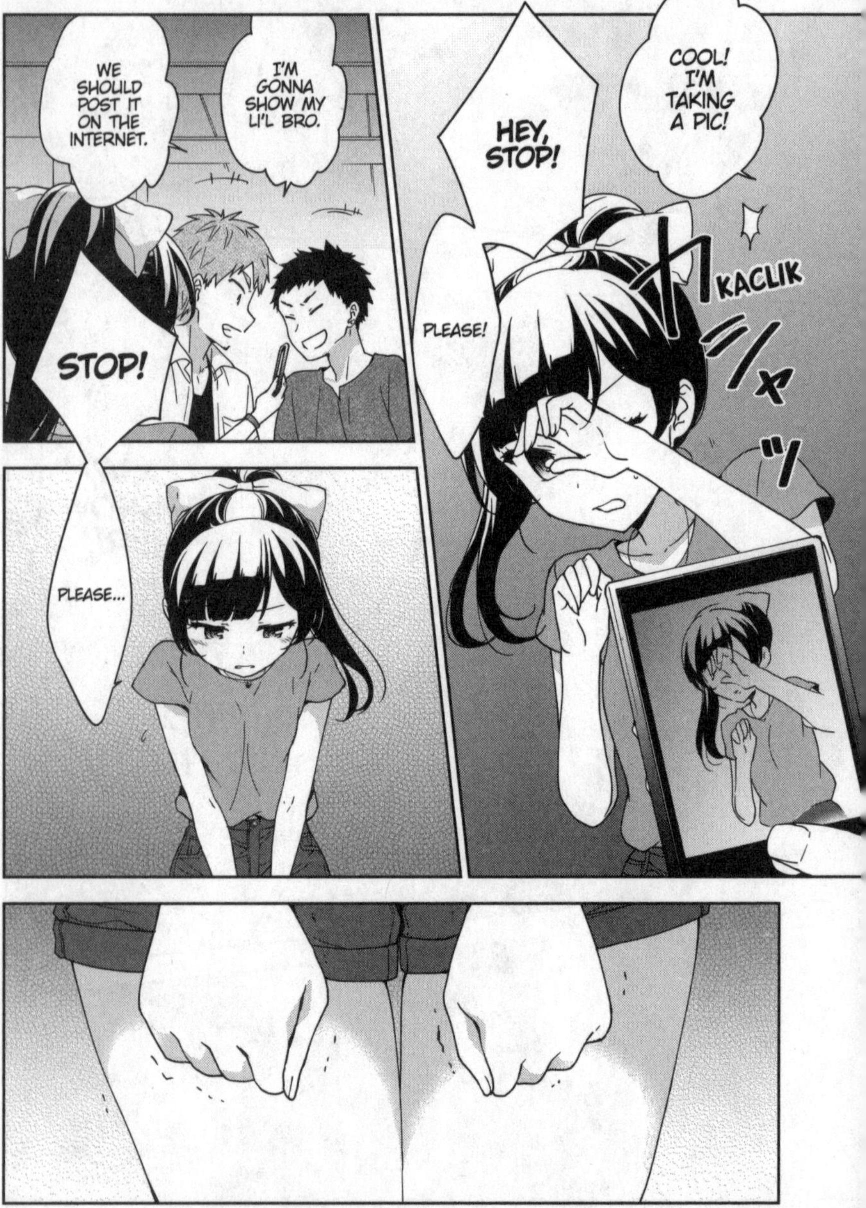
COOL! I'M TAKING A PIC!
HEY, STOP!
KACLIK
PLEASE!
I'M GONNA SHOW MY LI'L BRO.
WE SHOULD POST IT ON THE INTERNET.
STOP!
PLEASE...

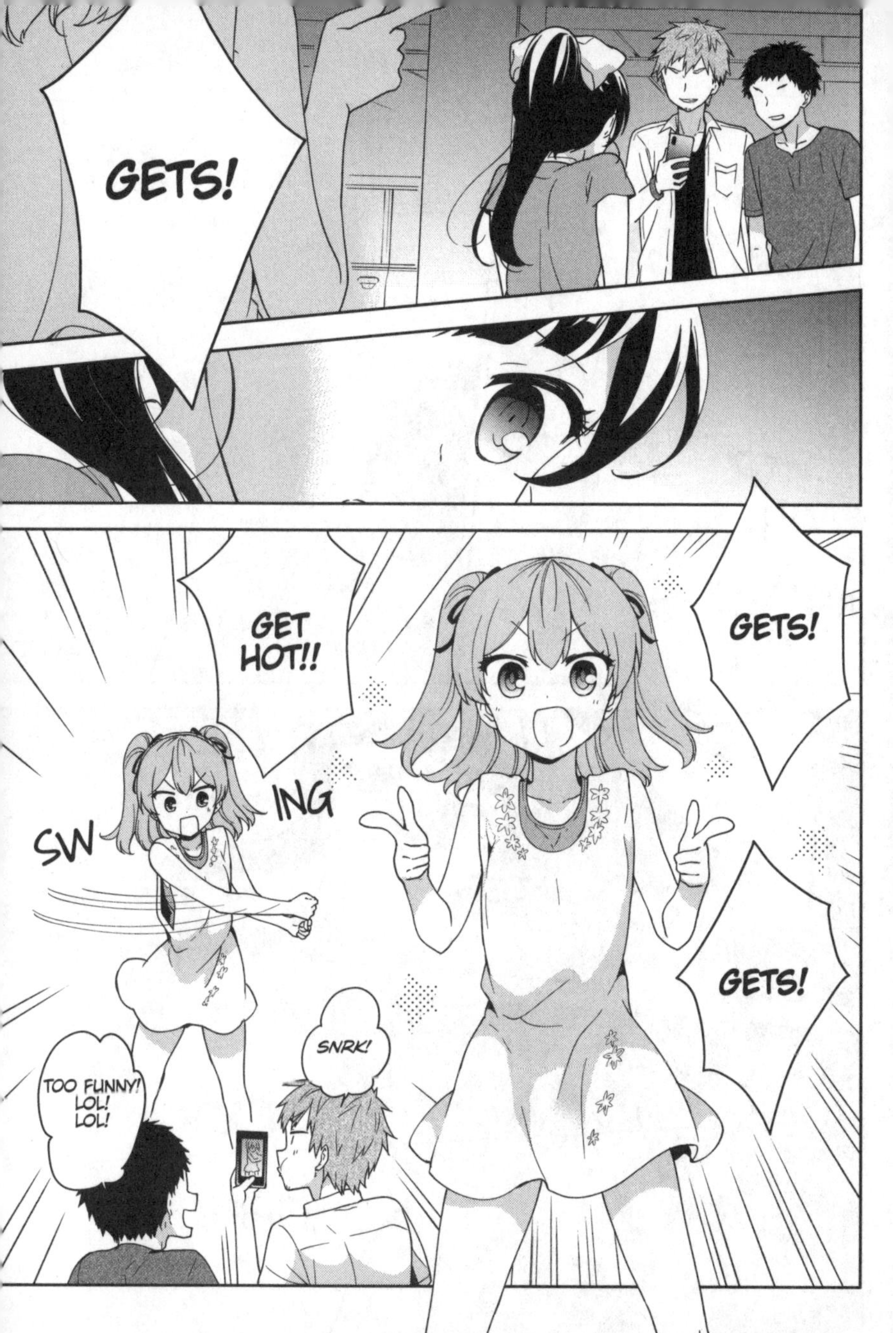
GETS!
GETS!
GET HOT!!
GETS!
SW ING
SNRK!
TOO FUNNY! LOL! LOL!

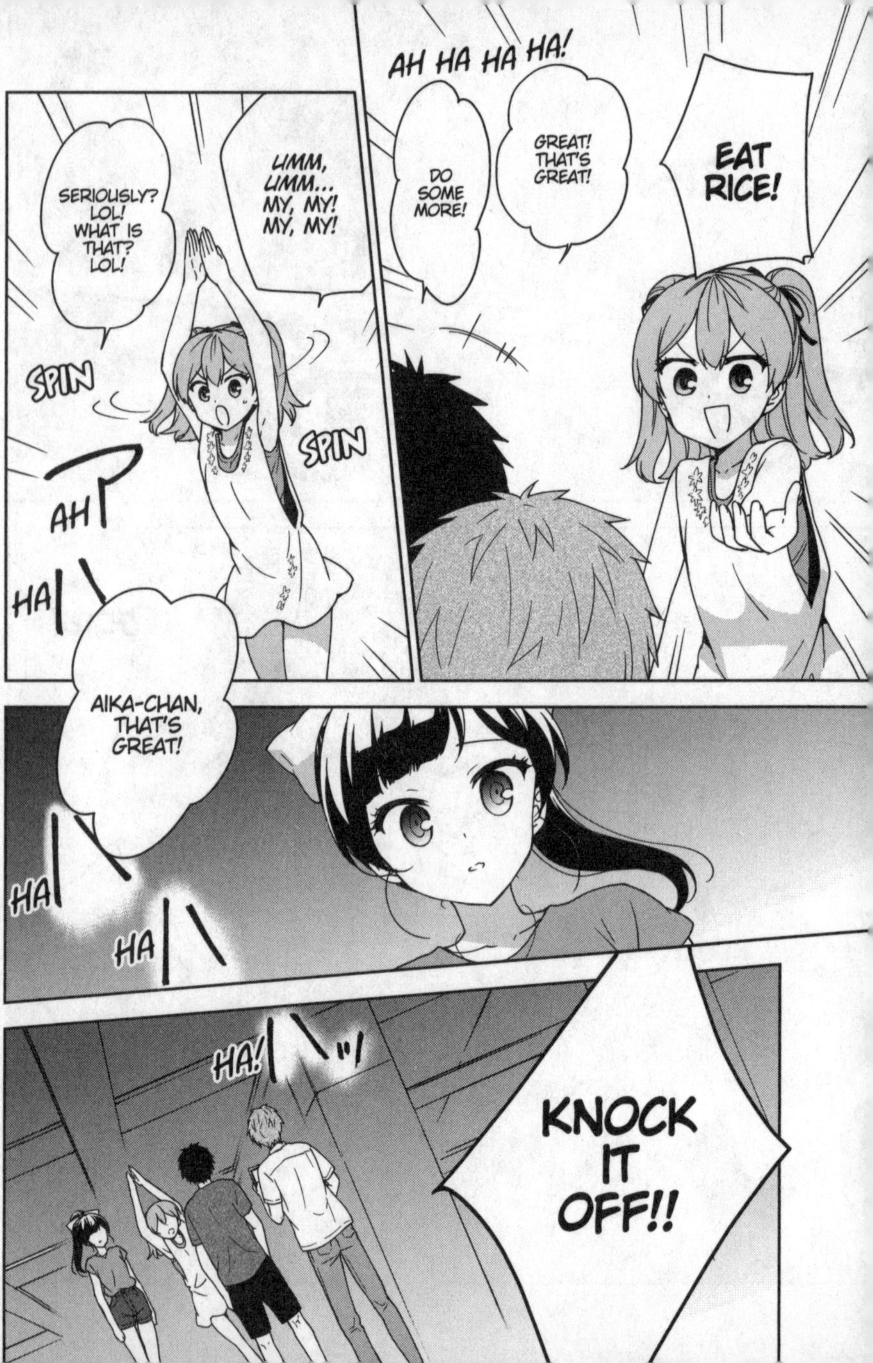
EAT RICE!
GREAT! THAT'S GREAT!
DO SOME MORE!
AH HA HA HA!
UMM, UMM... MY, MY! MY, MY!
SERIOUSLY? LOL! WHAT IS THAT? LOL!
SPIN
SPIN
AH
HA
AIKA-CHAN, THAT'S GREAT!
HA
HA
HA!
KNOCK IT OFF!!

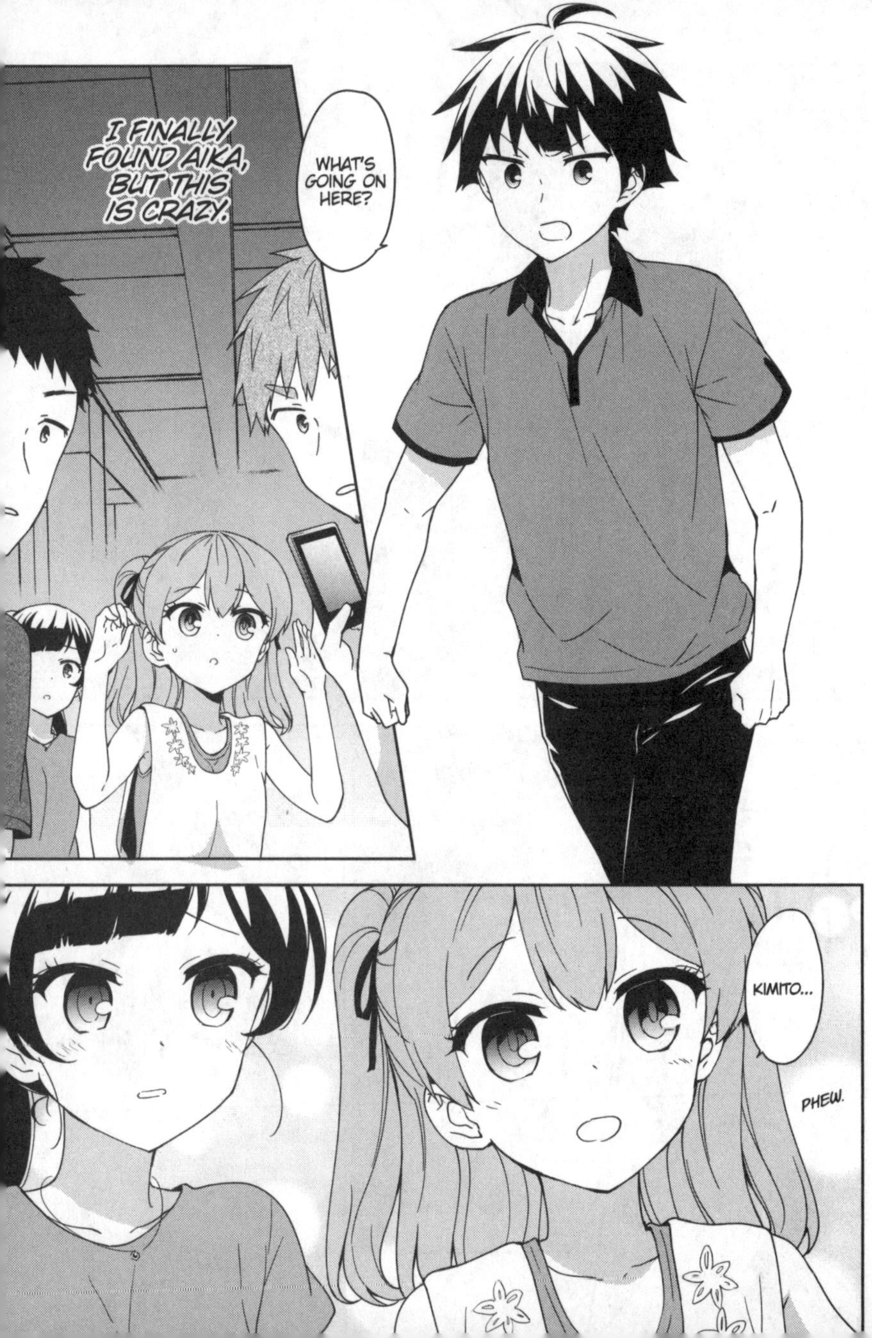
WHAT'S GOING ON HERE?
I FINALLY FOUND AIKA, BUT THIS IS CRAZY.
KIMITO...
PHEW.

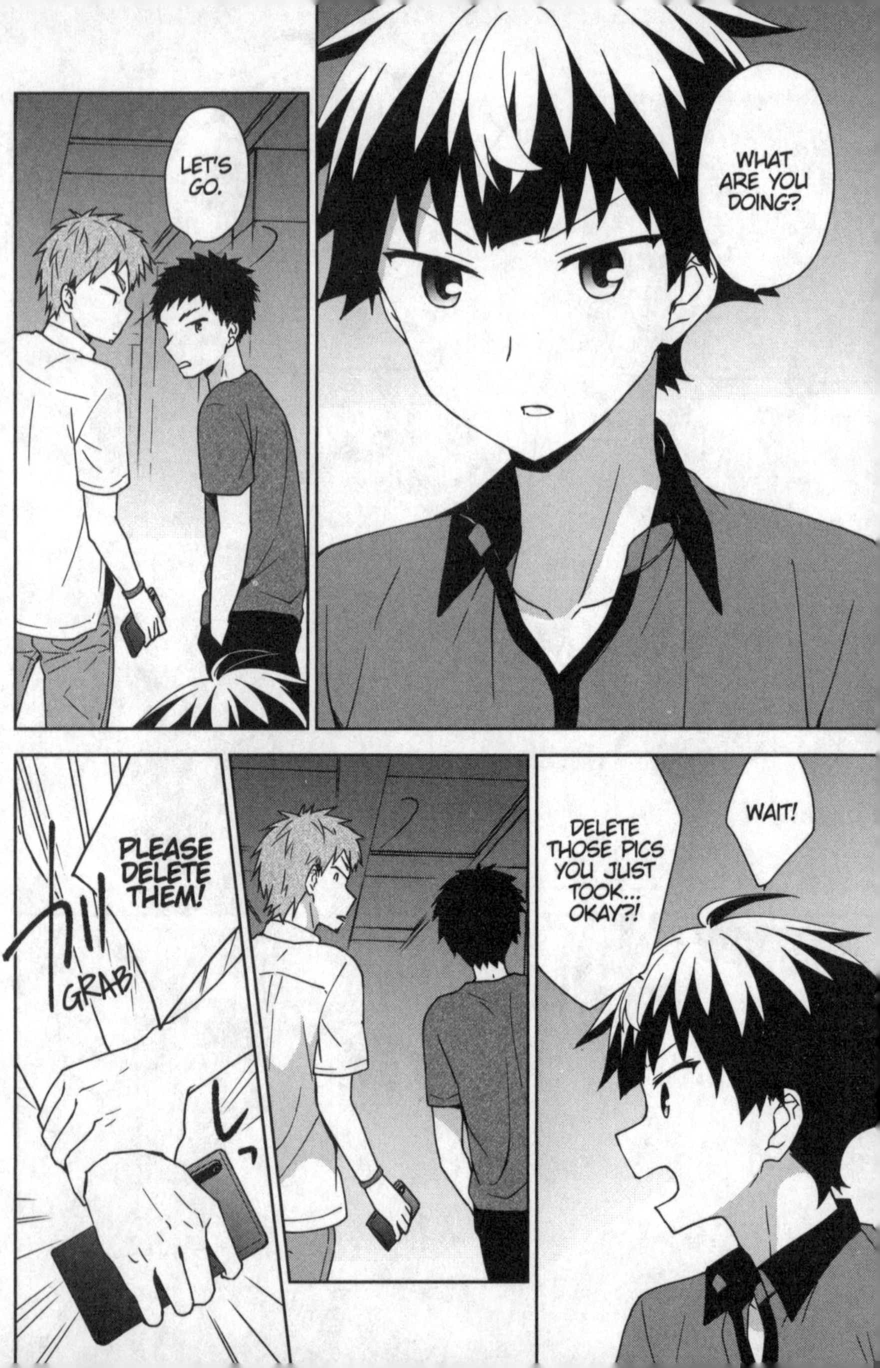
WHAT ARE YOU DOING?
LET'S GO.
WAIT!
DELETE THOSE PICS YOU JUST TOOK... OKAY?!
PLEASE DELETE THEM!
GRAB

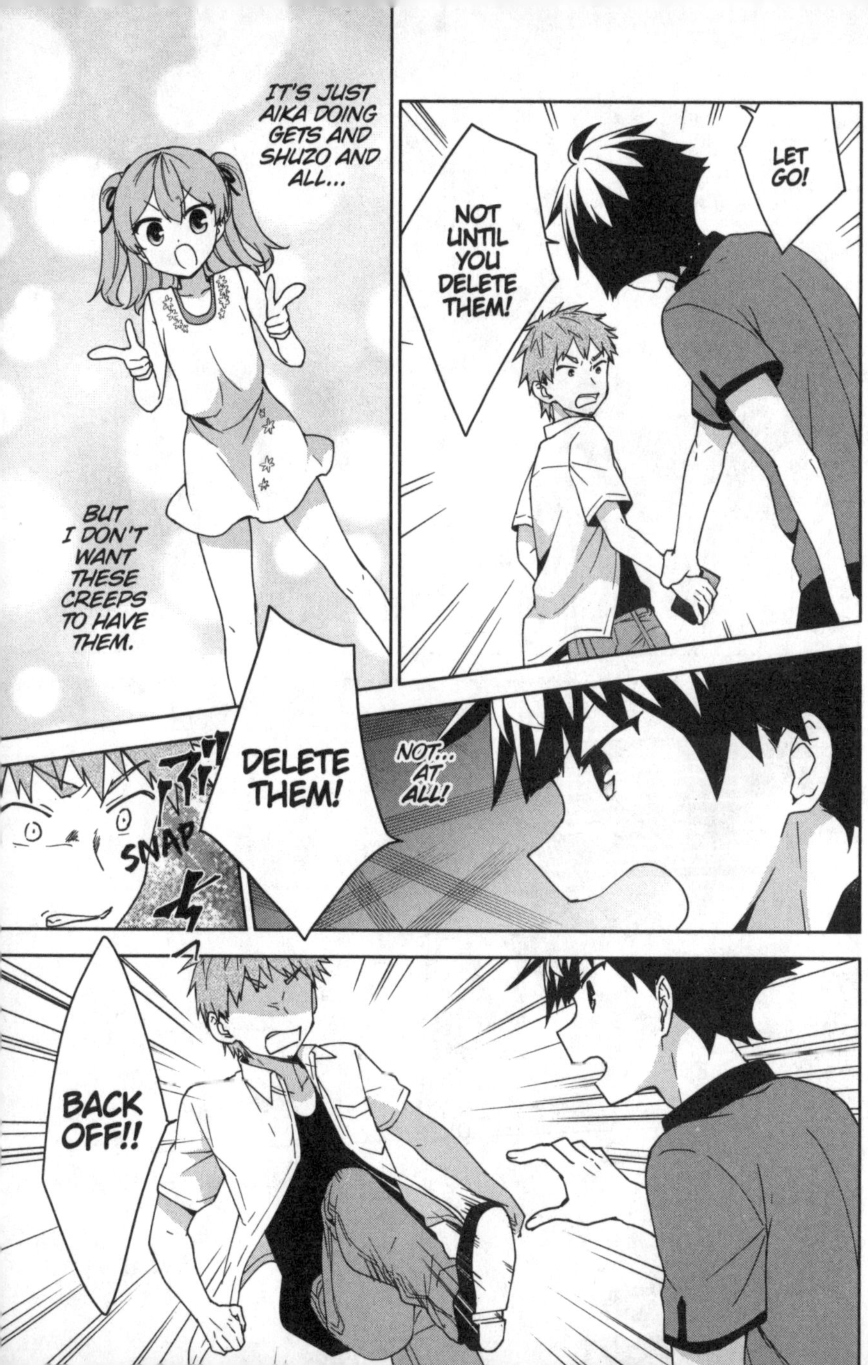

LET GO!
NOT UNTIL YOU DELETE THEM!
IT'S JUST AIKA DOING GETS AND SHUZO AND ALL...
BUT I DON'T WANT THESE CREEPS TO HAVE THEM.
NOT... AT ALL!
DELETE THEM!
SNAP
BACK OFF!!

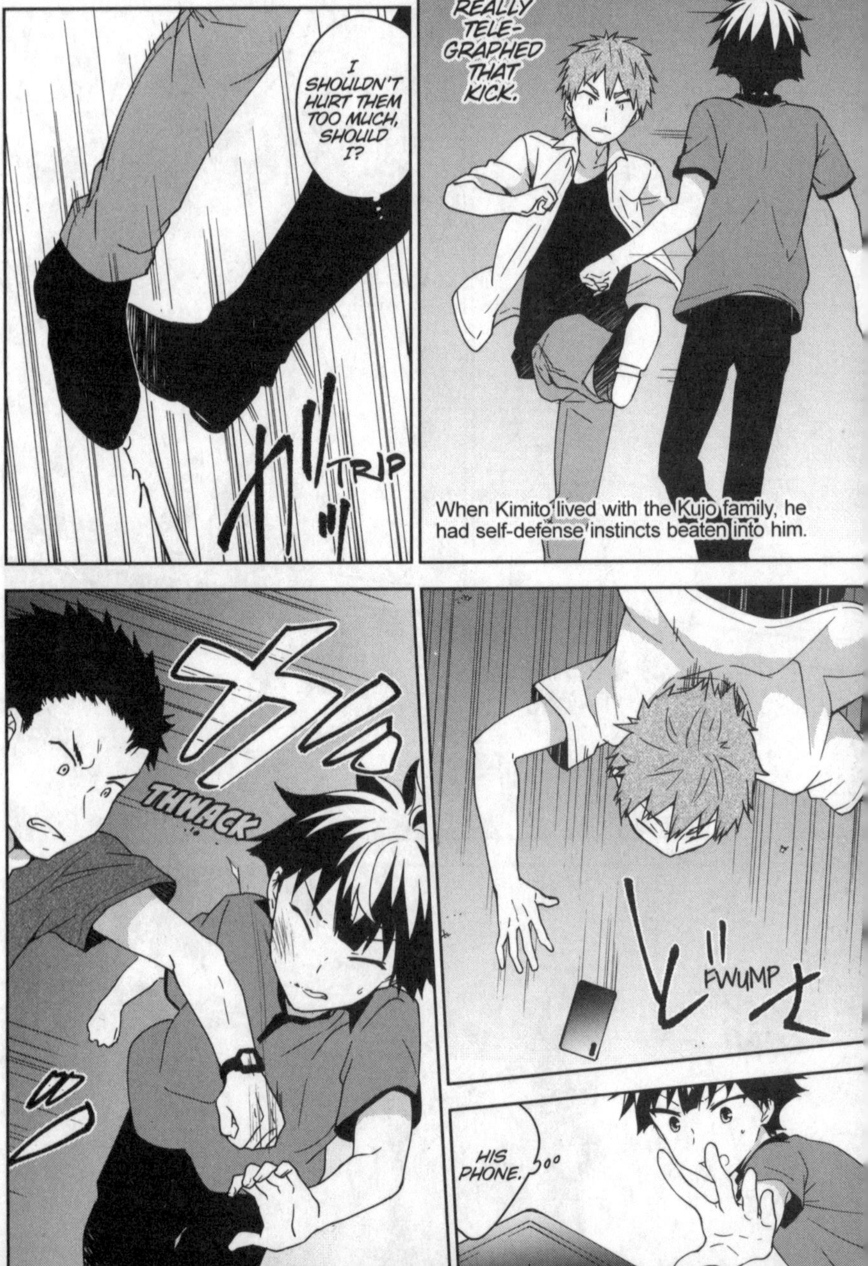
DODGe
HE REALLY TELE-GRAPHED THAT KICK.
When Kimito lived with the Kujo family, he had self-defense instincts beaten into him.
I SHOULDN'T HURT THEM TOO MUCH, SHOULD I?
TRIP
FWUMP
HIS PHONE.
THWACK

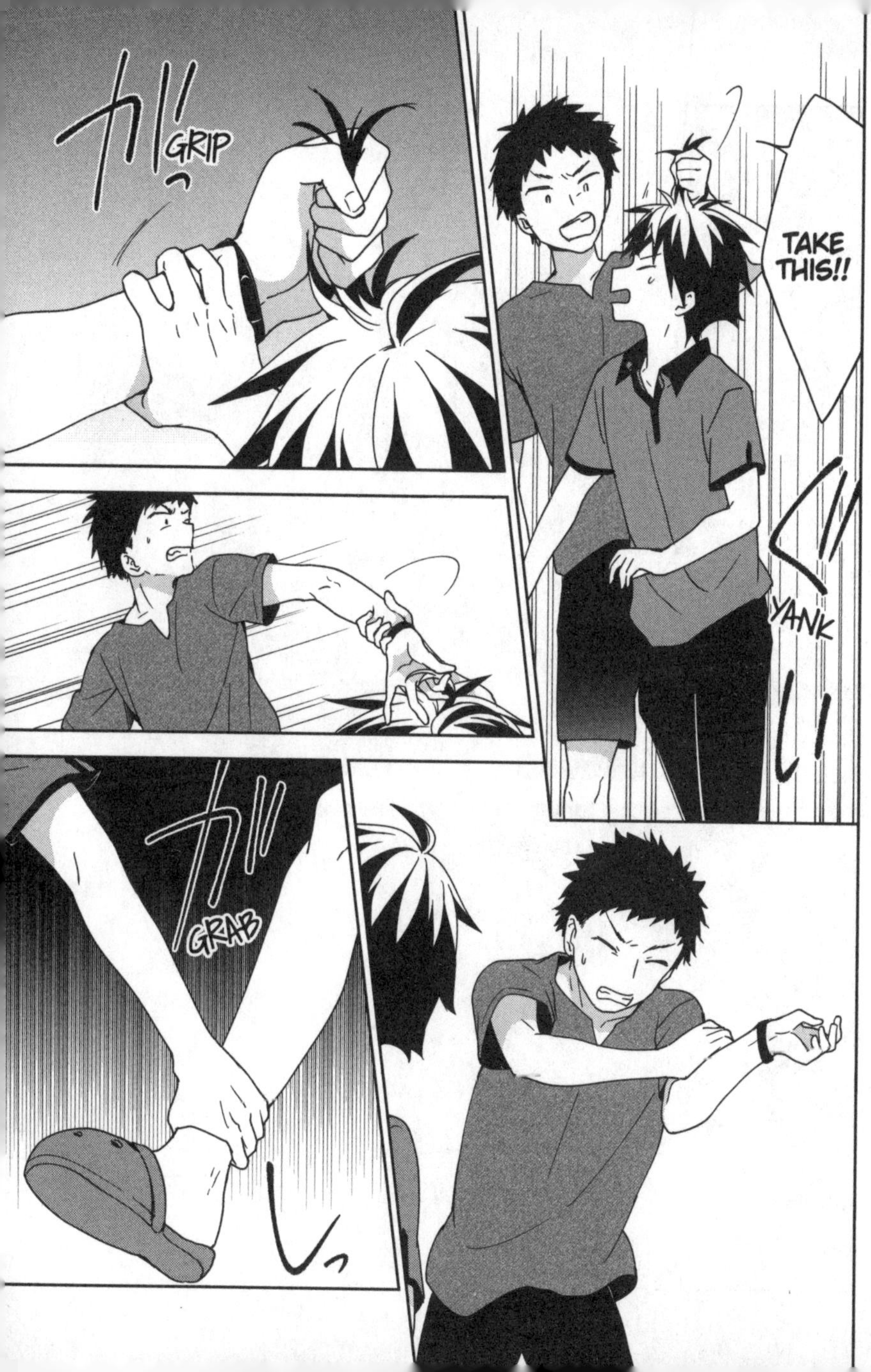
TAKE THIS!!
YANK
GRIP
GRAB

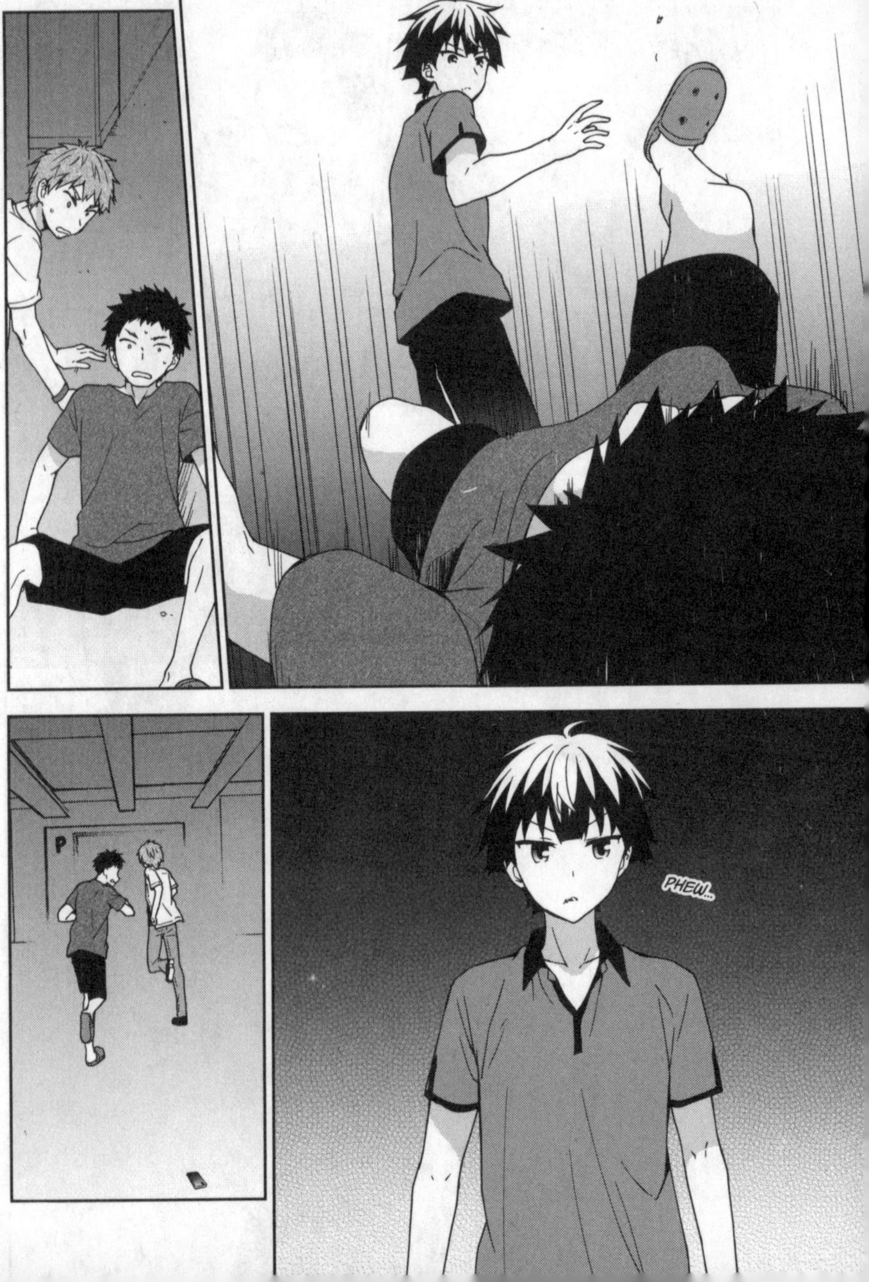
PHEW...

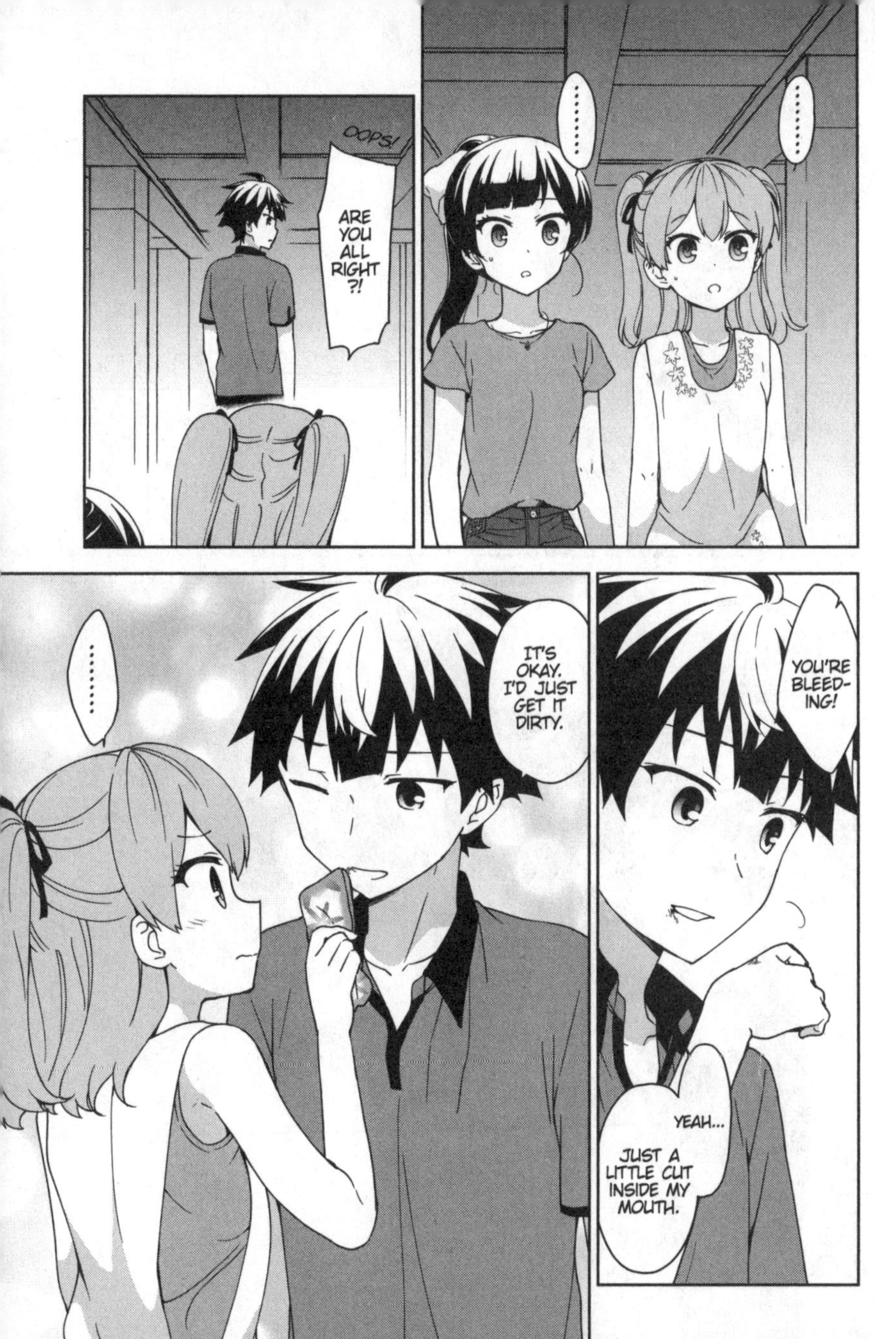
……
……
OOPS!
ARE YOU ALL RIGHT ?!
YOU'RE BLEED-ING!
YEAH...
JUST A LITTLE CUT INSIDE MY MOUTH.
IT'S OKAY. I'D JUST GET IT DIRTY.
……

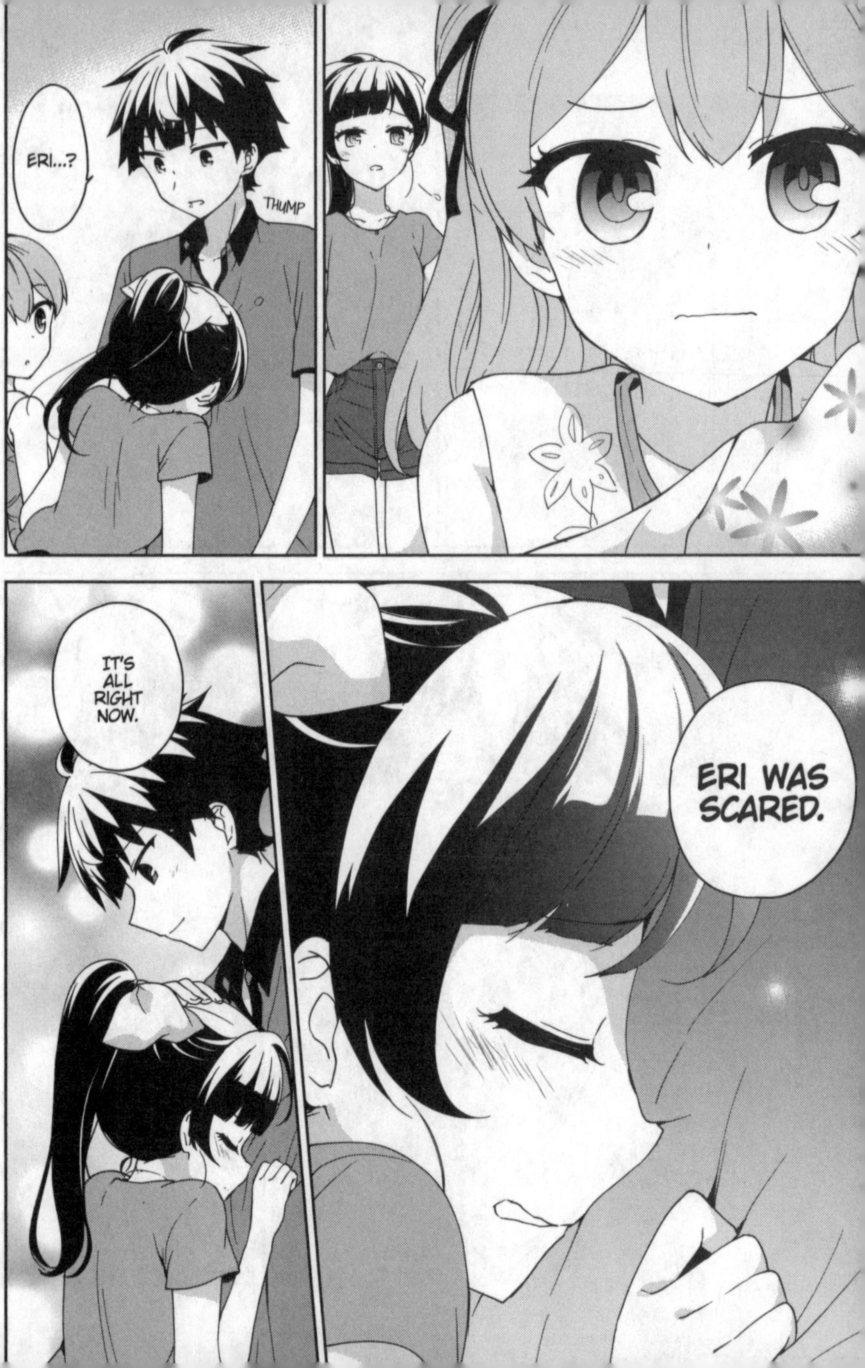
ERI...?
THUMP
ERI WAS SCARED.
IT'S ALL RIGHT NOW.

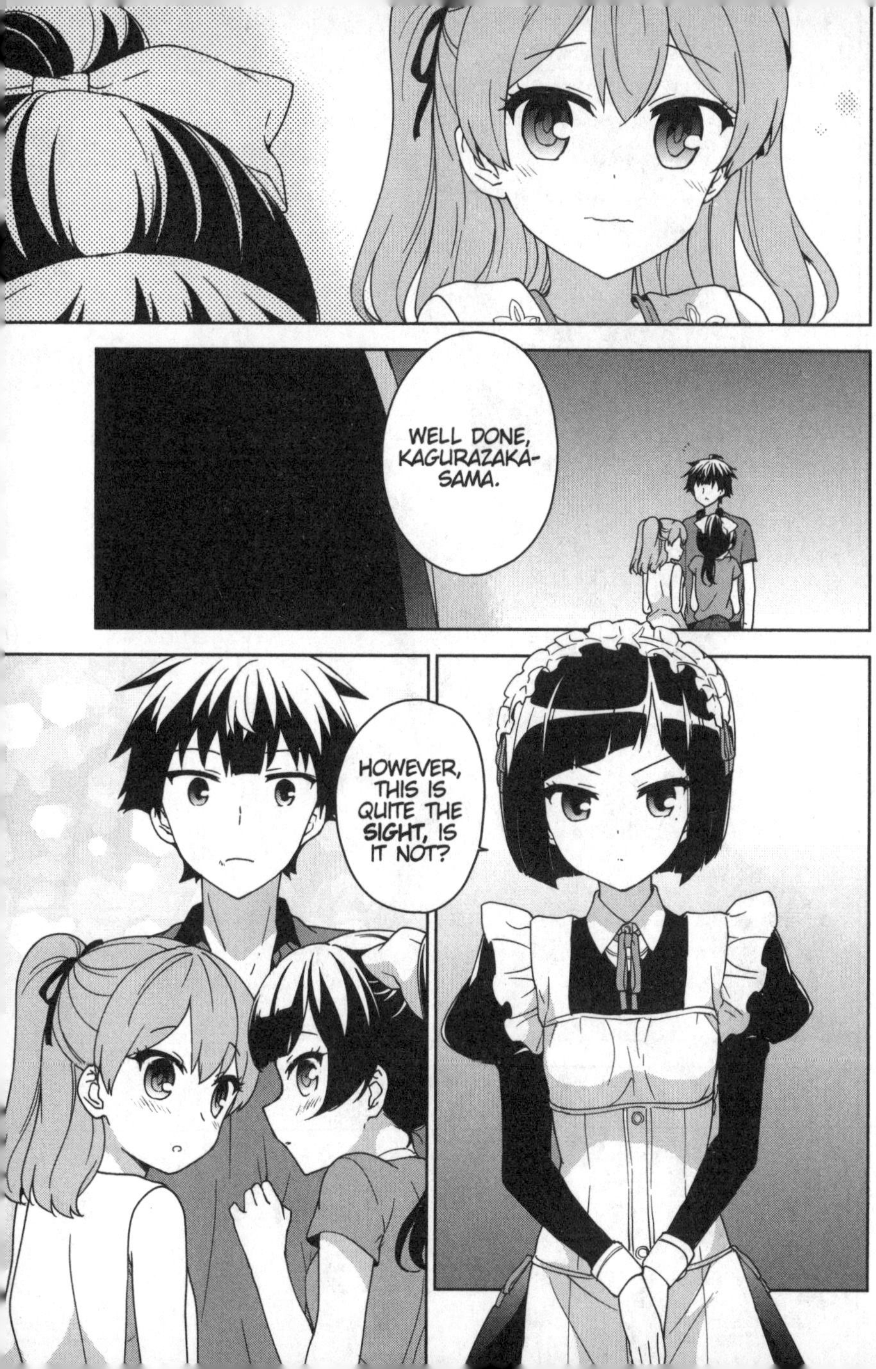
WELL DONE, KAGURAZAKA-SAMA.
HOWEVER, THIS IS QUITE THE SIGHT, IS IT NOT?

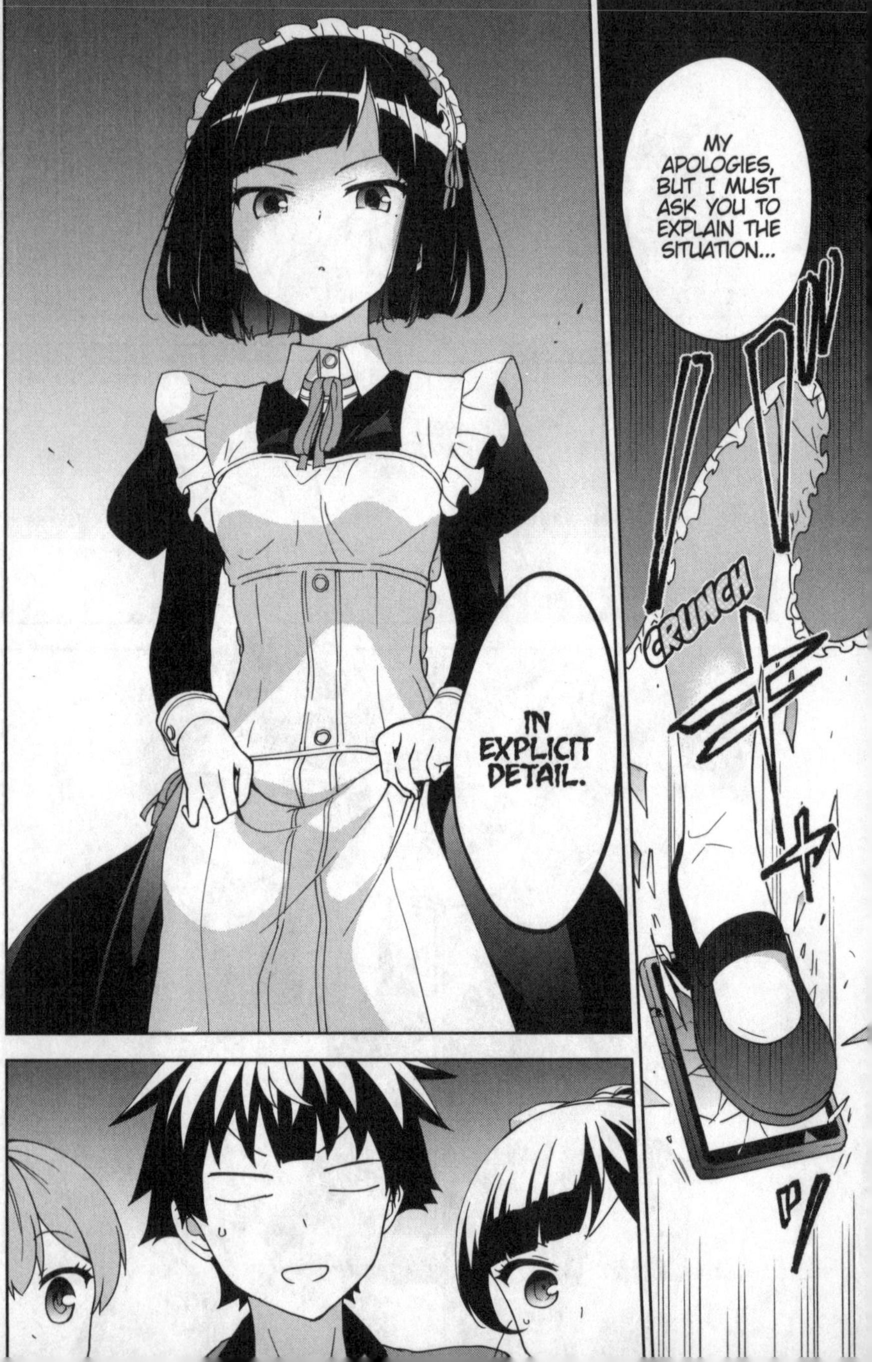
MY APOLOGIES, BUT I MUST ASK YOU TO EXPLAIN THE SITUATION...
CRUNCH
IN EXPLICIT DETAIL.

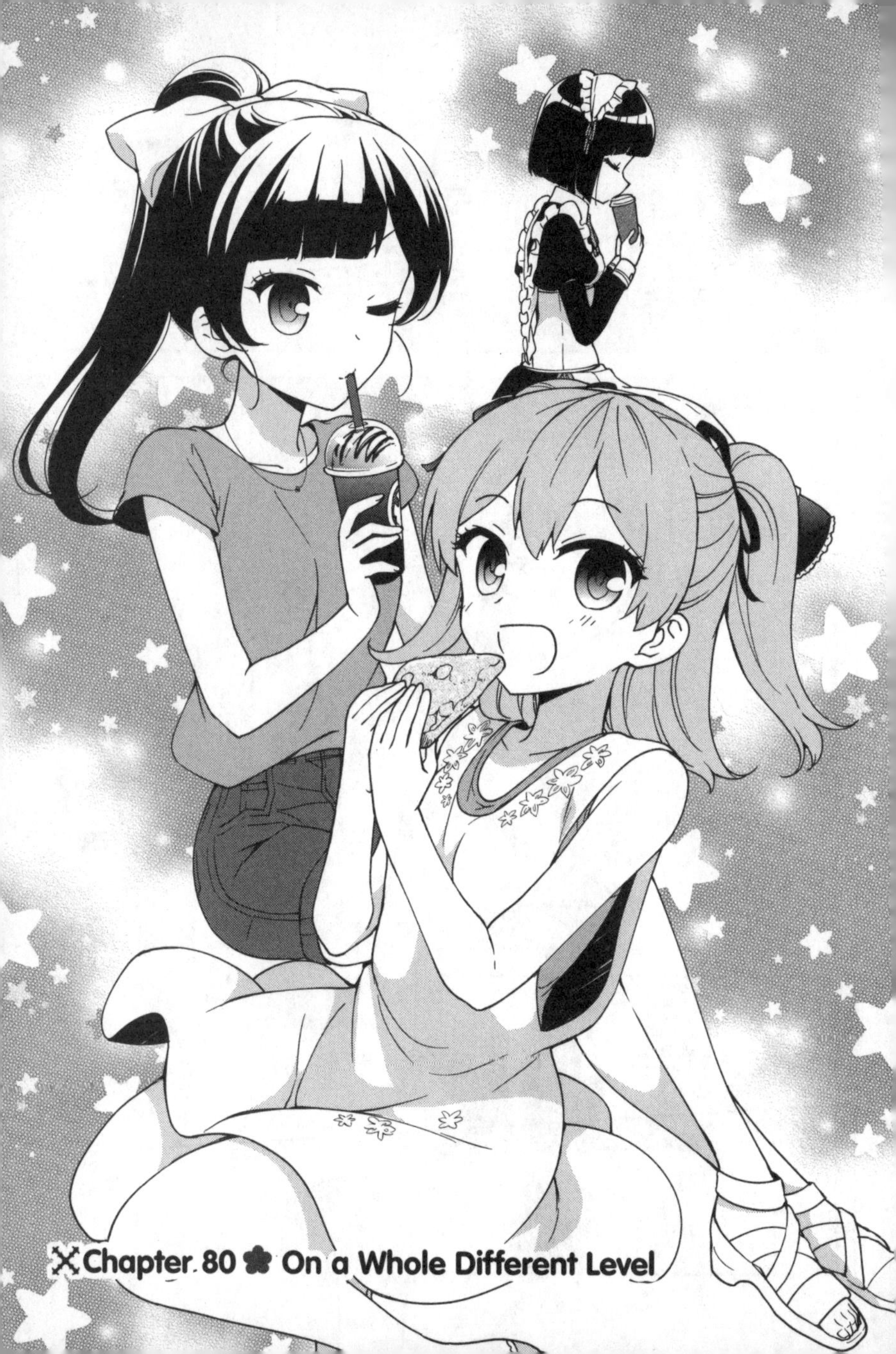

Chapter 80 ✿ On a Whole Different Level

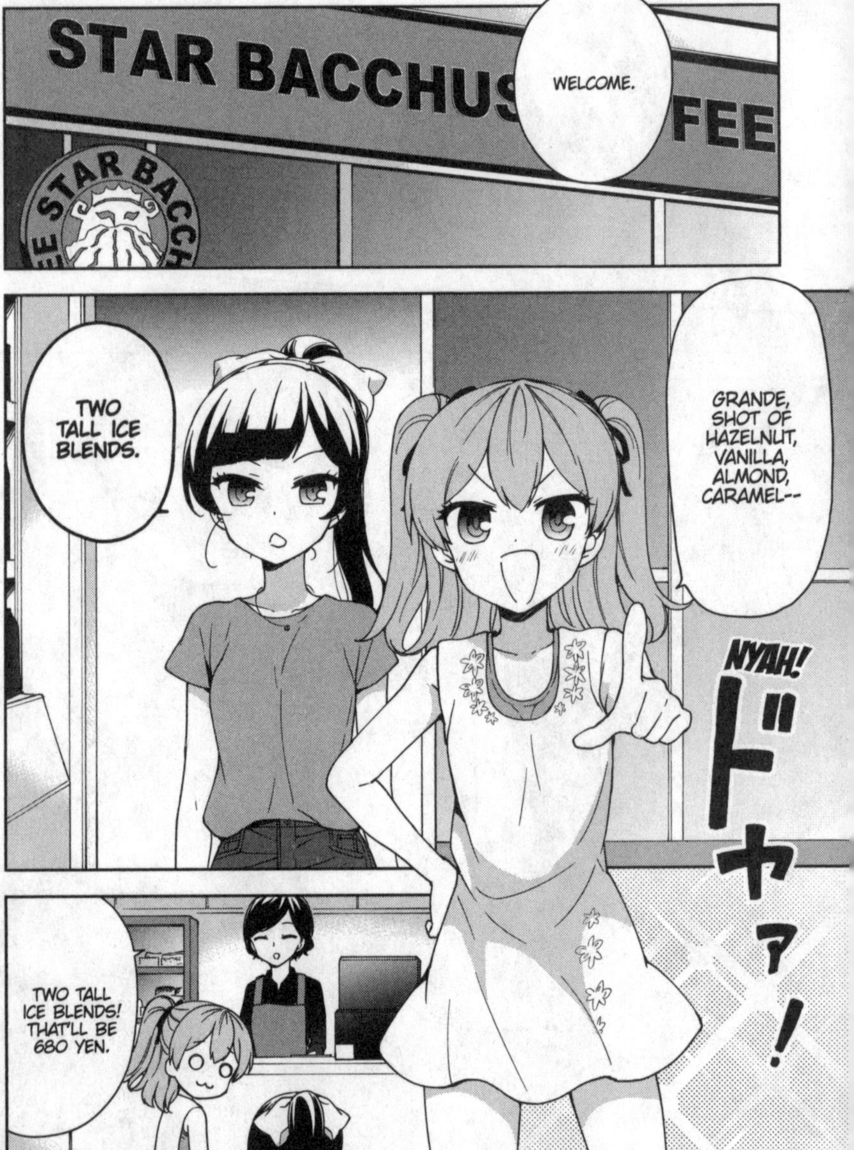
STAR BACCHUS
FEE
WELCOME.
GRANDE, SHOT OF HAZELNUT, VANILLA, ALMOND, CARAMEL--
NYAH!
ドヤァ!
TWO TALL ICE BLENDS.
TWO TALL ICE BLENDS! THAT'LL BE 680 YEN.

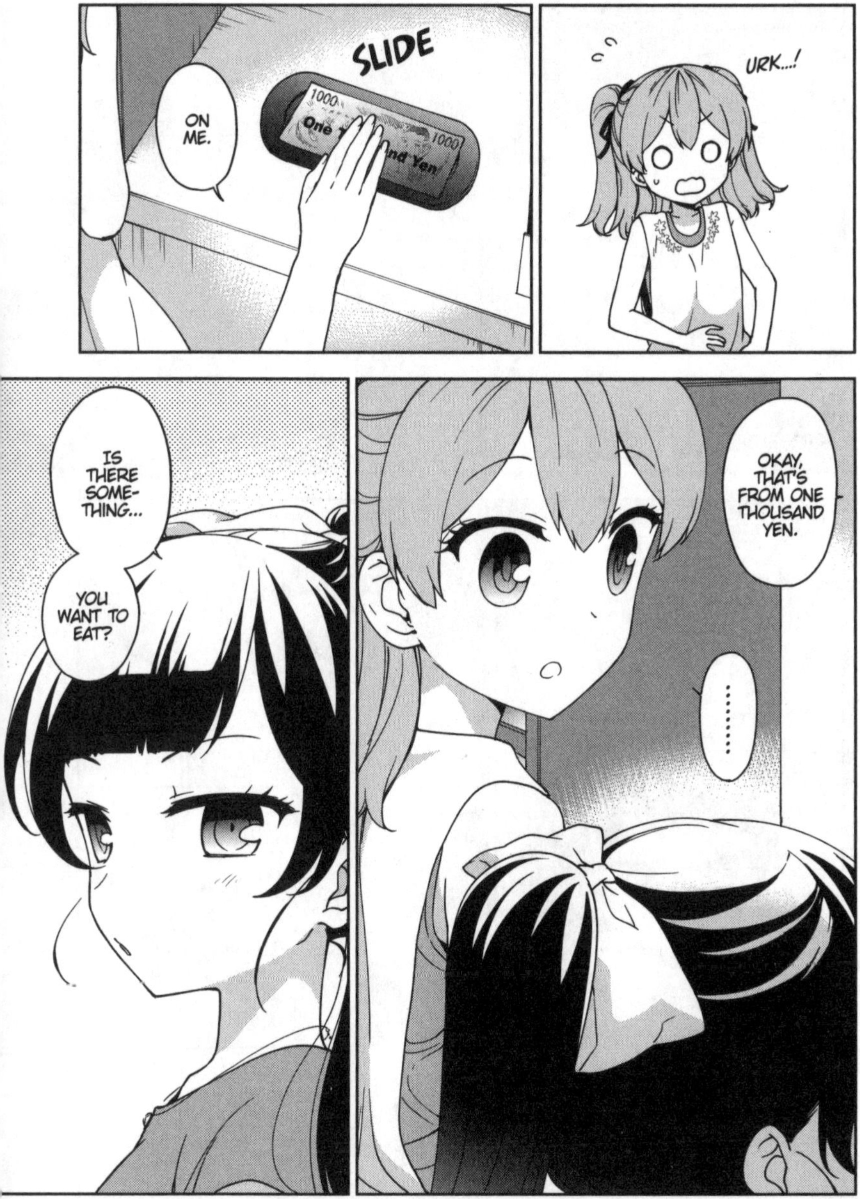
URK...!
SLIDE
ON ME.
OKAY, THAT'S FROM ONE THOUSAND YEN.
......
IS THERE SOME-THING...
YOU WANT TO EAT?

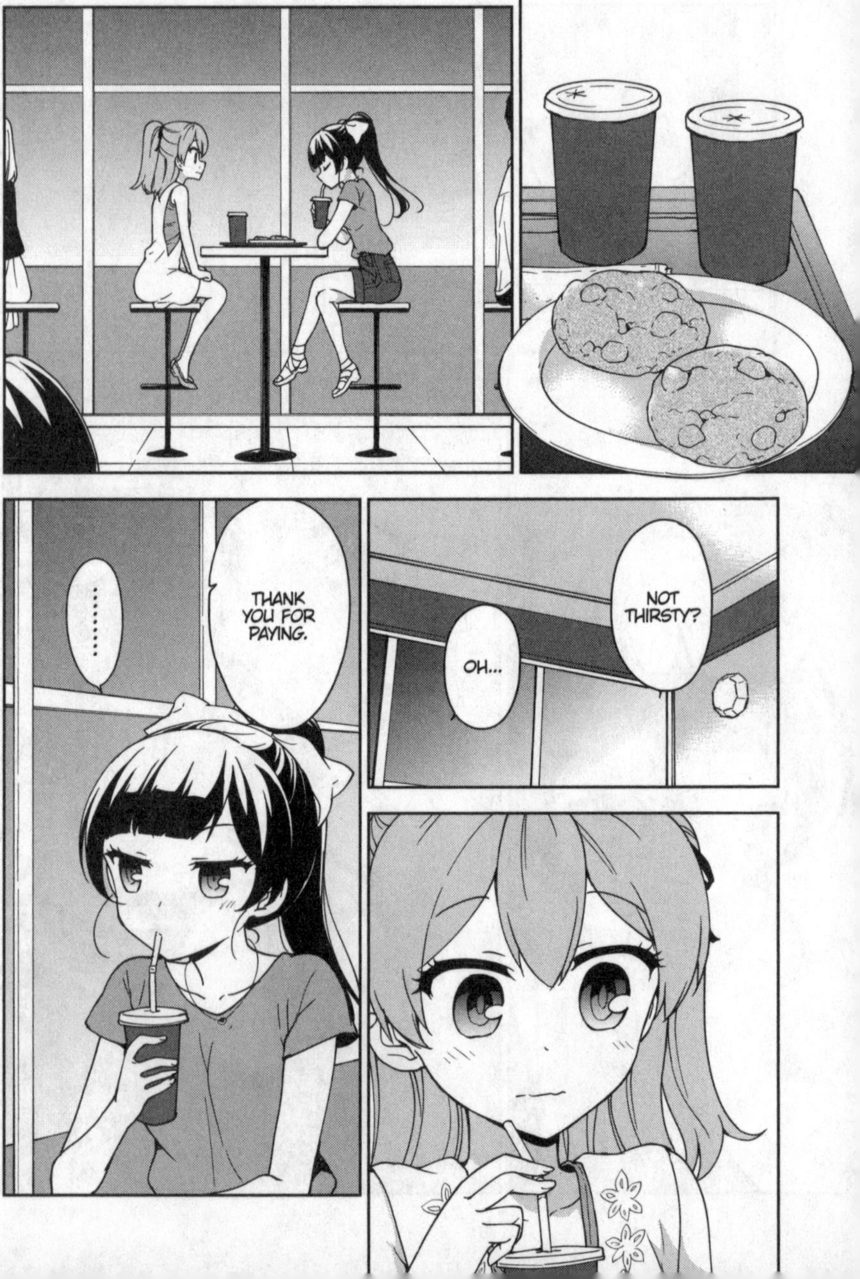
NOT THIRSTY?
OH...
THANK YOU FOR PAYING.
......

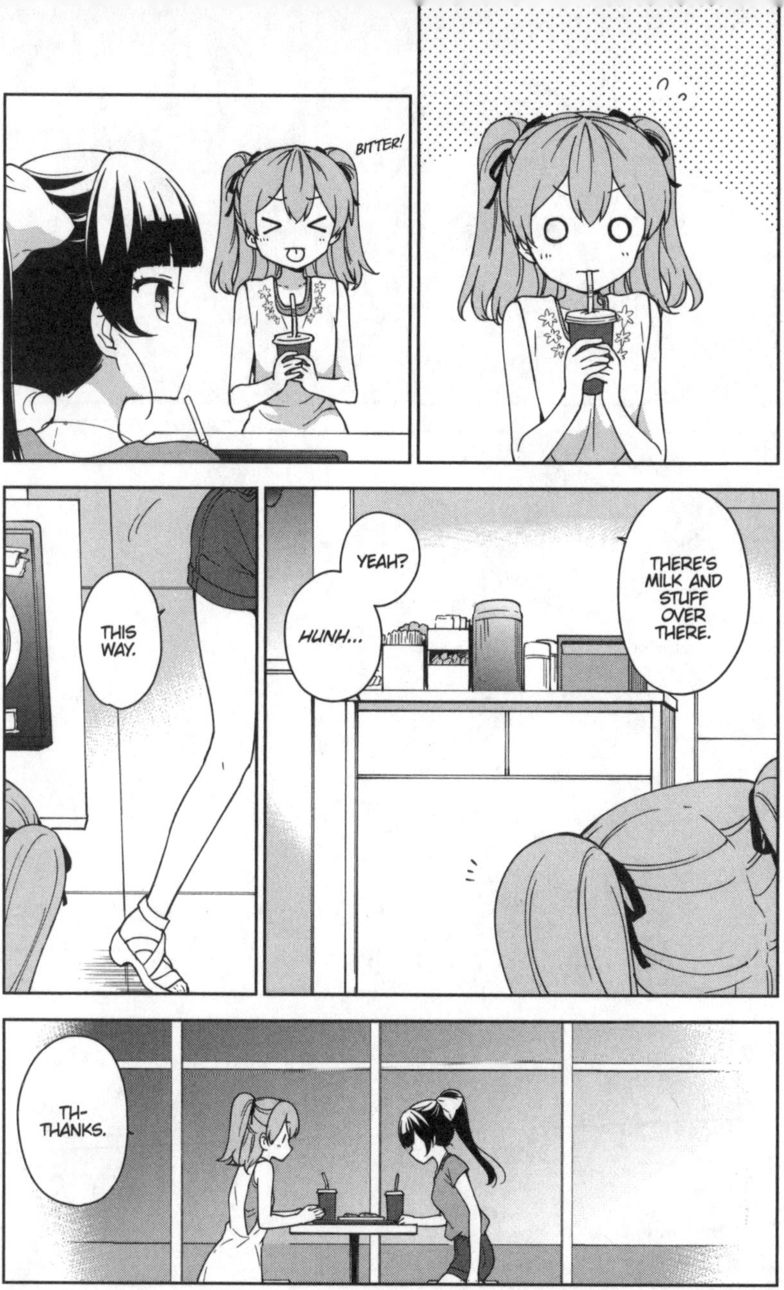
BITTER!
THERE'S MILK AND STUFF OVER THERE.
YEAH?
HUNH...
THIS WAY.
TH- THANKS.

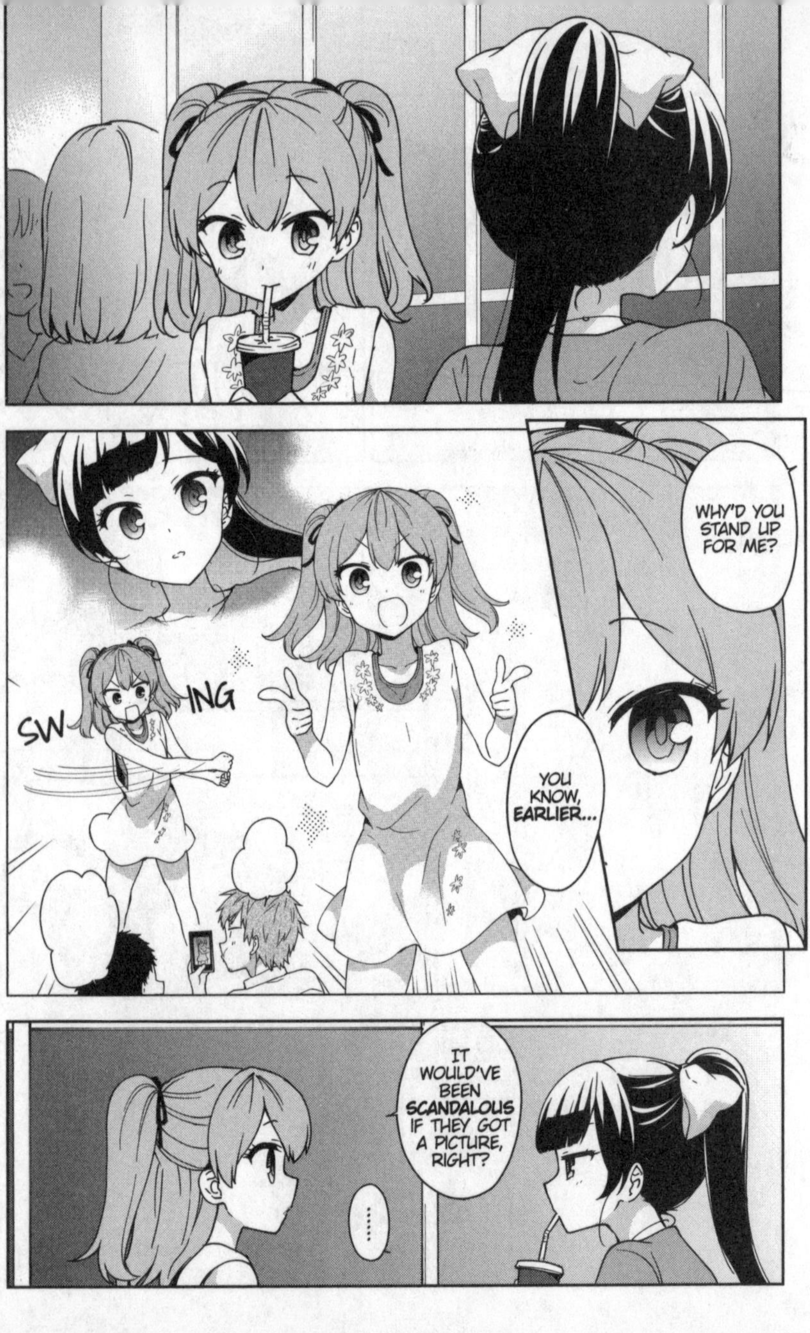
WHY'D YOU STAND UP FOR ME?
YOU KNOW, EARLIER...
SW ING
IT WOULD'VE BEEN SCANDALOUS IF THEY GOT A PICTURE, RIGHT?
......

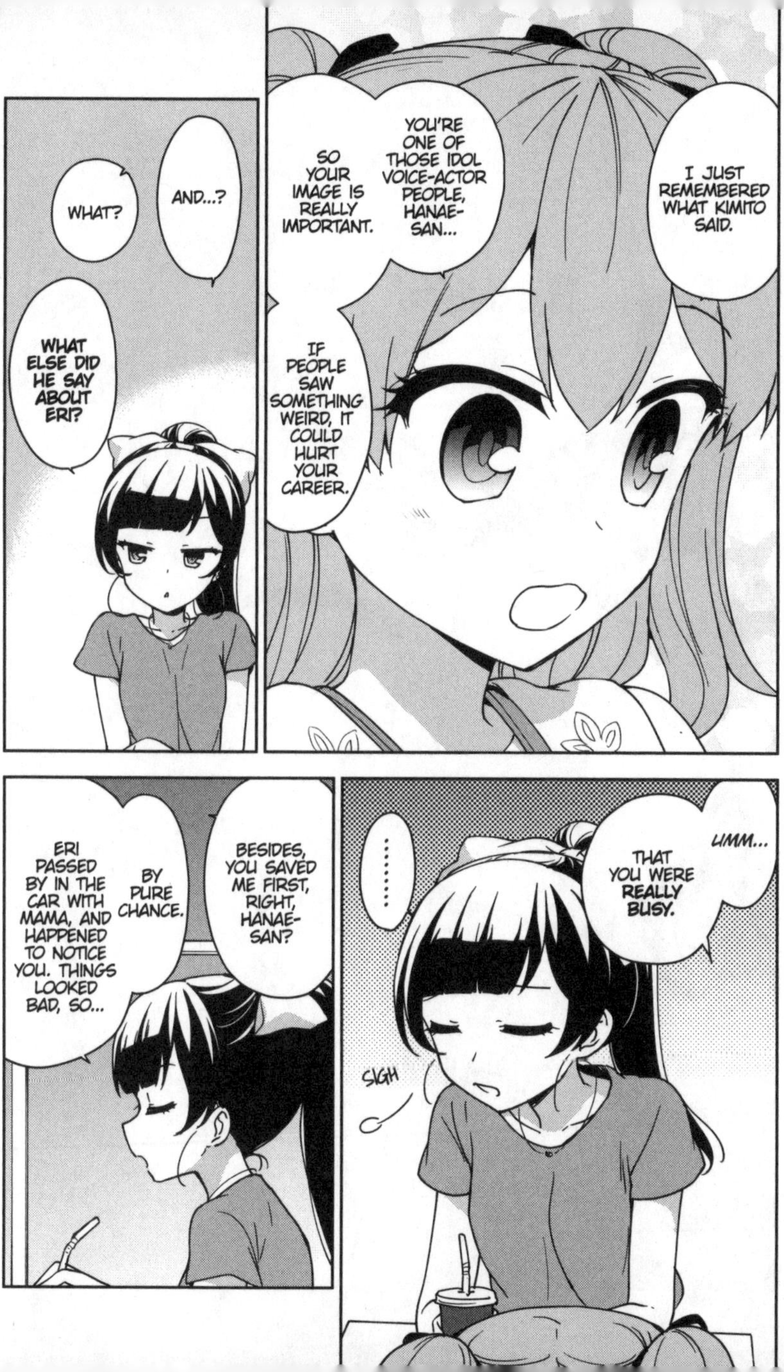

I JUST REMEMBERED WHAT KIMITO SAID.
YOU'RE ONE OF THOSE IDOL VOICE-ACTOR PEOPLE, HANAE-SAN...
SO YOUR IMAGE IS REALLY IMPORTANT.
IF PEOPLE SAW SOMETHING WEIRD, IT COULD HURT YOUR CAREER.
AND...?
WHAT?
WHAT ELSE DID HE SAY ABOUT ERI?
UMM...
THAT YOU WERE REALLY BUSY.
....
SIGH
BESIDES, YOU SAVED ME FIRST, RIGHT, HANAE-SAN?
BY PURE CHANCE.
ERI PASSED BY IN THE CAR WITH MAMA, AND HAPPENED TO NOTICE YOU. THINGS LOOKED BAD, SO...

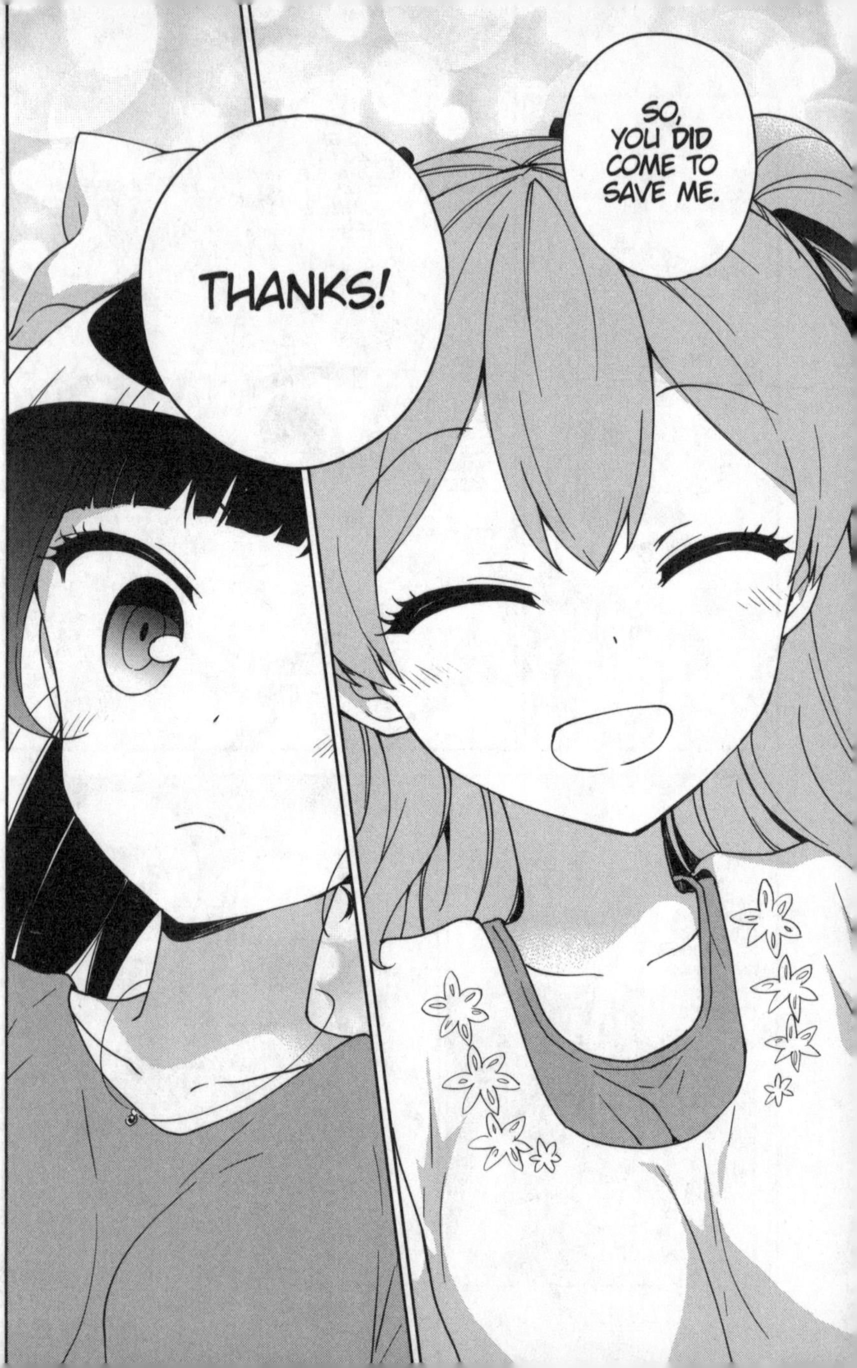
SO, YOU DID COME TO SAVE ME.
THANKS!

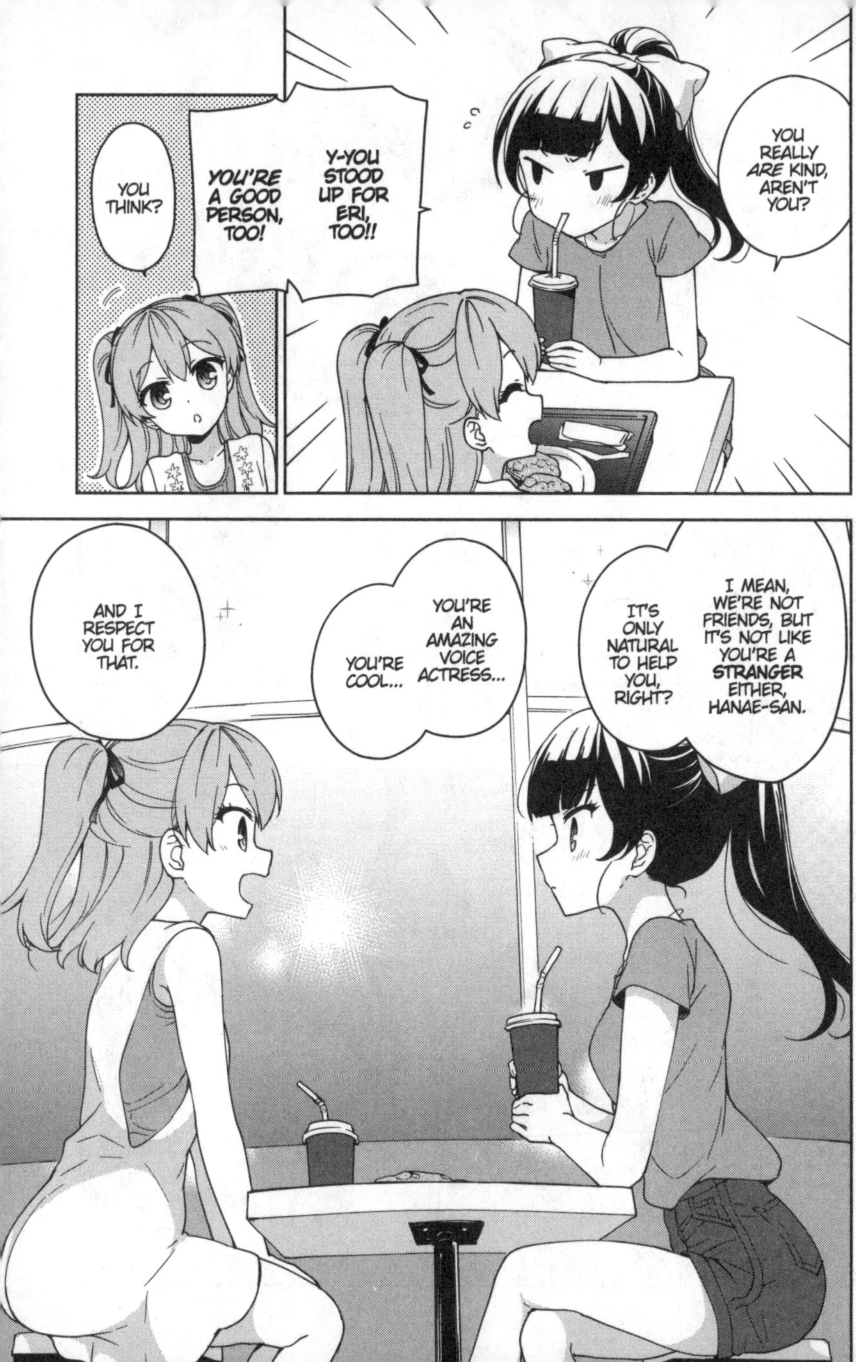
YOU REALLY ARE KIND, AREN'T YOU?
Y-YOU STOOD UP FOR ERI, TOO!!
YOU'RE A GOOD PERSON, TOO!
YOU THINK?
I MEAN, WE'RE NOT FRIENDS, BUT IT'S NOT LIKE YOU'RE A STRANGER EITHER, HANAE-SAN.
IT'S ONLY NATURAL TO HELP YOU, RIGHT?
YOU'RE AN AMAZING VOICE ACTRESS...
YOU'RE COOL...
AND I RESPECT YOU FOR THAT.

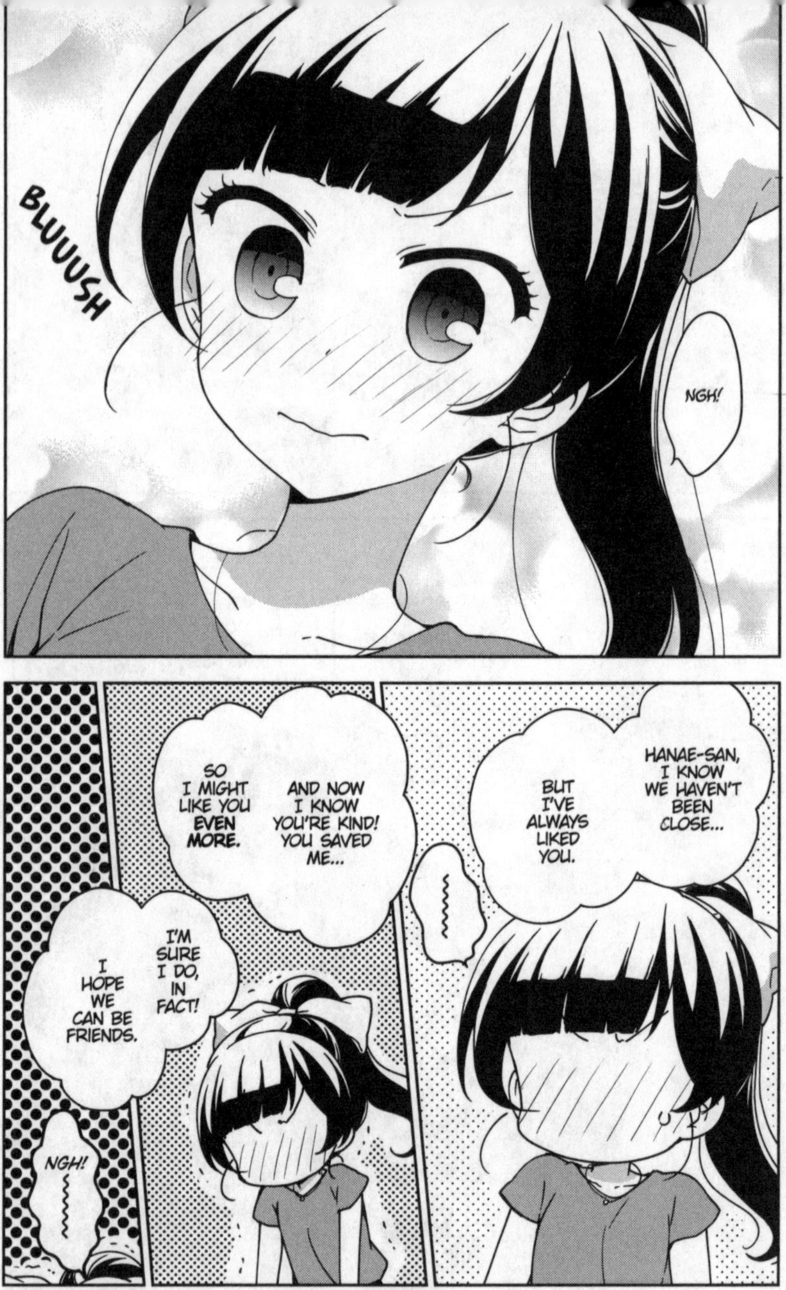
NGH!
BLUUUSH
HANAE-SAN, I KNOW WE HAVEN'T BEEN CLOSE...
BUT I'VE ALWAYS LIKED YOU.
AND NOW I KNOW YOU'RE KIND! YOU SAVED ME...
SO I MIGHT LIKE YOU EVEN MORE.
I'M SURE I DO, IN FACT!
I HOPE WE CAN BE FRIENDS.
NGH!

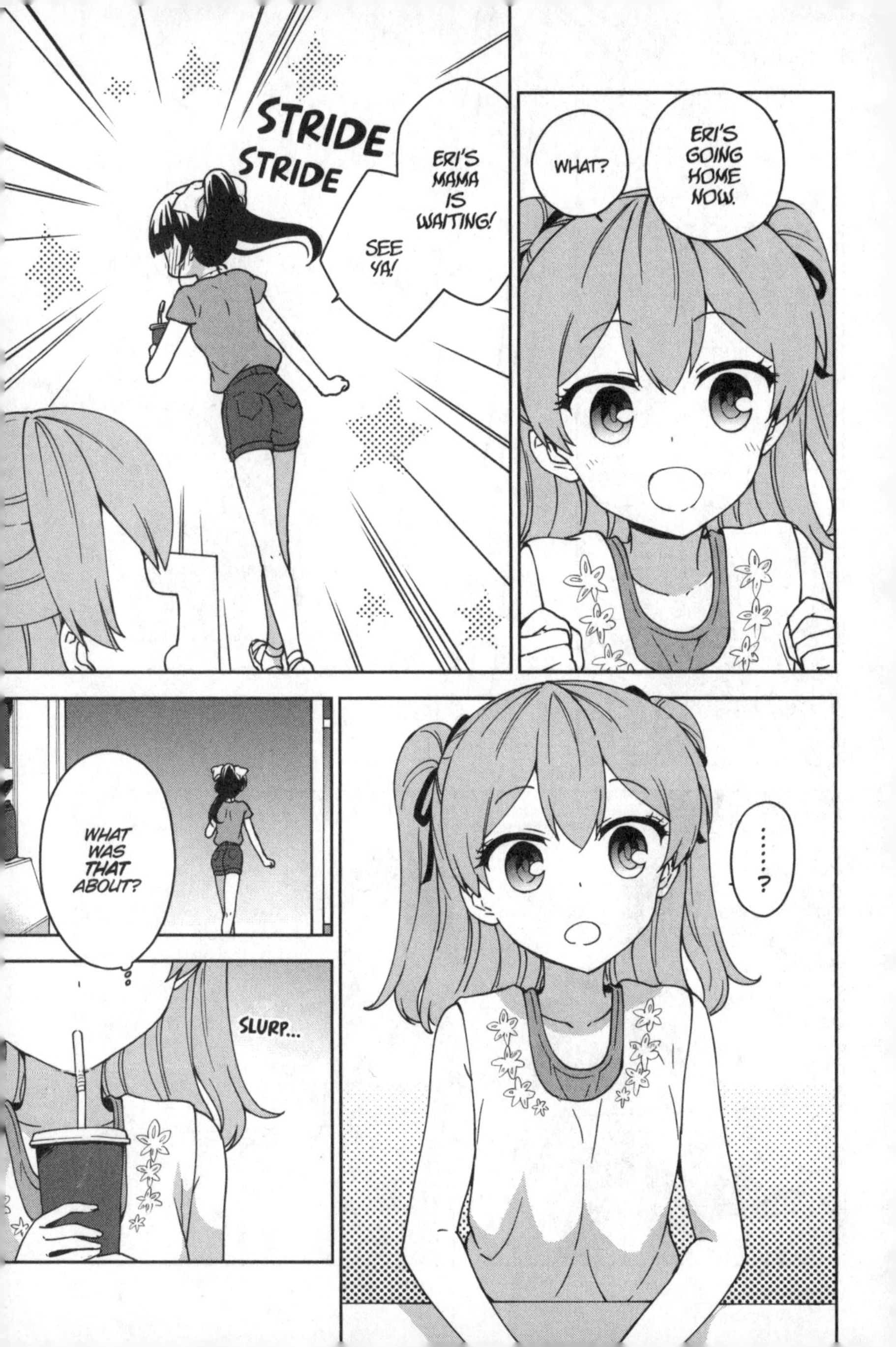

ERI'S GOING HOME NOW.
WHAT?
ERI'S MAMA IS WAITING!
SEE YA!
STRIDE STRIDE
......?
WHAT WAS THAT ABOUT?
SLURP...

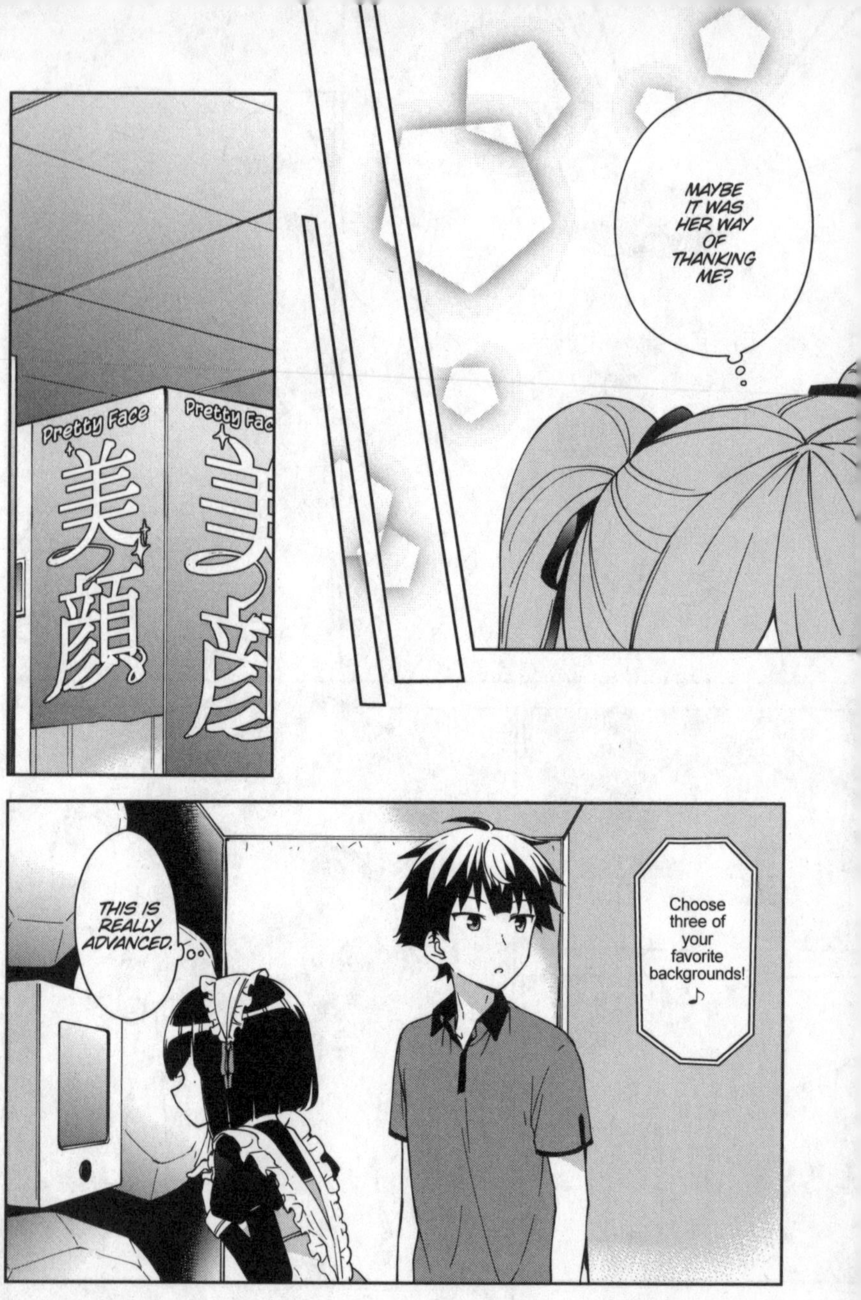
MAYBE IT WAS HER WAY OF THANKING ME?
Pretty Face
美顔
Choose three of your favorite backgrounds! ♪
THIS IS REALLY ADVANCED.

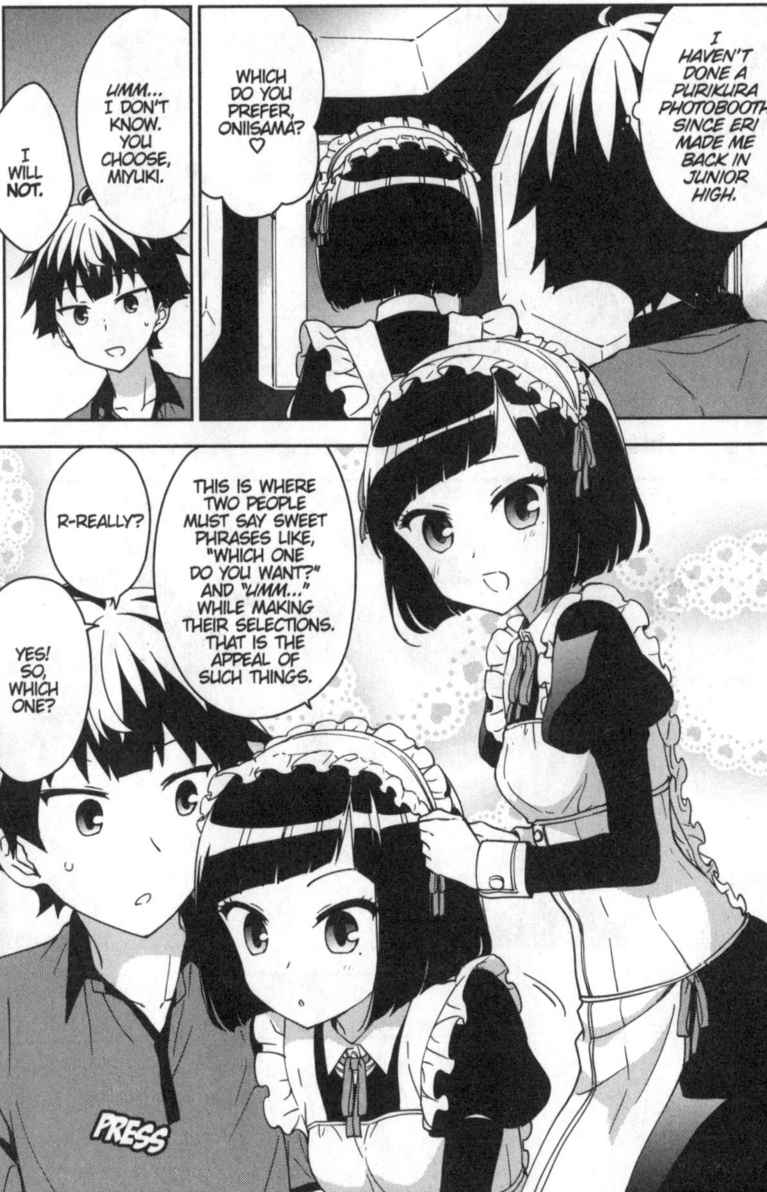
I HAVEN'T DONE A PURIKURA PHOTOBOOTH SINCE ERI MADE ME BACK IN JUNIOR HIGH.
WHICH DO YOU PREFER, ONIISAMA? ♡
UMM... I DON'T KNOW. YOU CHOOSE, MIYUKI.
I WILL NOT.
THIS IS WHERE TWO PEOPLE MUST SAY SWEET PHRASES LIKE, "WHICH ONE DO YOU WANT?" AND "UMM..." WHILE MAKING THEIR SELECTIONS. THAT IS THE APPEAL OF SUCH THINGS.
R-REALLY?
YES! SO, WHICH ONE?
PRESS

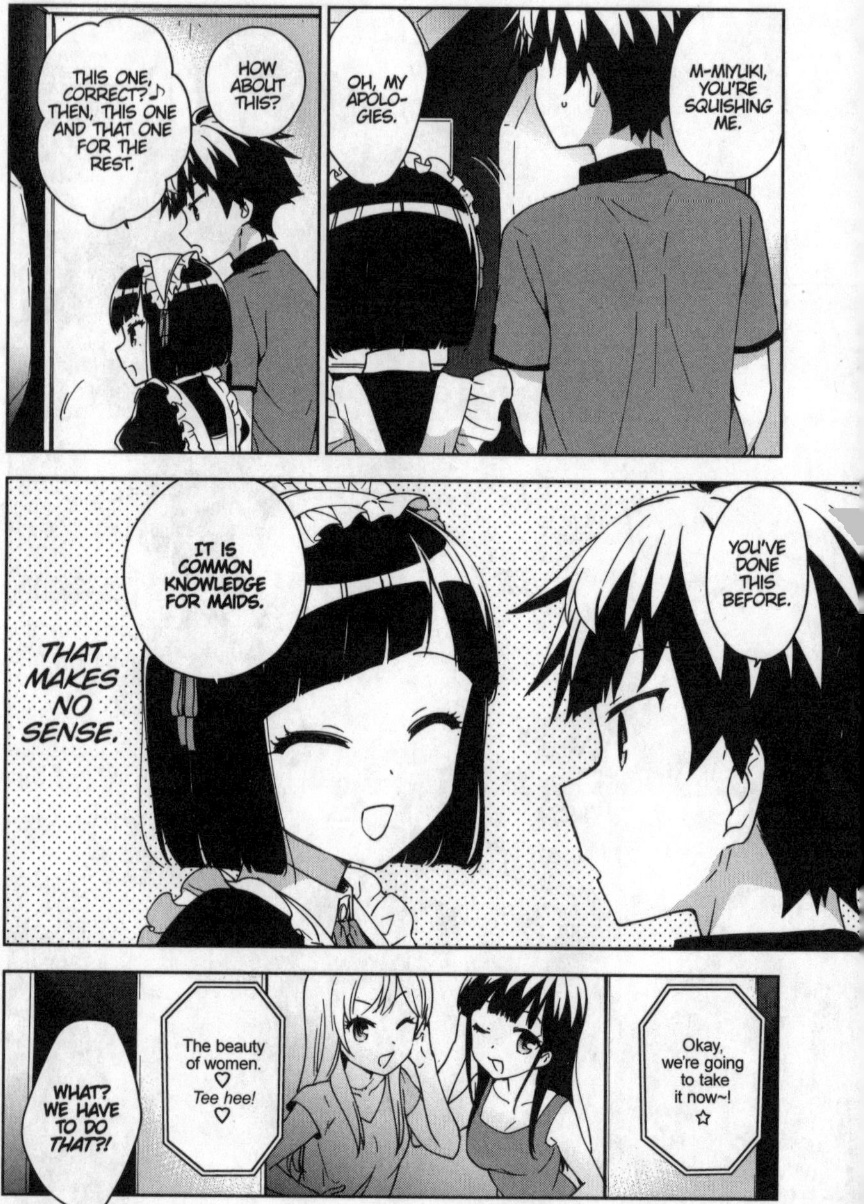
M-MIYUKI, YOU'RE SQUISHING ME.
OH, MY APOLOGIES.
HOW ABOUT THIS?
THIS ONE, CORRECT?♪ THEN, THIS ONE AND THAT ONE FOR THE REST.
YOU'VE DONE THIS BEFORE.
IT IS COMMON KNOWLEDGE FOR MAIDS.
THAT MAKES NO SENSE.
Okay, we're going to take it now~! ☆
The beauty of women. ♡ Tee hee! ♡
WHAT? WE HAVE TO DO THAT?!

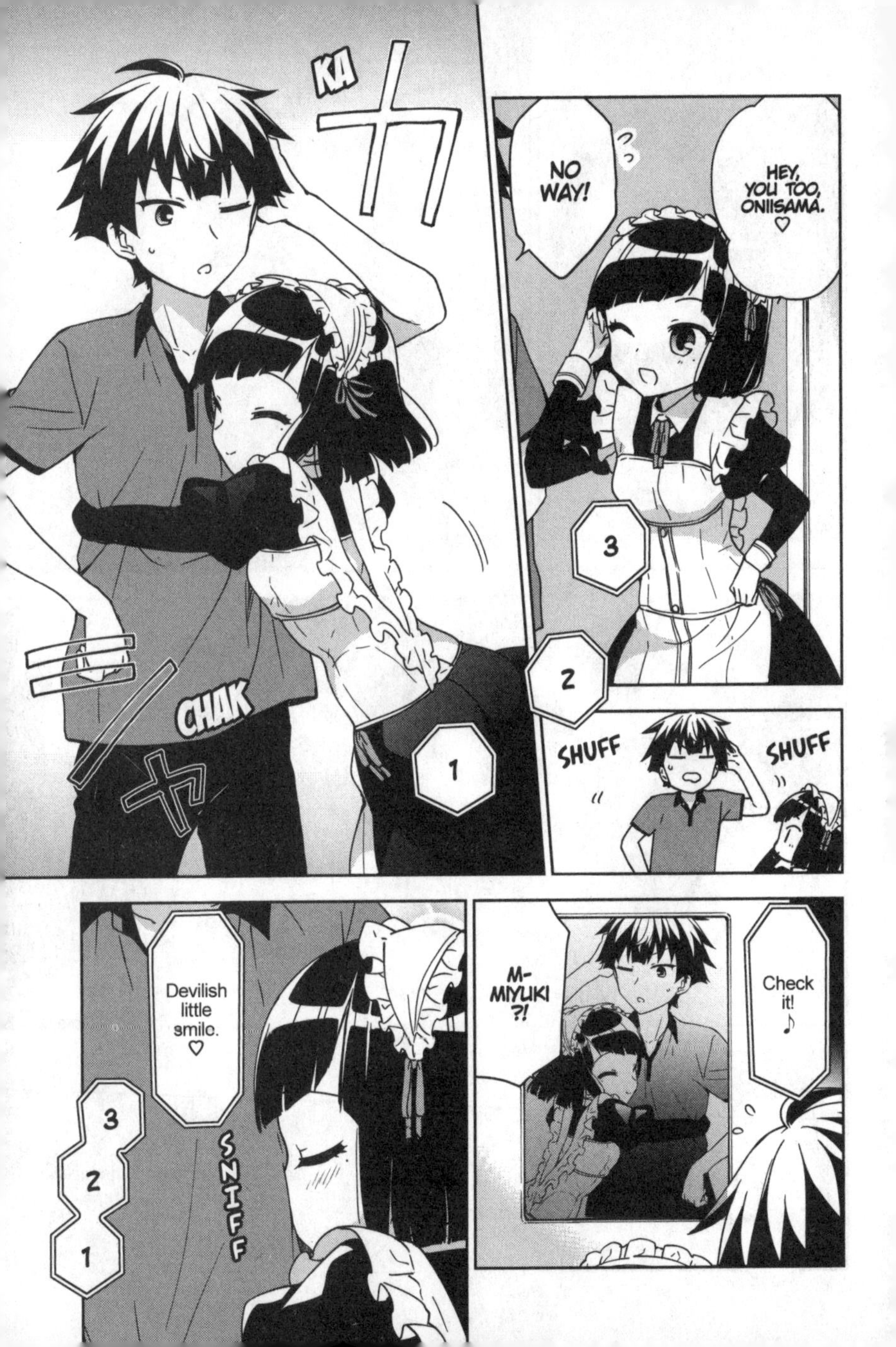
HEY, YOU TOO, ONIISAMA. ♡
NO WAY!
3
2
SHUFF
SHUFF
KA
カ
1
CHAK
Check it! ♪
M-MIYUKI ?!
Devilish little smile. ♡
3
2
1
SNIFF

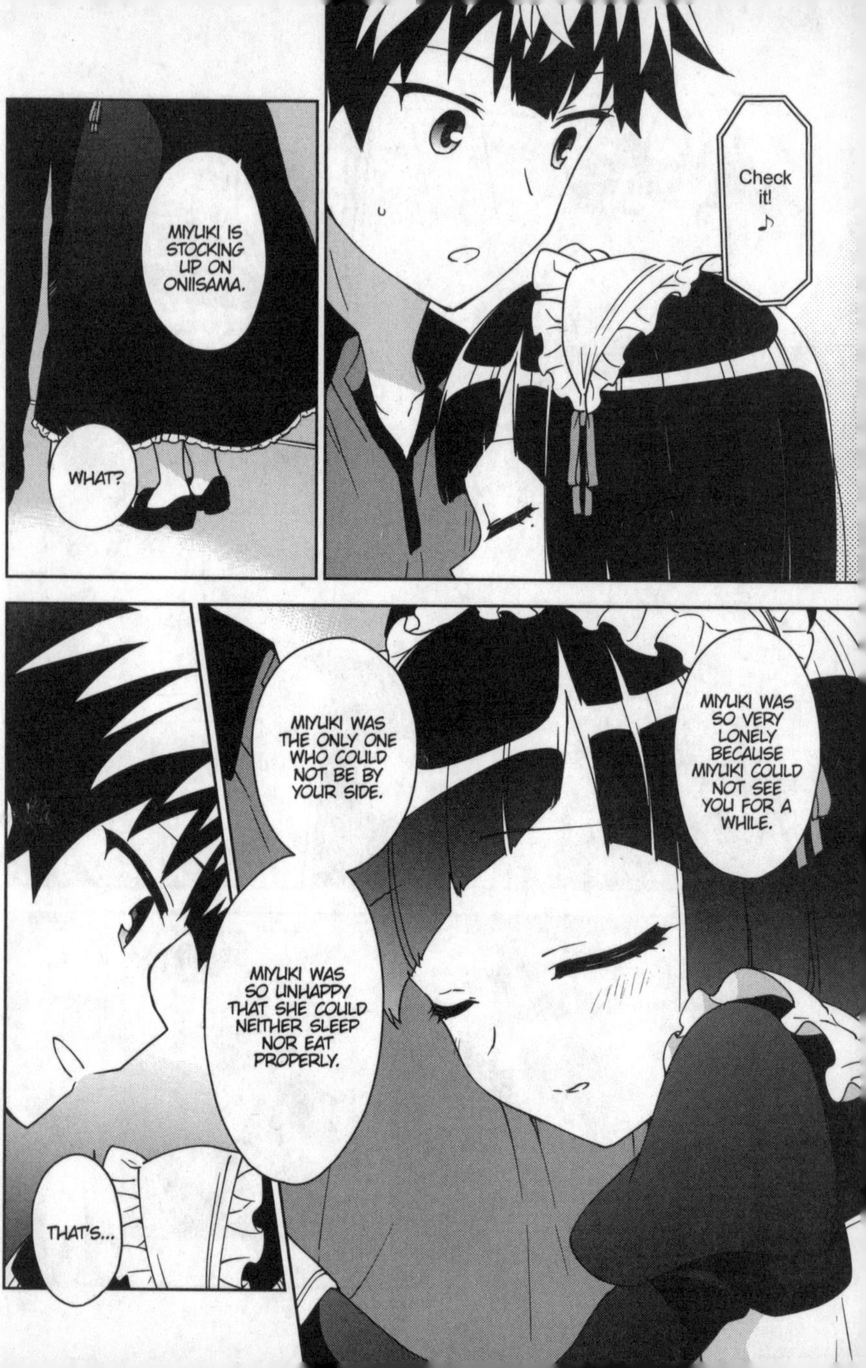
Check it! ♪
MIYUKI IS STOCKING UP ON ONIISAMA.
WHAT?
MIYUKI WAS SO VERY LONELY BECAUSE MIYUKI COULD NOT SEE YOU FOR A WHILE.
MIYUKI WAS THE ONLY ONE WHO COULD NOT BE BY YOUR SIDE.
MIYUKI WAS SO UNHAPPY THAT SHE COULD NEITHER SLEEP NOR EAT PROPERLY.
THAT'S...

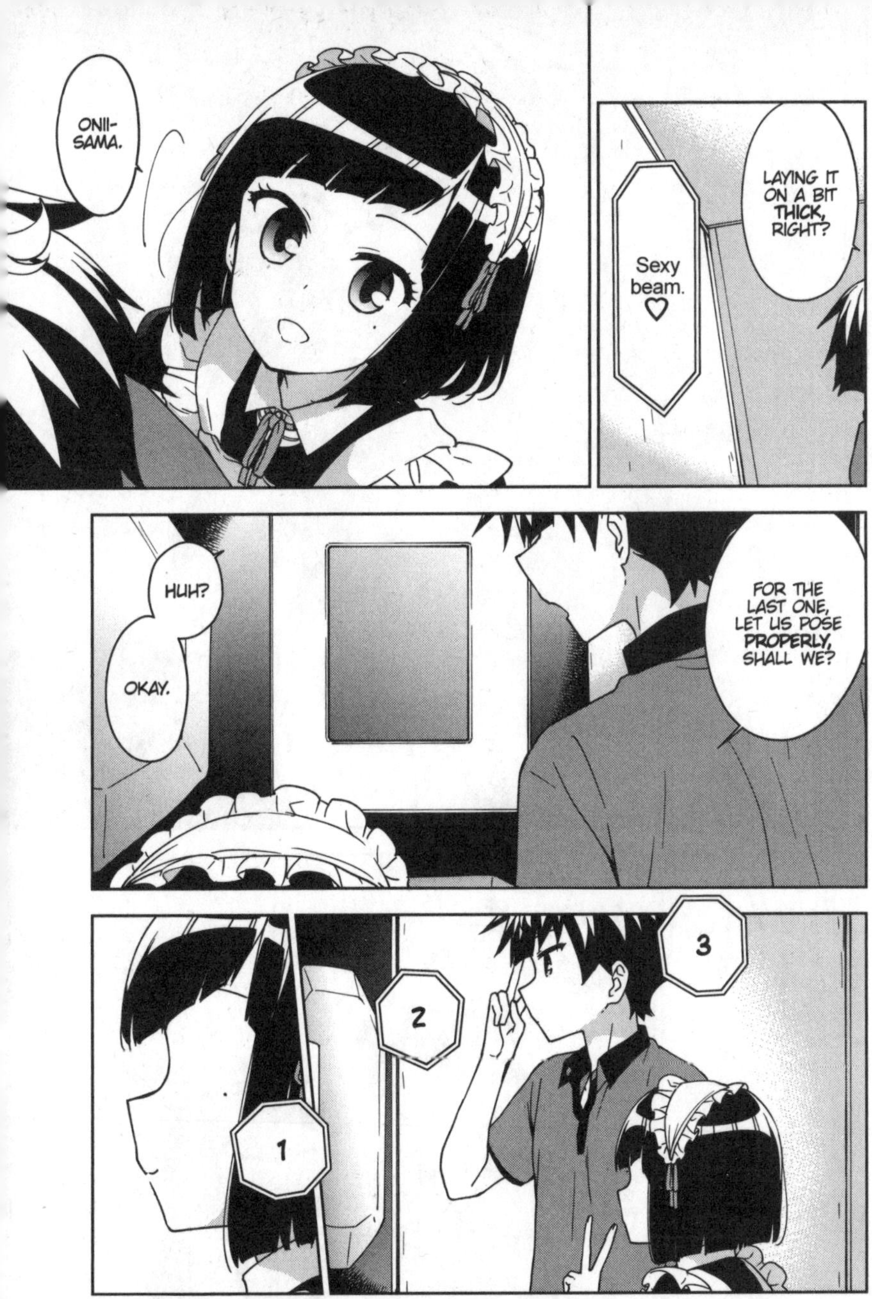
LAYING IT ON A BIT THICK, RIGHT?
Sexy beam. ♡
ONII-SAMA.
FOR THE LAST ONE, LET US POSE PROPERLY, SHALL WE?
HUH?
OKAY.
3
2
1

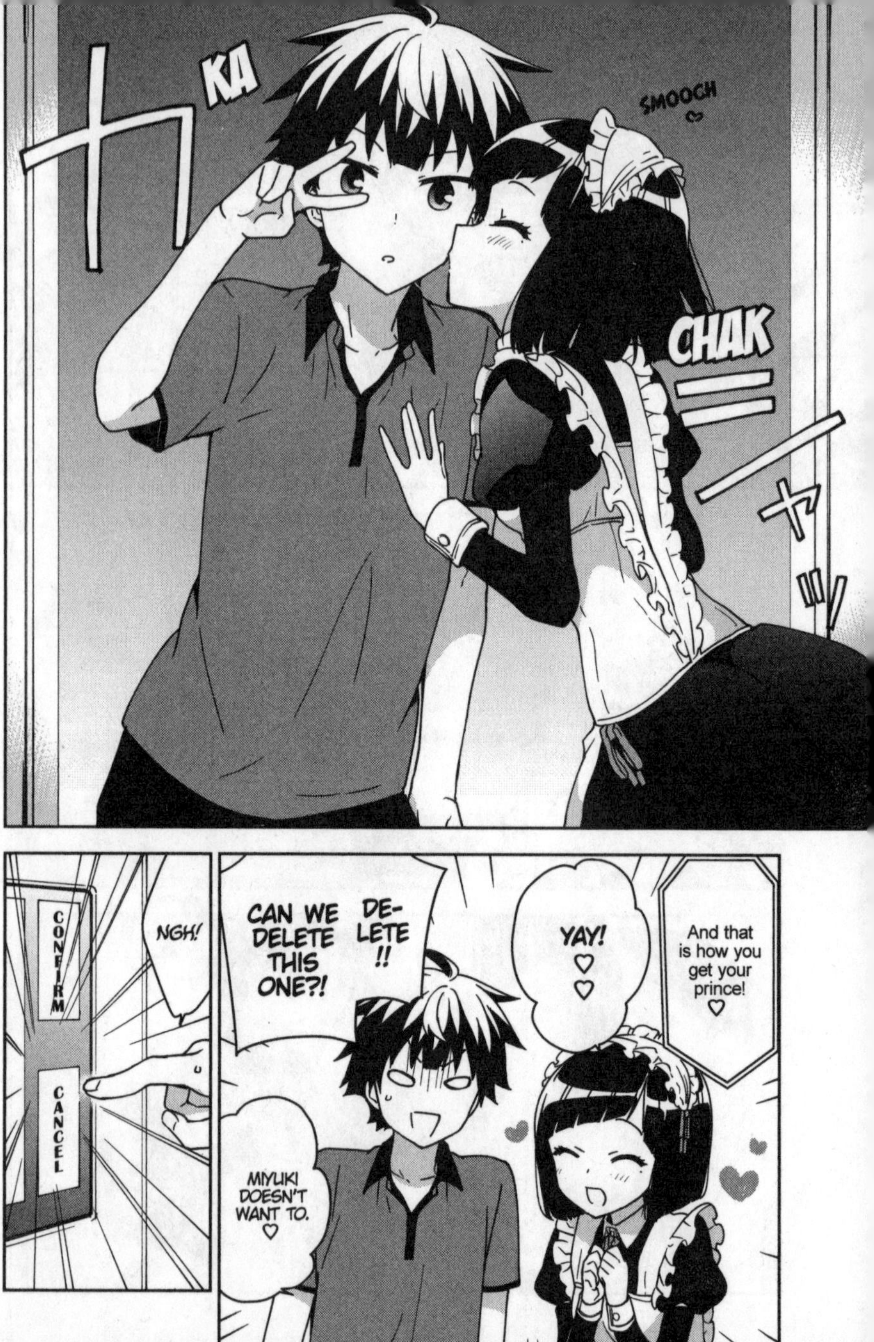

KA
SMOOCH ♡
CHAK
And that is how you get your prince! ♡
YAY! ♡ ♡
DE-LETE !!
CAN WE DELETE THIS ONE?!
MIYUKI DOESN'T WANT TO. ♡
NGH!
CONFIRM
CANCEL

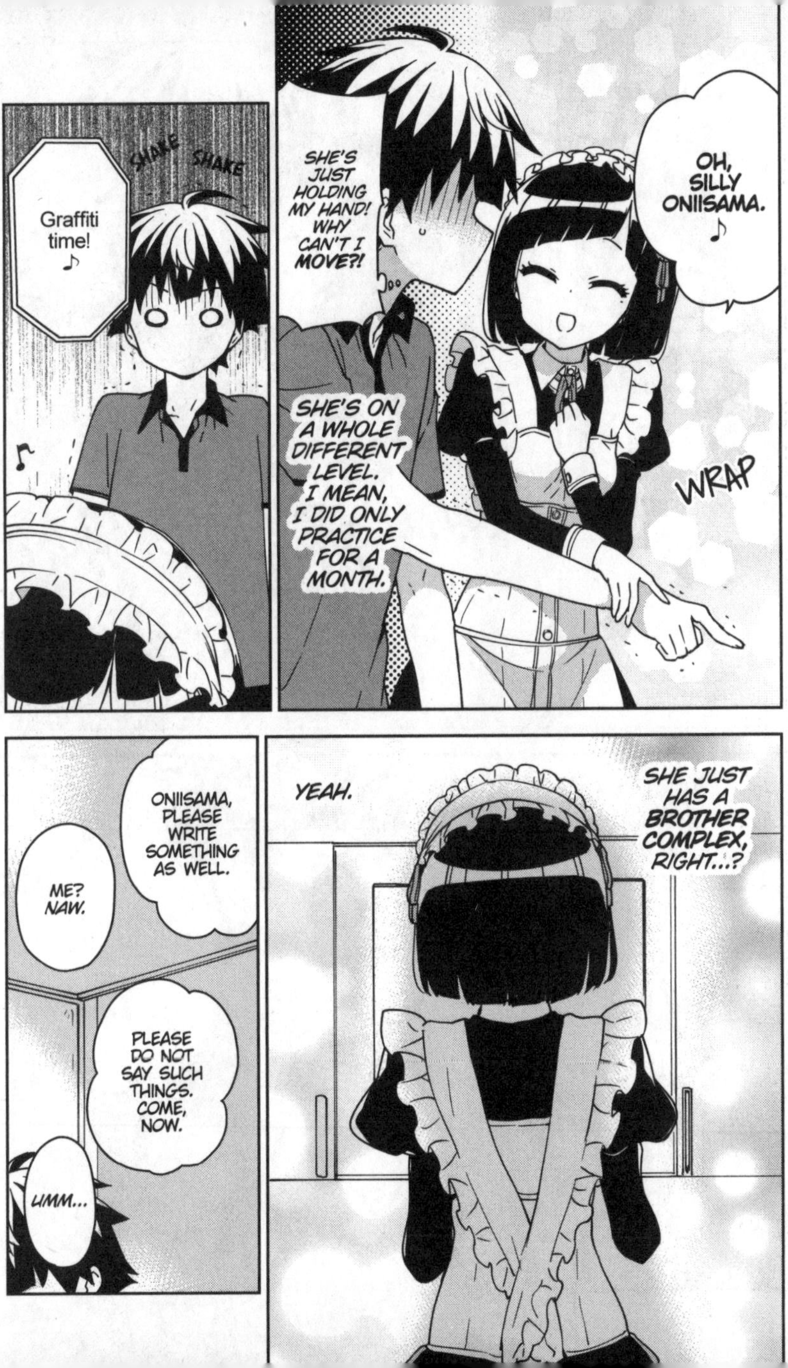
OH, SILLY ONIISAMA. ♪
SHE'S JUST HOLDING MY HAND! WHY CAN'T I MOVE?!
SHE'S ON A WHOLE DIFFERENT LEVEL. I MEAN, I DID ONLY PRACTICE FOR A MONTH.
WRAP
SHAKE
SHAKE
Graffiti time! ♪
♪
SHE JUST HAS A BROTHER COMPLEX, RIGHT...?
YEAH.
ONIISAMA, PLEASE WRITE SOMETHING AS WELL.
ME? NAW.
PLEASE DO NOT SAY SUCH THINGS. COME, NOW.
UMM...

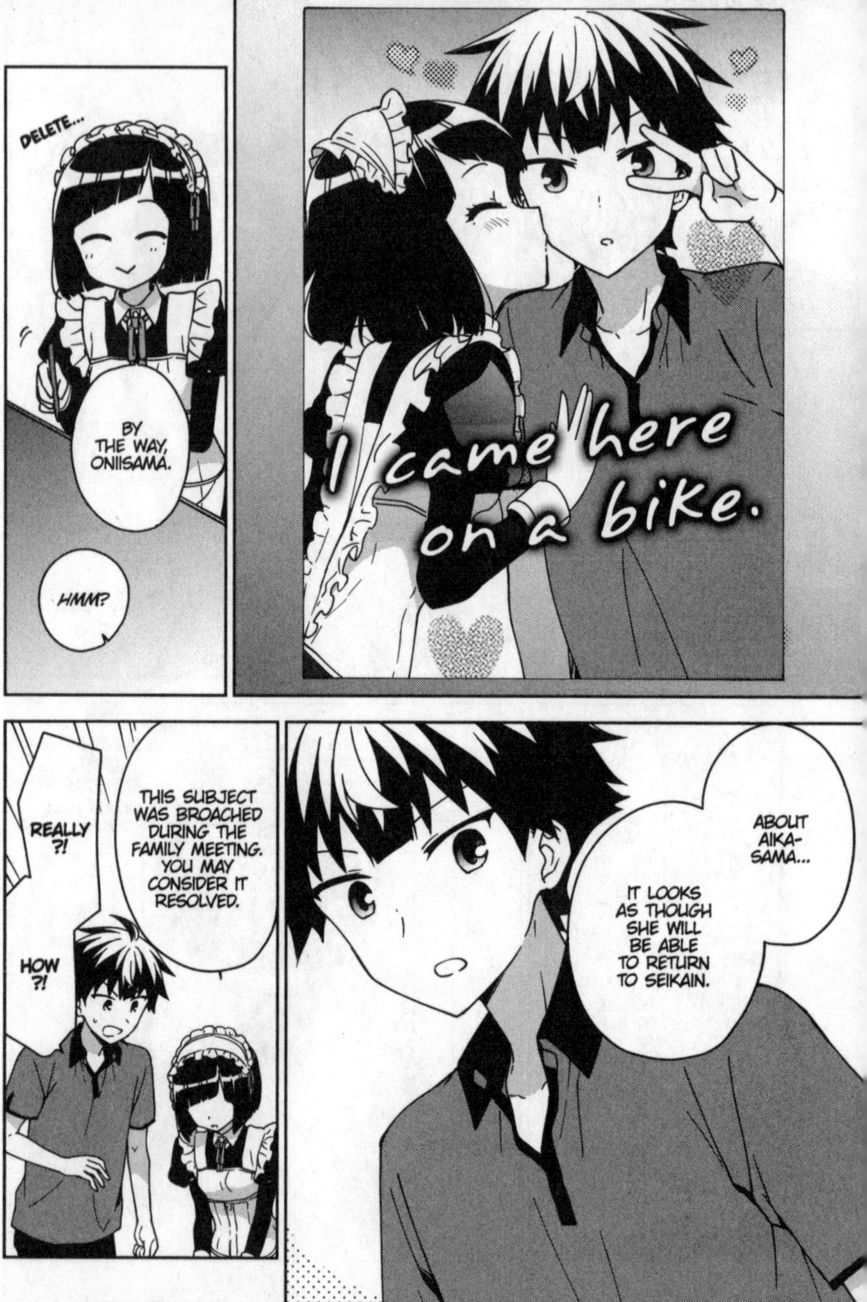
I came here on a bike.
DELETE...
BY THE WAY, ONIISAMA.
HMM?
ABOUT AIKA-SAMA...
IT LOOKS AS THOUGH SHE WILL BE ABLE TO RETURN TO SEIKAIN.
THIS SUBJECT WAS BROACHED DURING THE FAMILY MEETING. YOU MAY CONSIDER IT RESOLVED.
REALLY ?!
HOW ?!

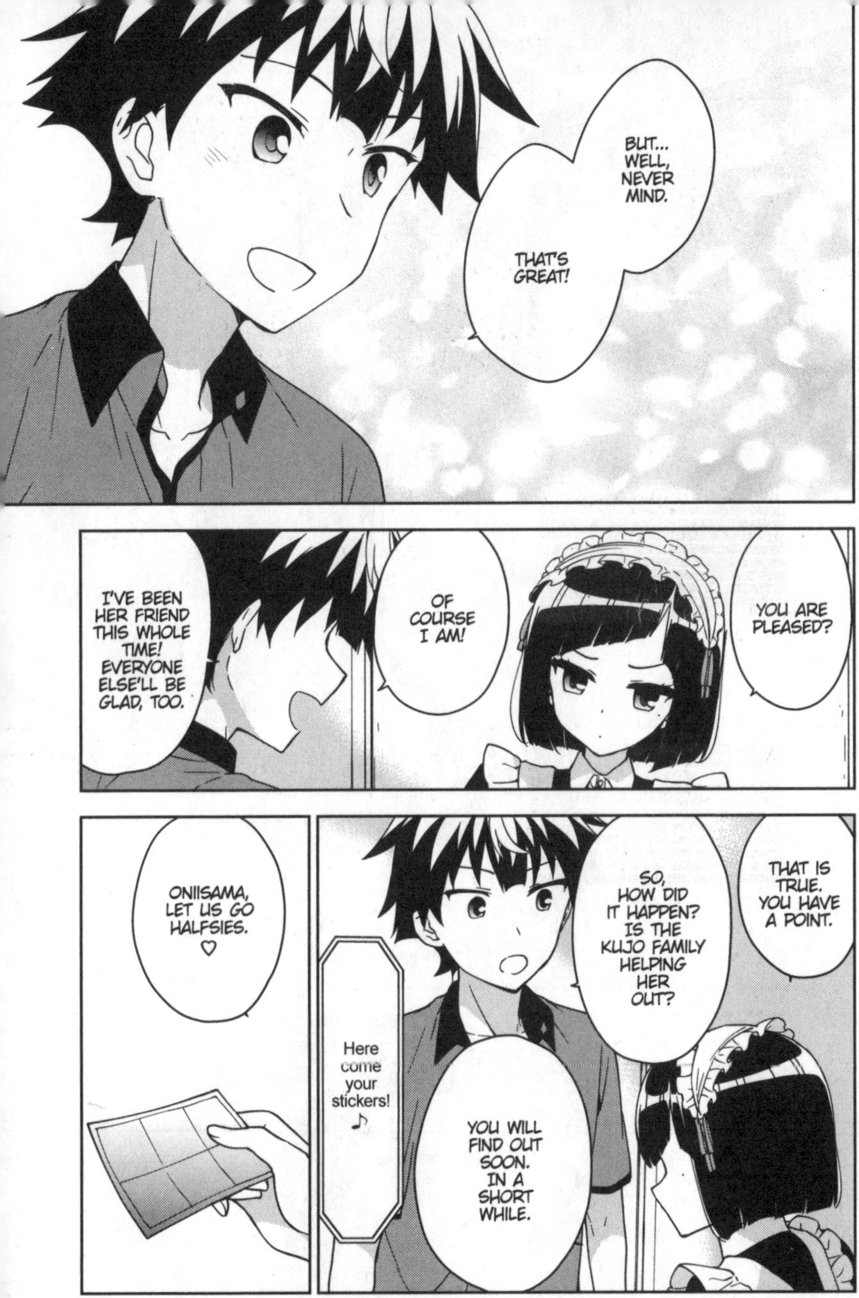
BUT... WELL, NEVER MIND.
THAT'S GREAT!
YOU ARE PLEASED?
OF COURSE I AM!
I'VE BEEN HER FRIEND THIS WHOLE TIME! EVERYONE ELSE'LL BE GLAD, TOO.
THAT IS TRUE. YOU HAVE A POINT.
SO, HOW DID IT HAPPEN? IS THE KUJO FAMILY HELPING HER OUT?
YOU WILL FIND OUT SOON. IN A SHORT WHILE.
Here come your stickers! ♪
ONIISAMA, LET US GO HALFSIES. ♡

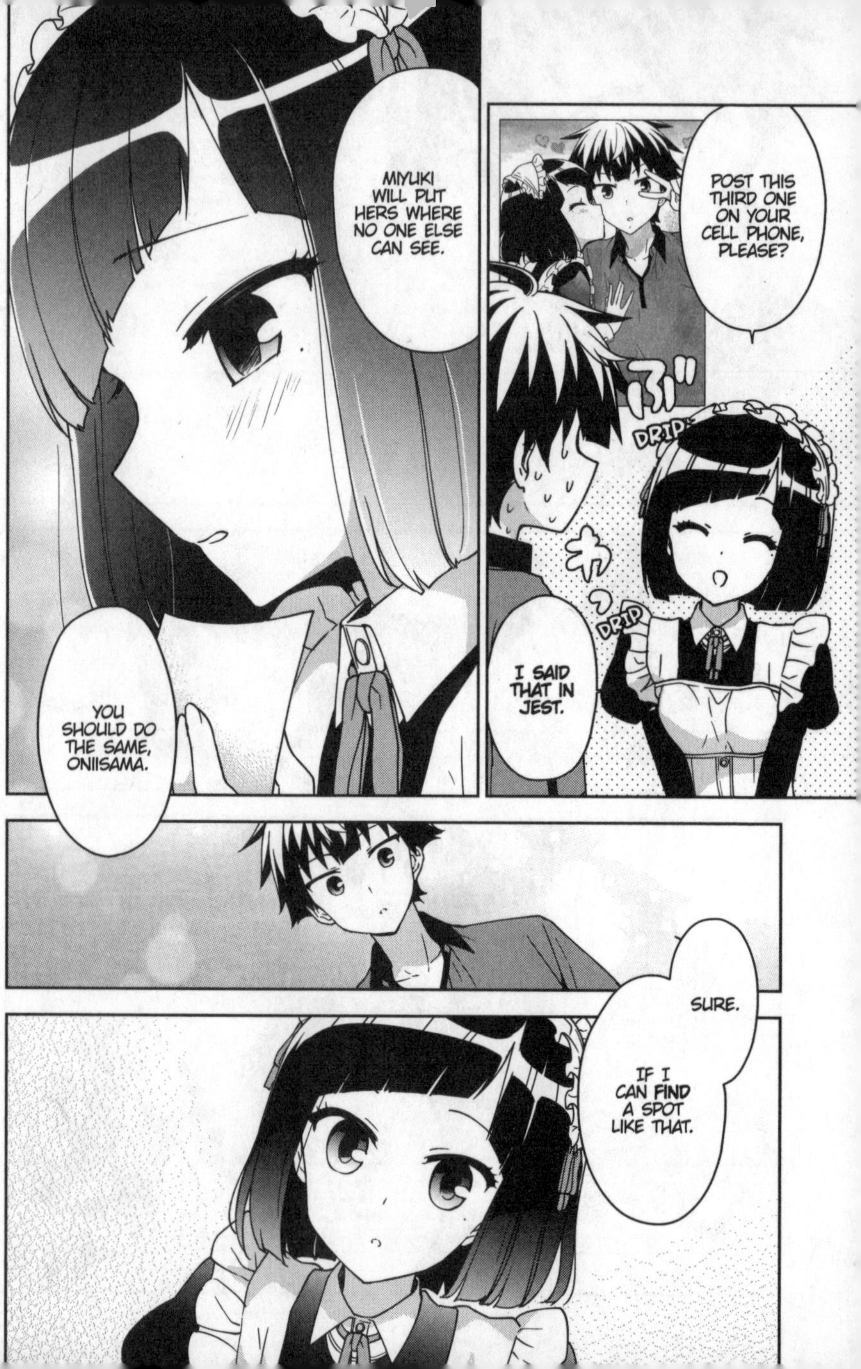
POST THIS THIRD ONE ON YOUR CELL PHONE, PLEASE?
DRIP
DRIP
I SAID THAT IN JEST.
MIYUKI WILL PUT HERS WHERE NO ONE ELSE CAN SEE.
YOU SHOULD DO THE SAME, ONIISAMA.
SURE.
IF I CAN FIND A SPOT LIKE THAT.

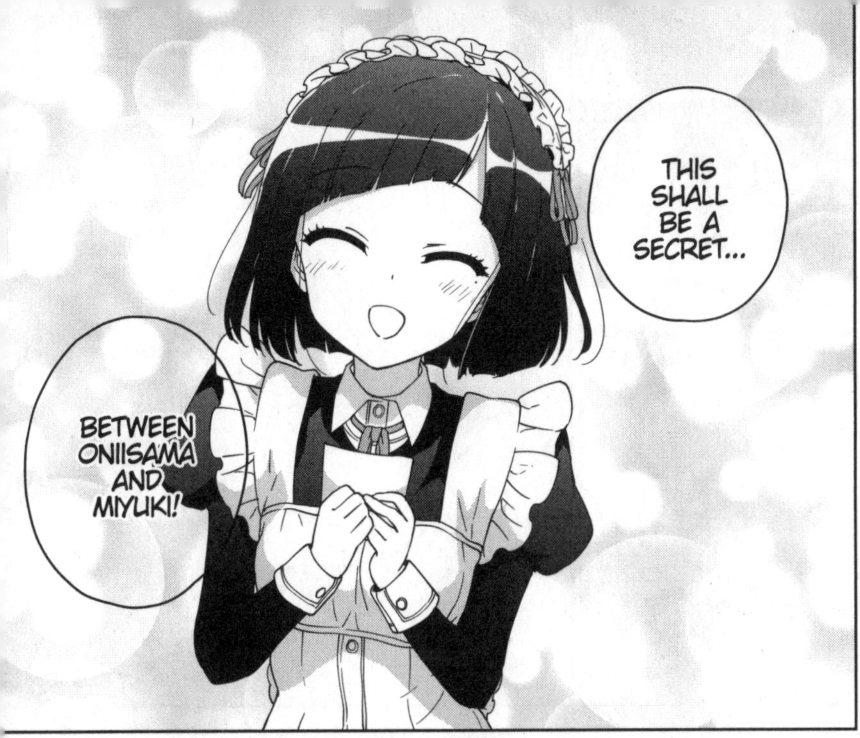
THIS SHALL BE A SECRET...
BETWEEN ONIISAMA AND MIYUKI!
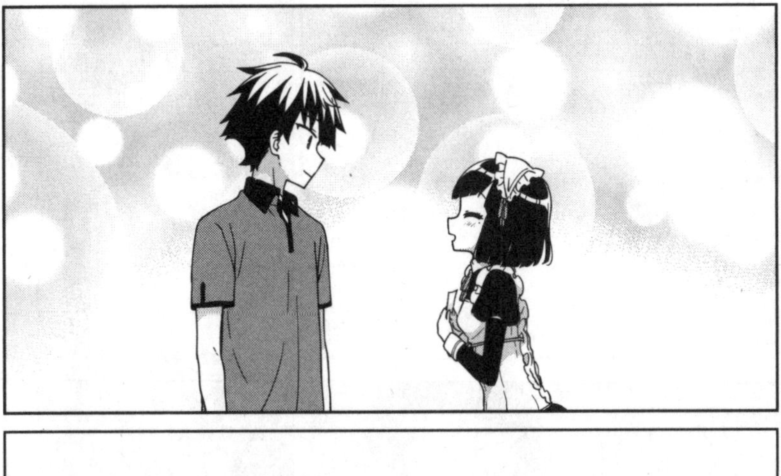

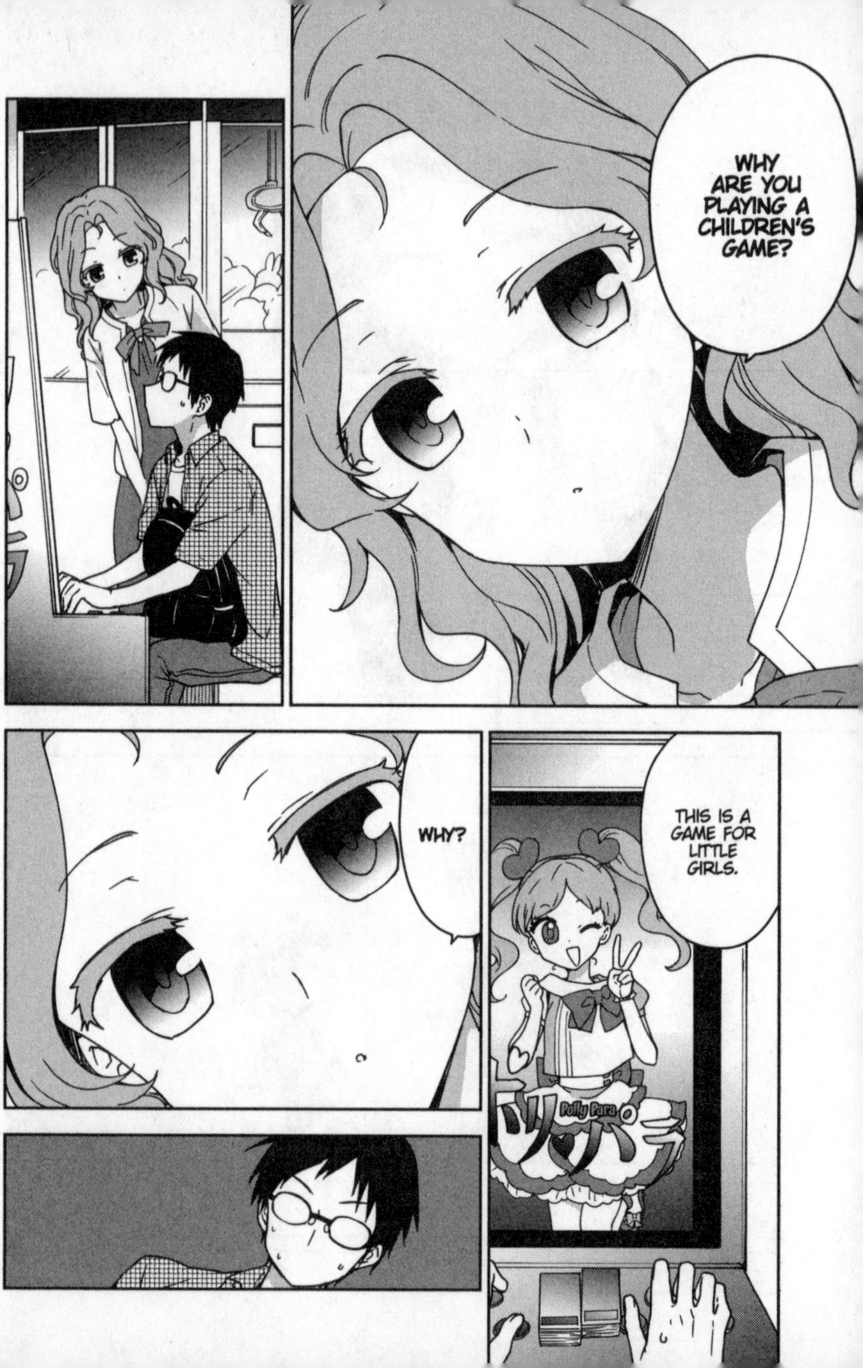
WHY ARE YOU PLAYING A CHILDREN'S GAME?
THIS IS A GAME FOR LITTLE GIRLS.
Polly Para
WHY?

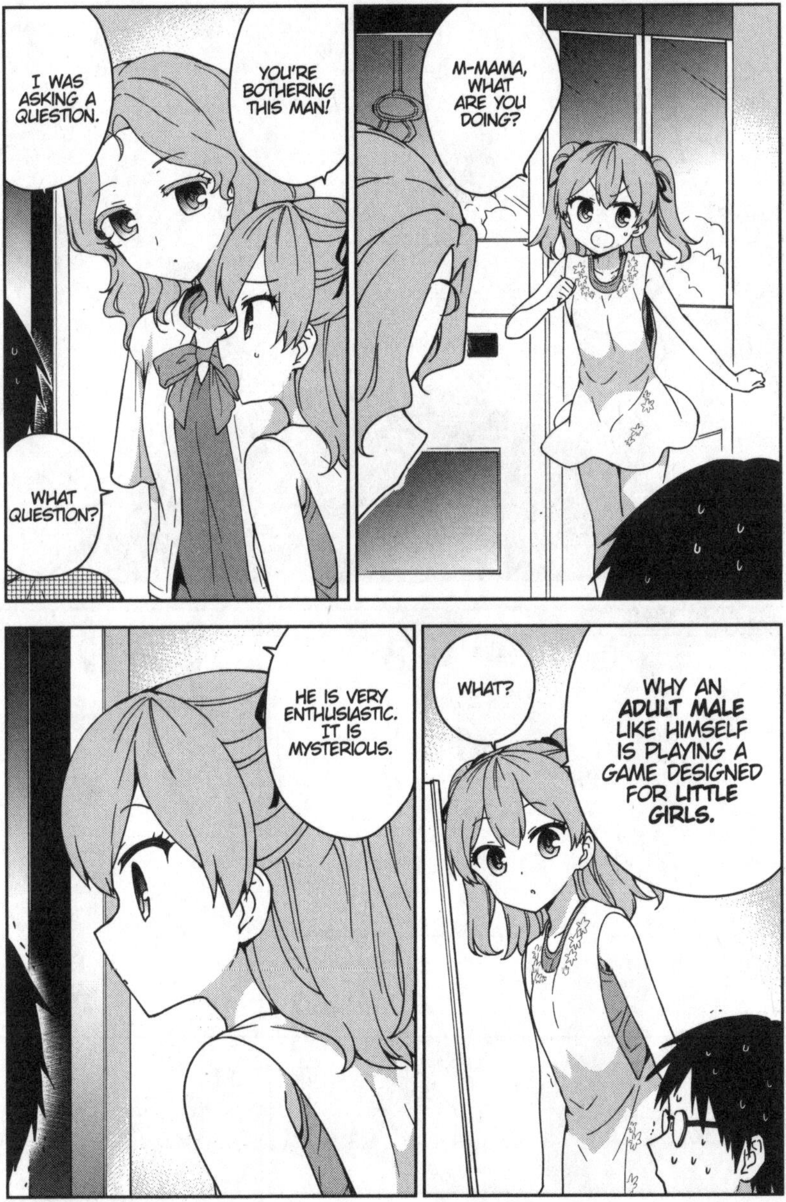
M-MAMA, WHAT ARE YOU DOING?
YOU'RE BOTHERING THIS MAN!
I WAS ASKING A QUESTION.
WHAT QUESTION?
WHY AN ADULT MALE LIKE HIMSELF IS PLAYING A GAME DESIGNED FOR LITTLE GIRLS.
WHAT?
HE IS VERY ENTHUSIASTIC. IT IS MYSTERIOUS.

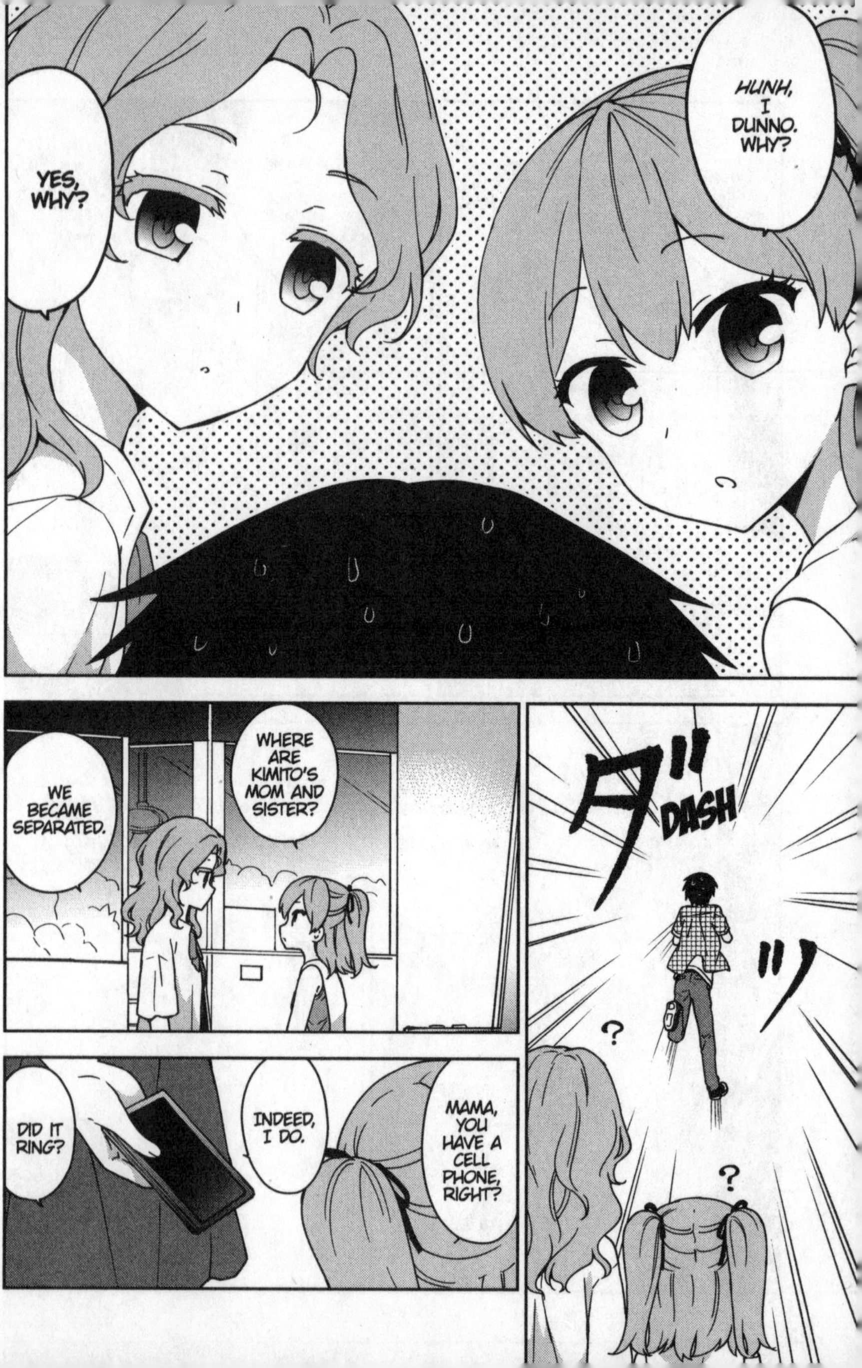
HUNH, I DUNNO. WHY?
YES, WHY?
ダッ
DASH
ッ
?
?
WHERE ARE KIMITO'S MOM AND SISTER?
WE BECAME SEPARATED.
MAMA, YOU HAVE A CELL PHONE, RIGHT?
INDEED, I DO.
DID IT RING?

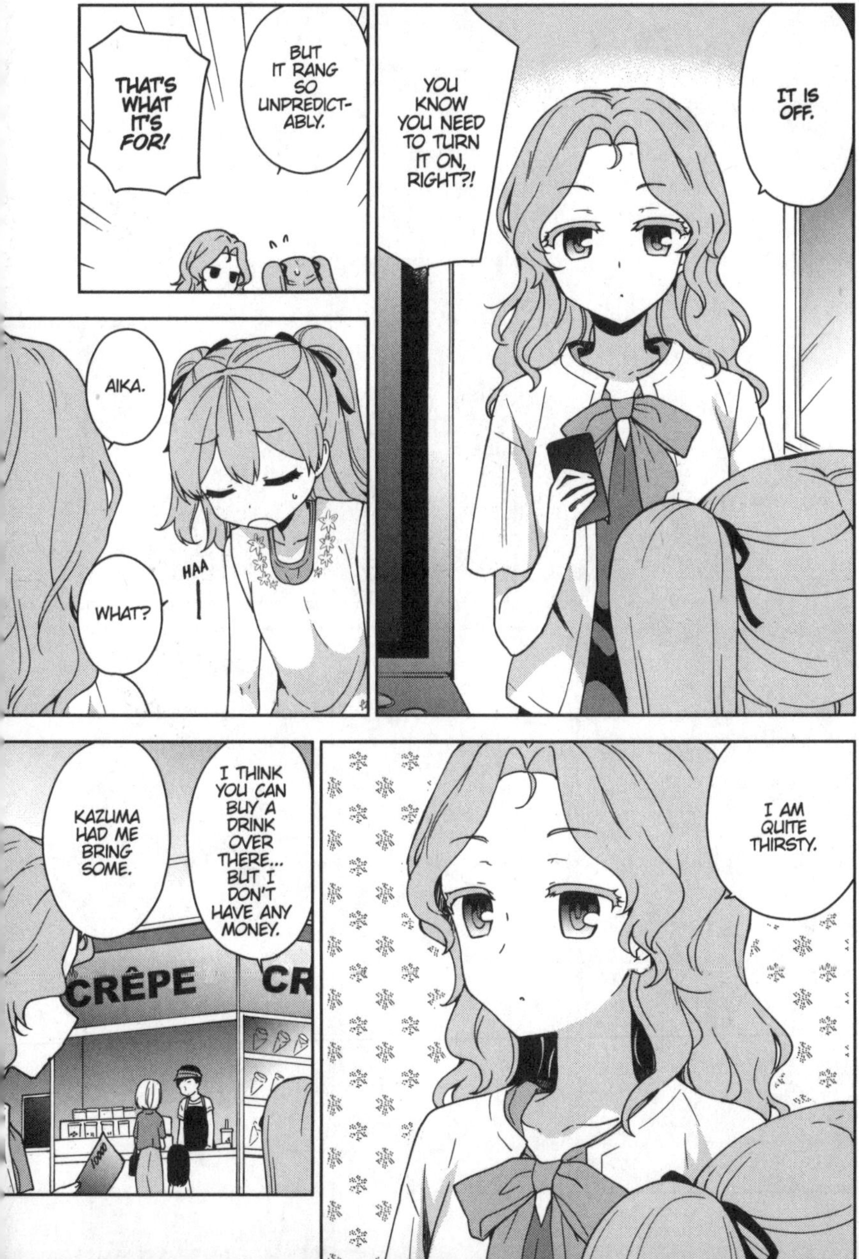
IT IS OFF.
YOU KNOW YOU NEED TO TURN IT ON, RIGHT?!
BUT IT RANG SO UNPREDICT-ABLY.
THAT'S WHAT IT'S FOR!
AIKA.
HAA
WHAT?
I AM QUITE THIRSTY.
I THINK YOU CAN BUY A DRINK OVER THERE... BUT I DON'T HAVE ANY MONEY.
KAZUMA HAD ME BRING SOME.
CRÊPE
CR

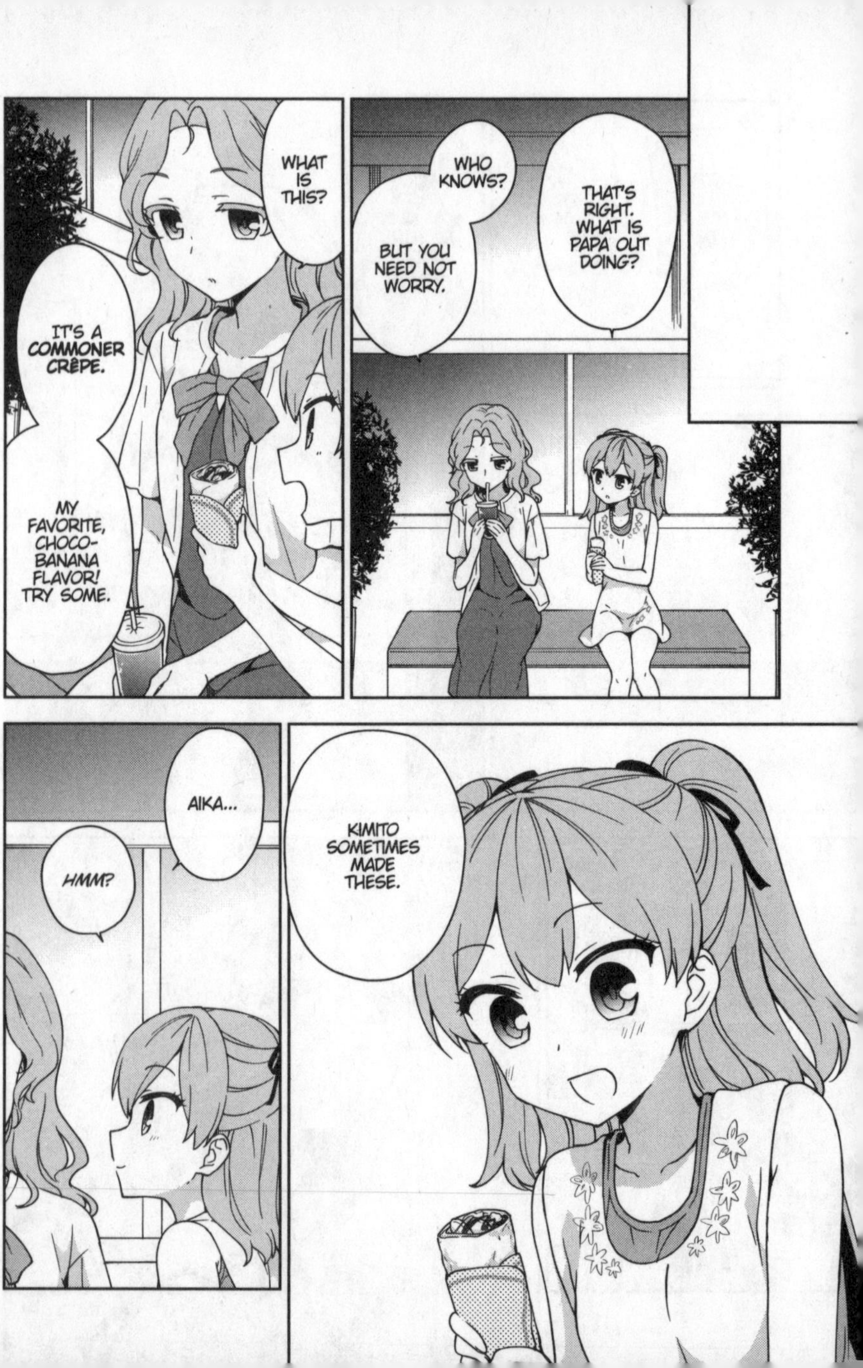
THAT'S RIGHT. WHAT IS PAPA OUT DOING?
WHO KNOWS?
BUT YOU NEED NOT WORRY.
WHAT IS THIS?
IT'S A COMMONER CRÊPE.
MY FAVORITE, CHOCO-BANANA FLAVOR! TRY SOME.
KIMITO SOMETIMES MADE THESE.
AIKA...
HMM?

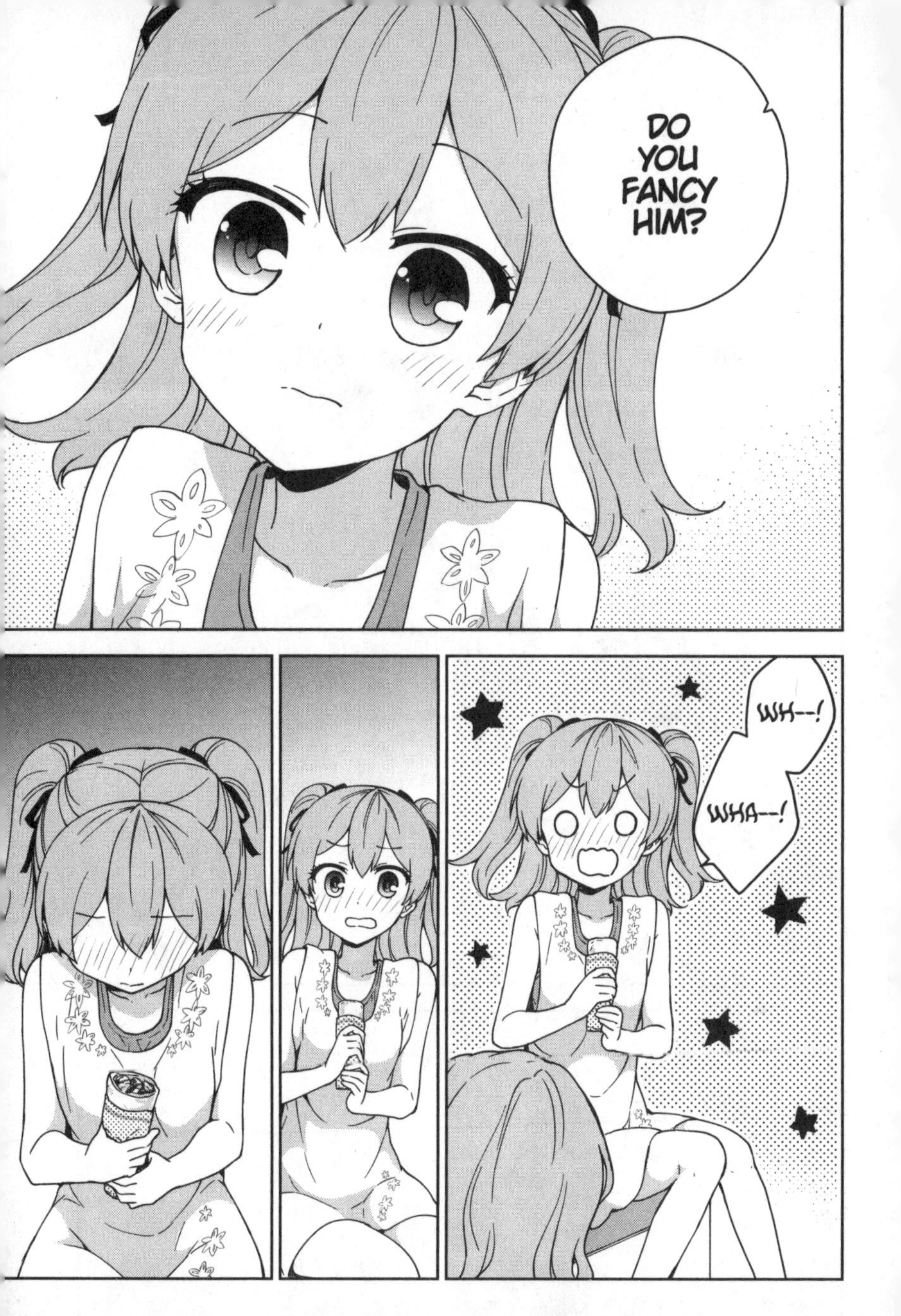
DO YOU FANCY HIM?
WH--!
WHA--!

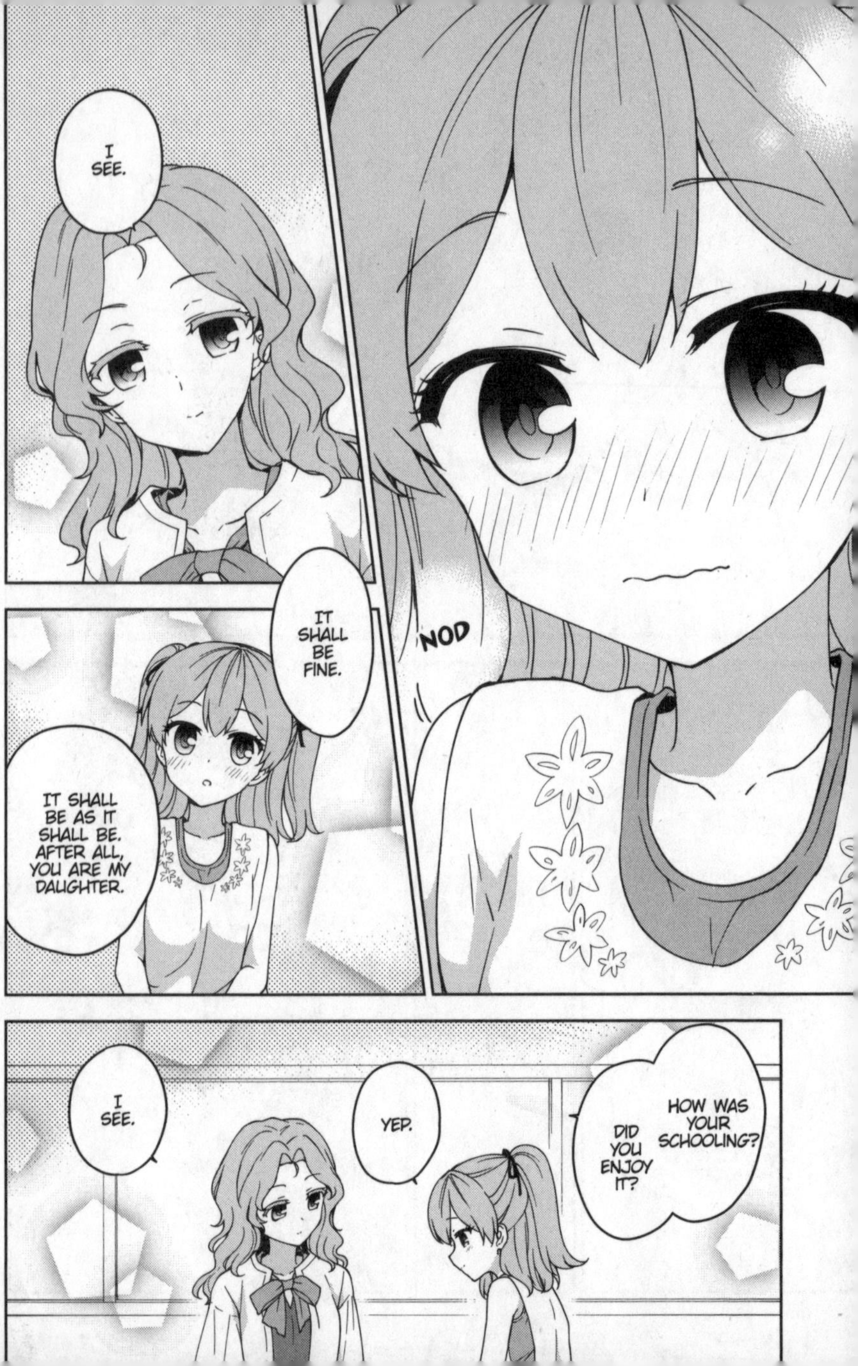
NOD
I SEE.
IT SHALL BE FINE.
IT SHALL BE AS IT SHALL BE. AFTER ALL, YOU ARE MY DAUGHTER.
HOW WAS YOUR SCHOOLING?
DID YOU ENJOY IT?
YEP.
I SEE.

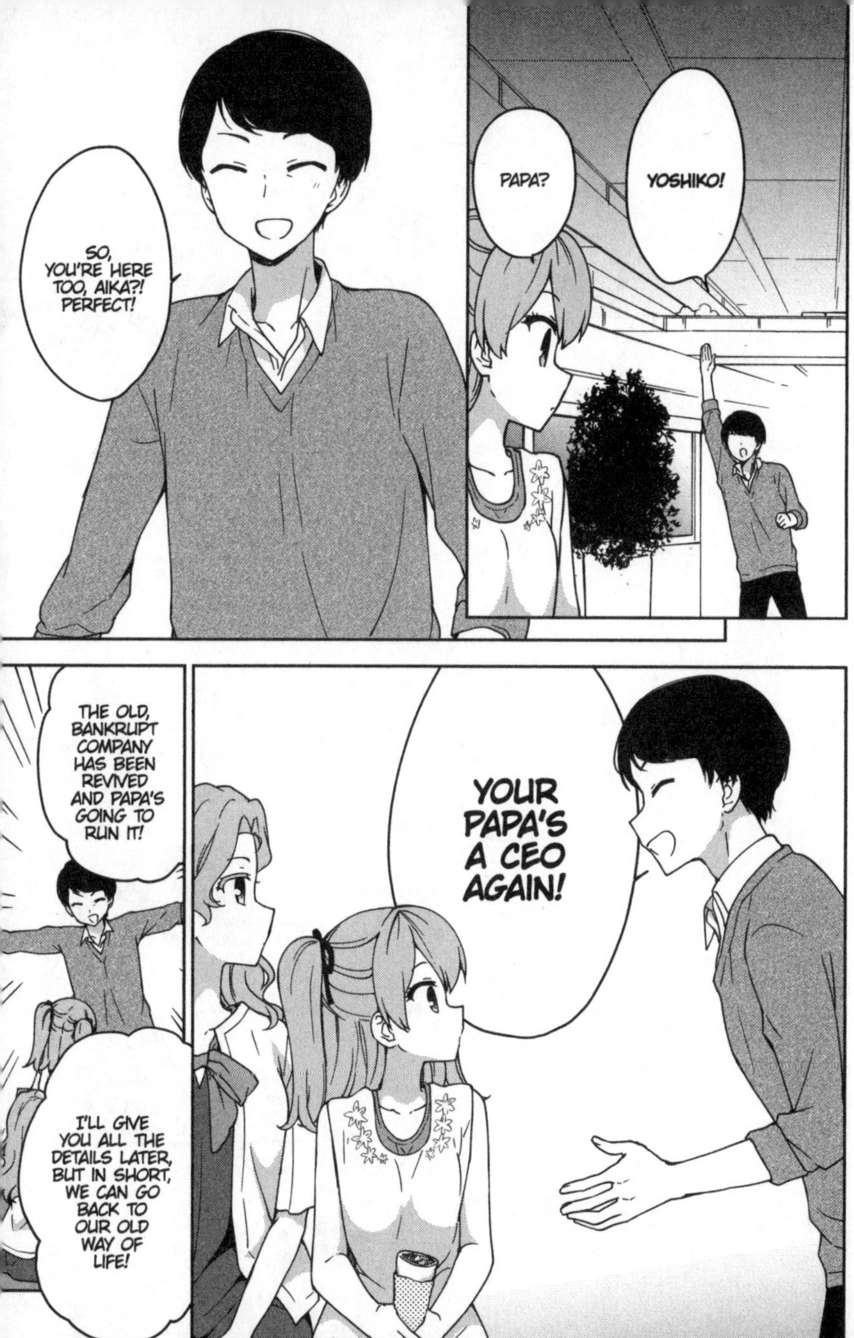
YOSHIKO!
PAPA?
SO, YOU'RE HERE TOO, AIKA?! PERFECT!
YOUR PAPA'S A CEO AGAIN!
THE OLD, BANKRUPT COMPANY HAS BEEN REVIVED AND PAPA'S GOING TO RUN IT!
I'LL GIVE YOU ALL THE DETAILS LATER, BUT IN SHORT, WE CAN GO BACK TO OUR OLD WAY OF LIFE!

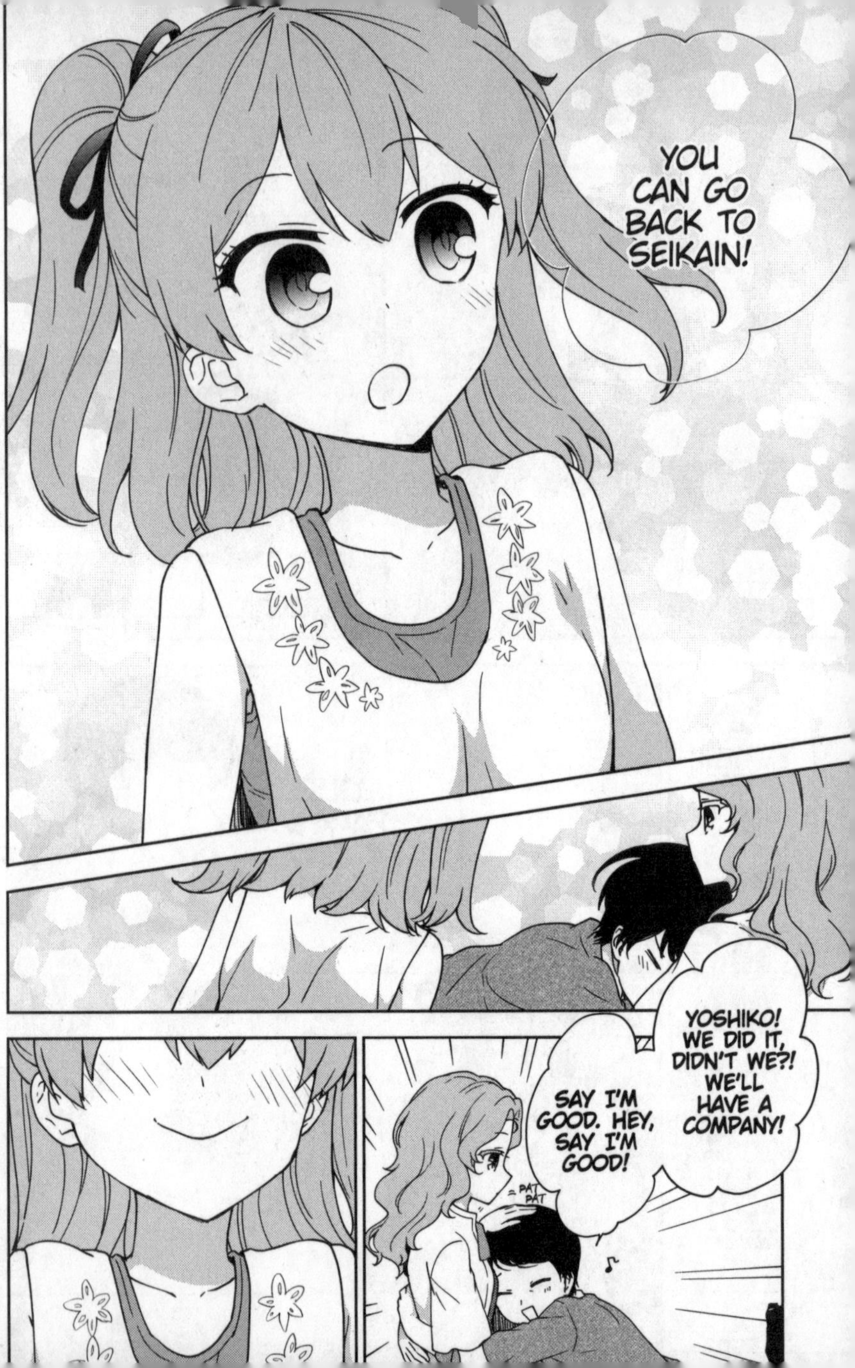
YOU CAN GO BACK TO SEIKAIN!
YOSHIKO! WE DID IT, DIDN'T WE?! WE'LL HAVE A COMPANY!
SAY I'M GOOD. HEY, SAY I'M GOOD!
PAT PAT

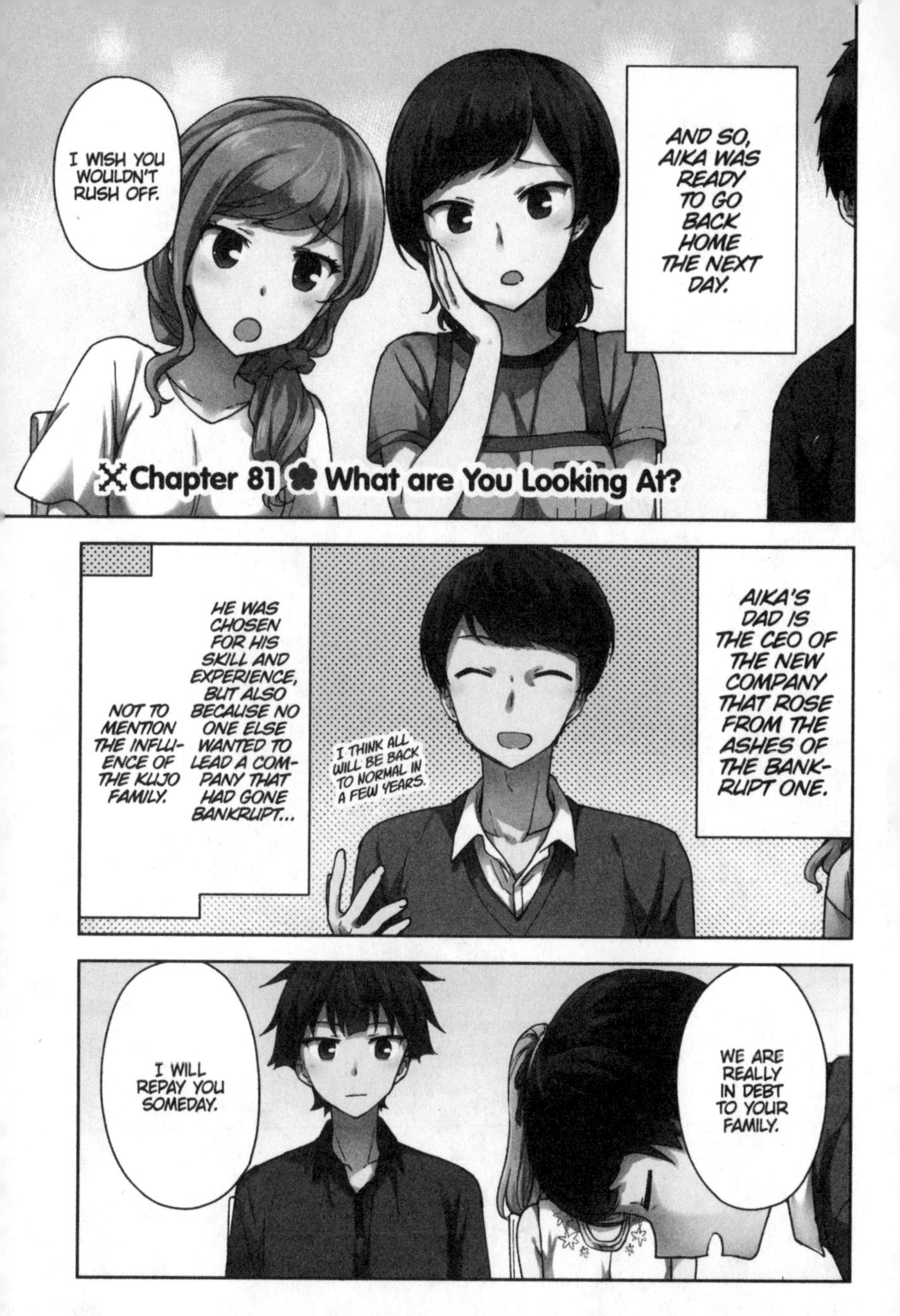
AND SO, AIKA WAS READY TO GO BACK HOME THE NEXT DAY.
I WISH YOU WOULDN'T RUSH OFF.
Chapter 81 What are You Looking At?
AIKA'S DAD IS THE CEO OF THE NEW COMPANY THAT ROSE FROM THE ASHES OF THE BANKRUPT ONE.
HE WAS CHOSEN FOR HIS SKILL AND EXPERIENCE, BUT ALSO BECAUSE NO ONE ELSE WANTED TO LEAD A COMPANY THAT HAD GONE BANKRUPT...
NOT TO MENTION THE INFLUENCE OF THE KUJO FAMILY.
I THINK ALL WILL BE BACK TO NORMAL IN A FEW YEARS.
WE ARE REALLY IN DEBT TO YOUR FAMILY.
I WILL REPAY YOU SOMEDAY.

Chapter 81 ✿ What are You Looking At?

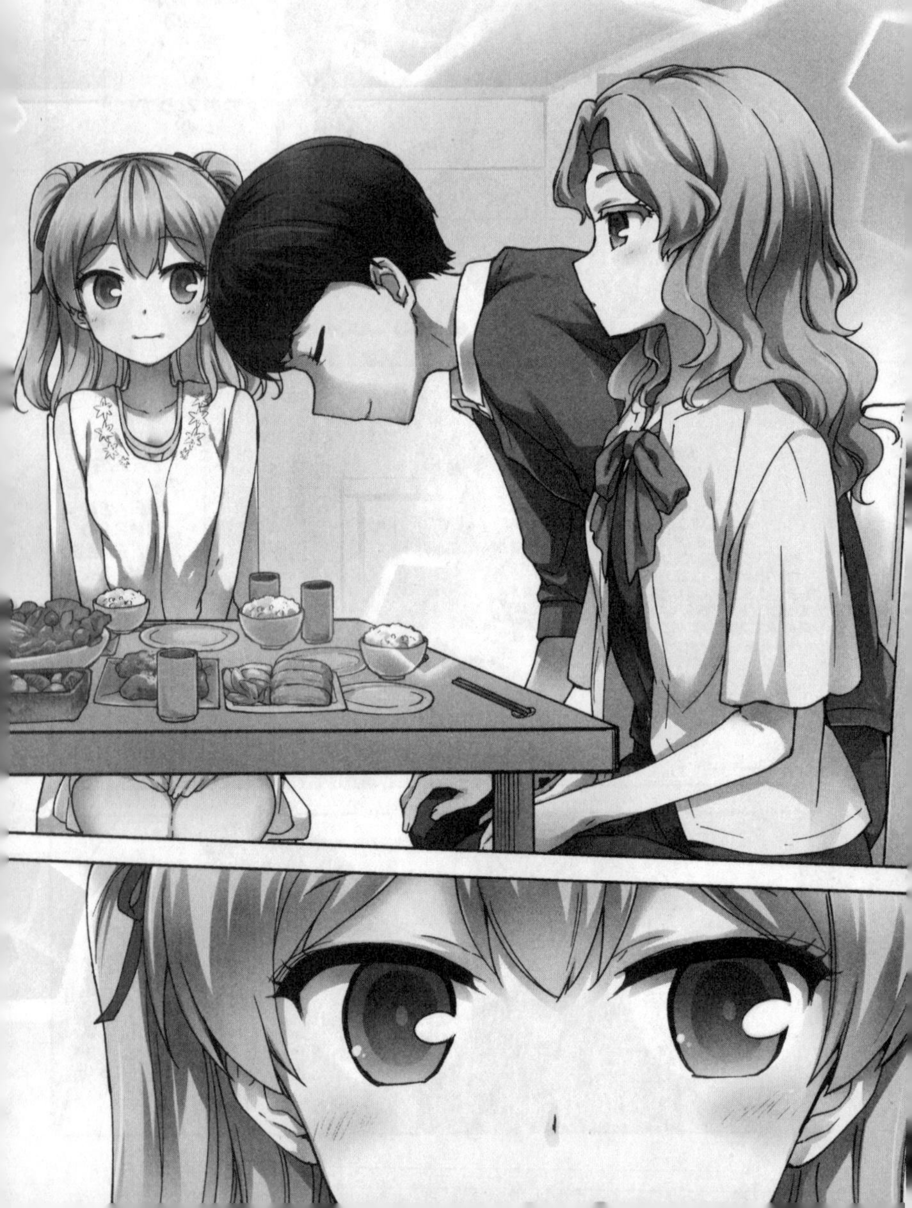

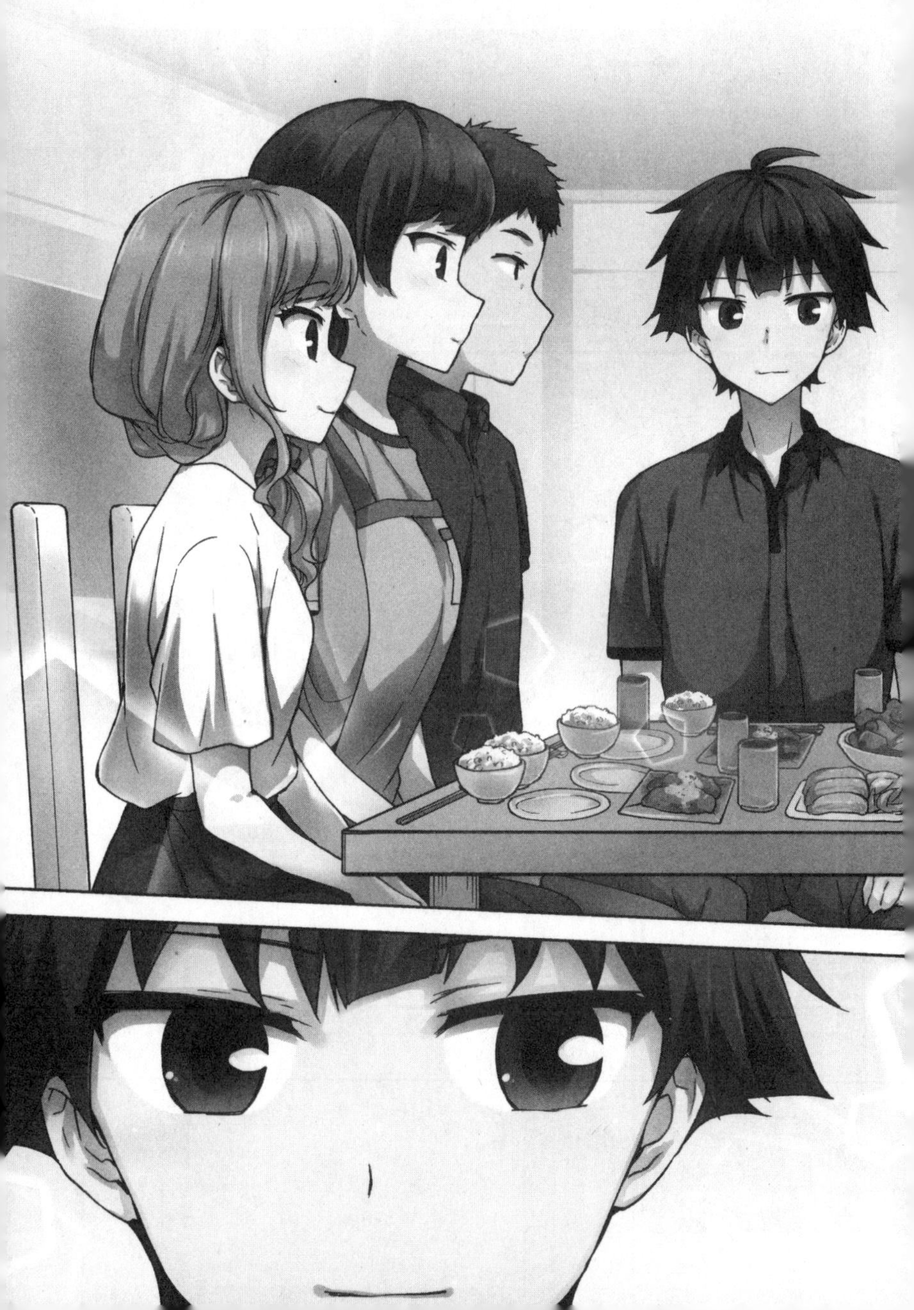

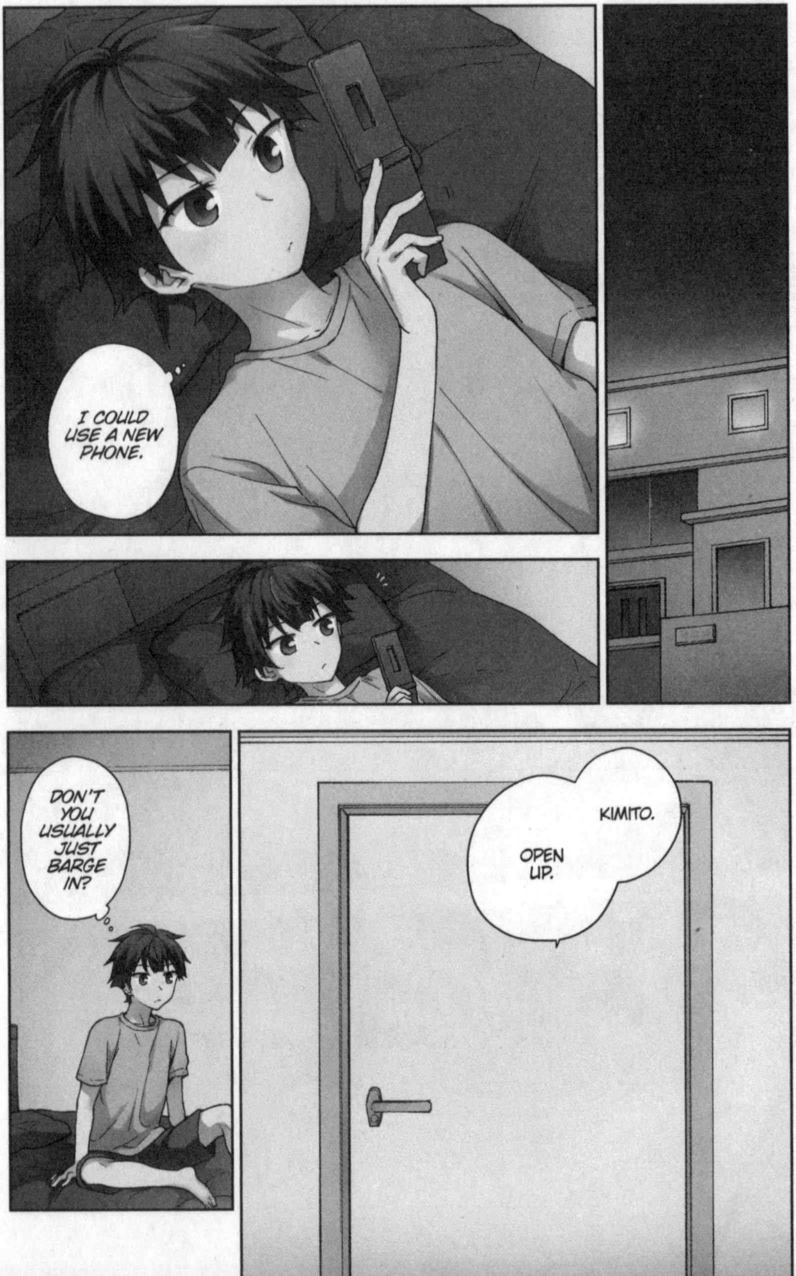
I COULD USE A NEW PHONE.
KIMITO.
OPEN UP.
DON'T YOU USUALLY JUST BARGE IN?

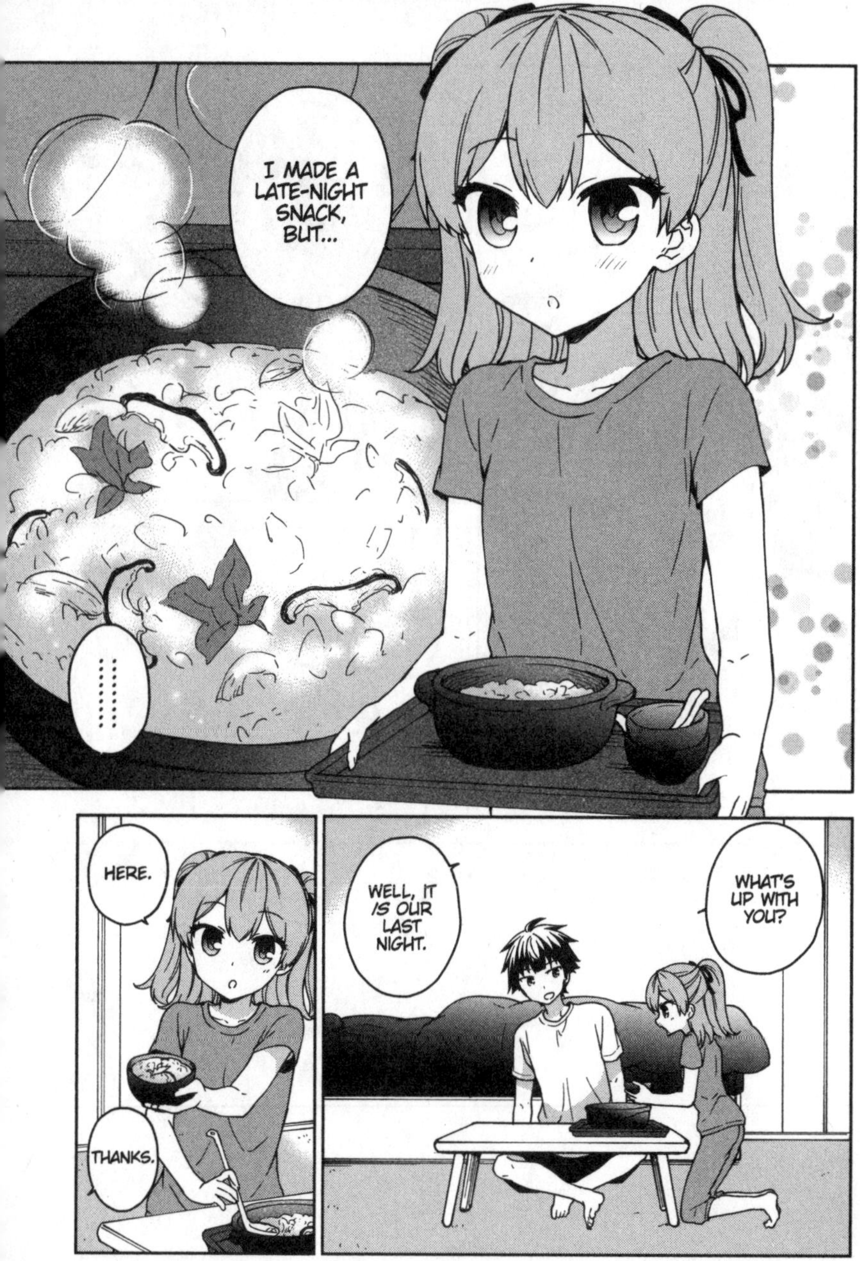
I MADE A LATE-NIGHT SNACK, BUT...
......
WHAT'S UP WITH YOU?
WELL, IT IS OUR LAST NIGHT.
HERE.
THANKS.

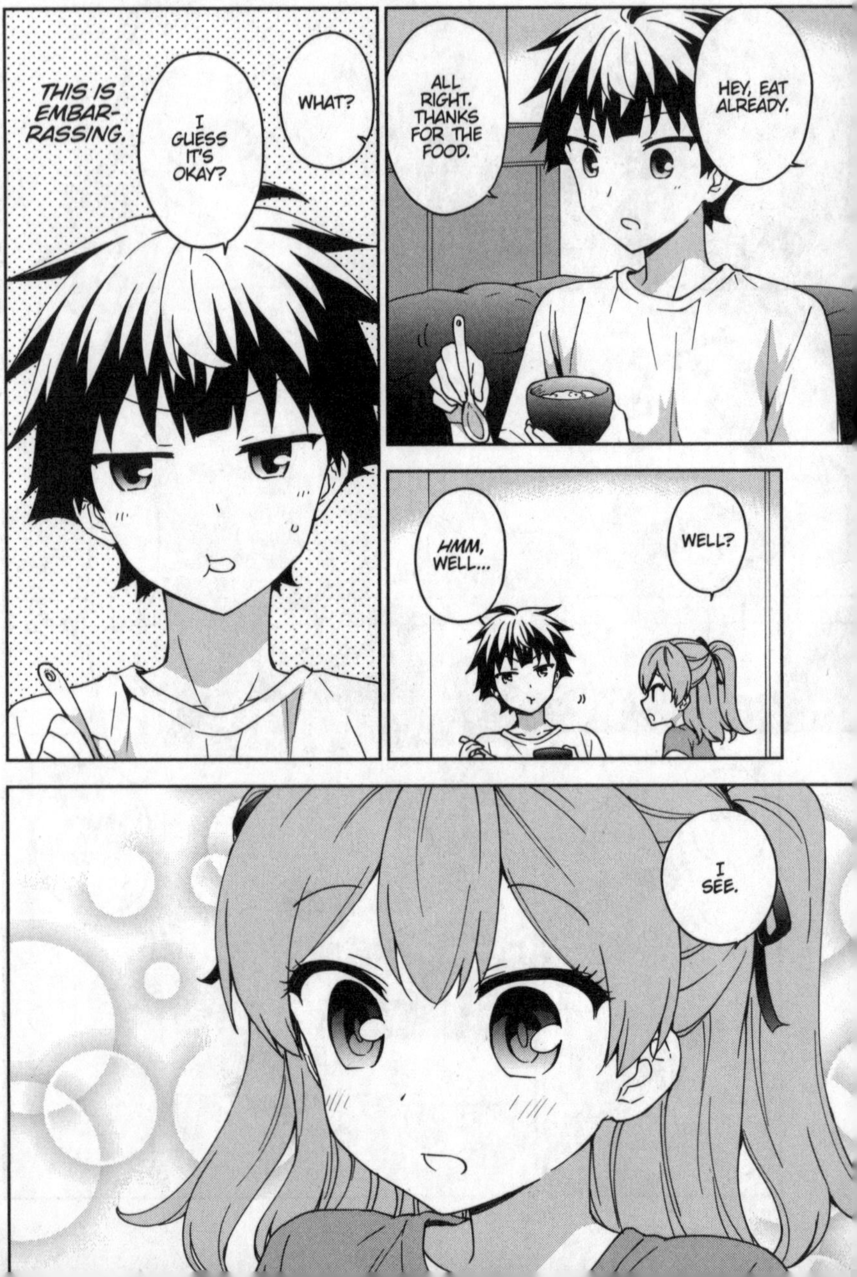
HEY, EAT ALREADY.
ALL RIGHT. THANKS FOR THE FOOD.
WELL?
HMM, WELL...
WHAT?
I GUESS IT'S OKAY?
THIS IS EMBAR-RASSING.
I SEE.

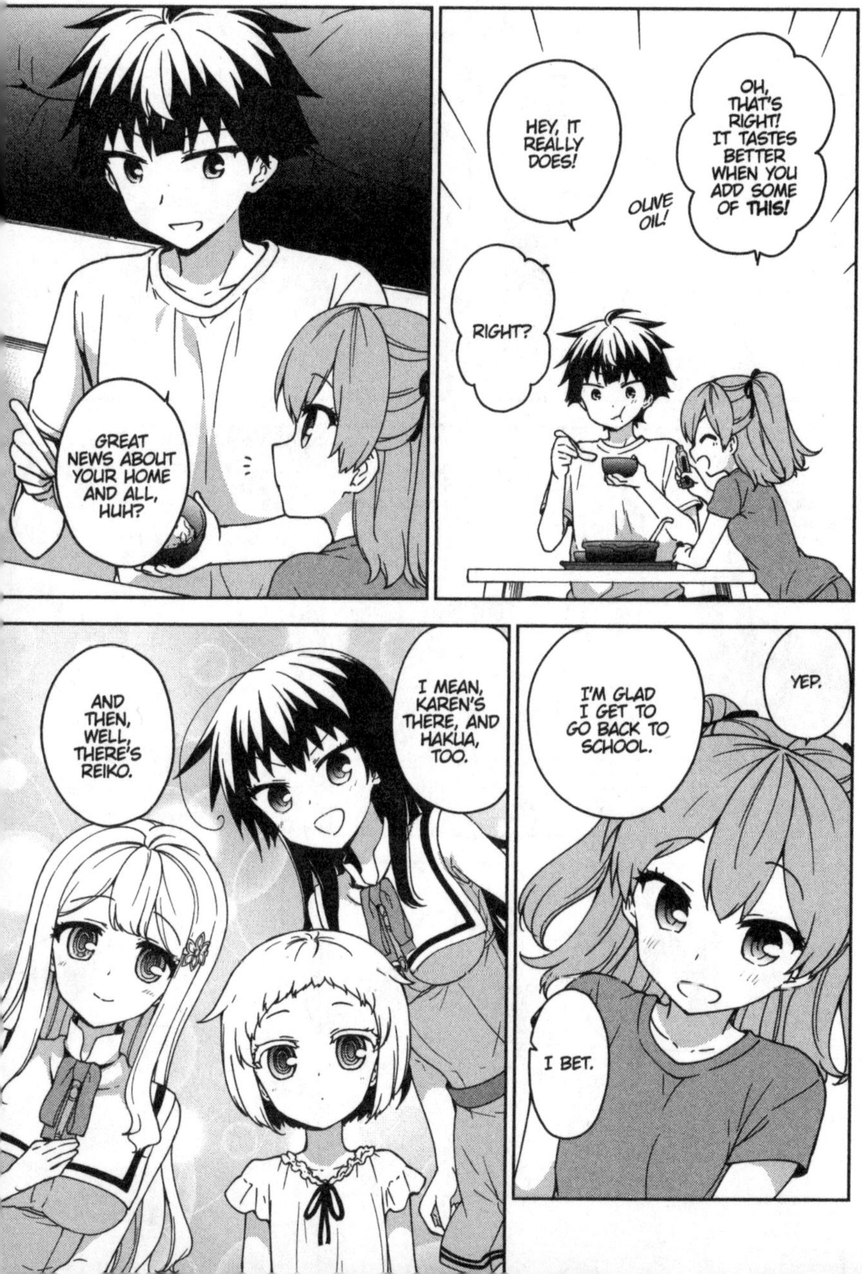
OH, THAT'S RIGHT! IT TASTES BETTER WHEN YOU ADD SOME OF THIS!
OLIVE OIL!
HEY, IT REALLY DOES!
RIGHT?
GREAT NEWS ABOUT YOUR HOME AND ALL, HUH?
YEP.
I'M GLAD I GET TO GO BACK TO SCHOOL.
I BET.
I MEAN, KAREN'S THERE, AND HAKUA, TOO.
AND THEN, WELL, THERE'S REIKO.

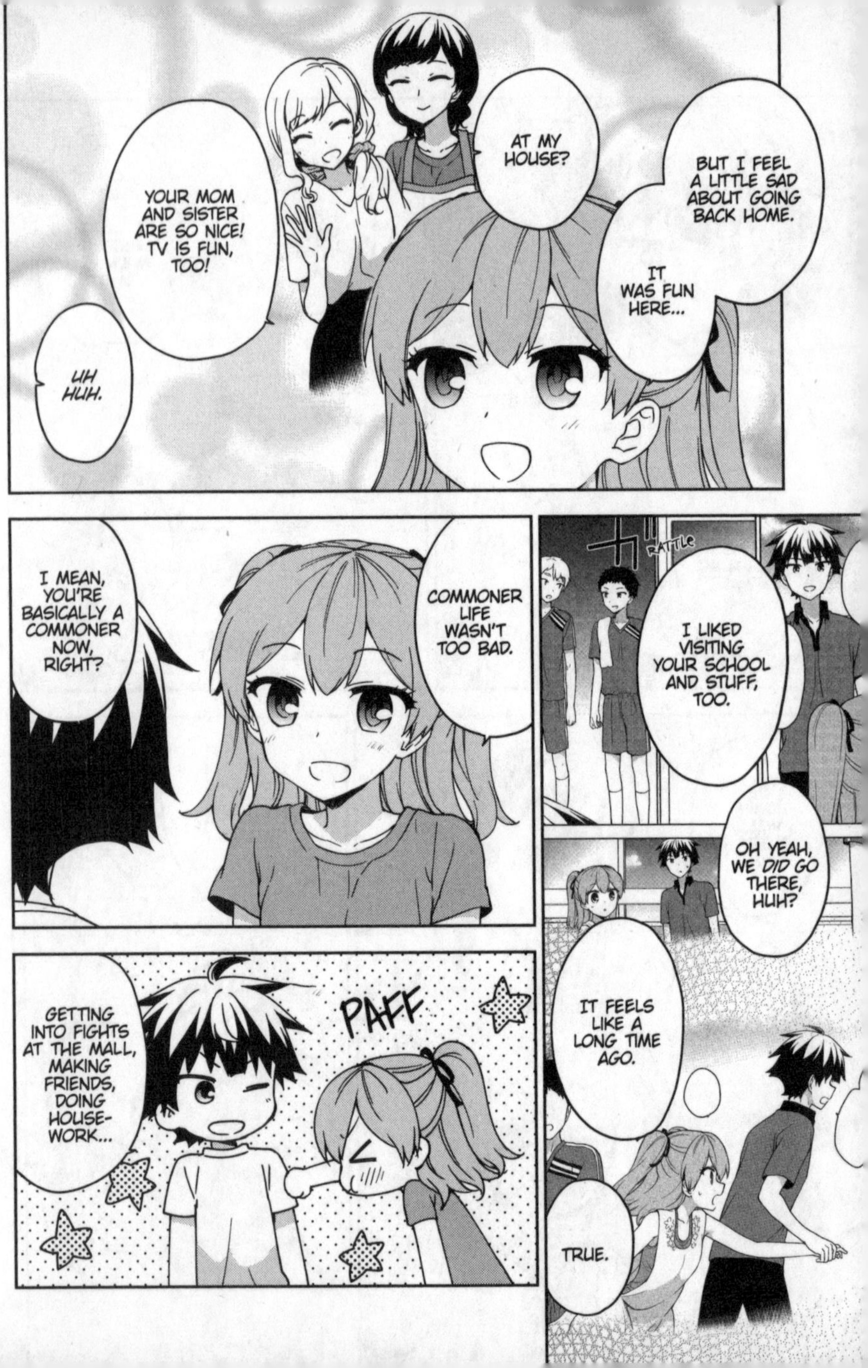
BUT I FEEL A LITTLE SAD ABOUT GOING BACK HOME.
IT WAS FUN HERE...
AT MY HOUSE?
YOUR MOM AND SISTER ARE SO NICE! TV IS FUN, TOO!
UH HUH.
RATTLE
I LIKED VISITING YOUR SCHOOL AND STUFF, TOO.
COMMONER LIFE WASN'T TOO BAD.
I MEAN, YOU'RE BASICALLY A COMMONER NOW, RIGHT?
OH YEAH, WE *DID* GO THERE, HUH?
IT FEELS LIKE A LONG TIME AGO.
TRUE.
PAFF
GETTING INTO FIGHTS AT THE MALL, MAKING FRIENDS, DOING HOUSE-WORK...

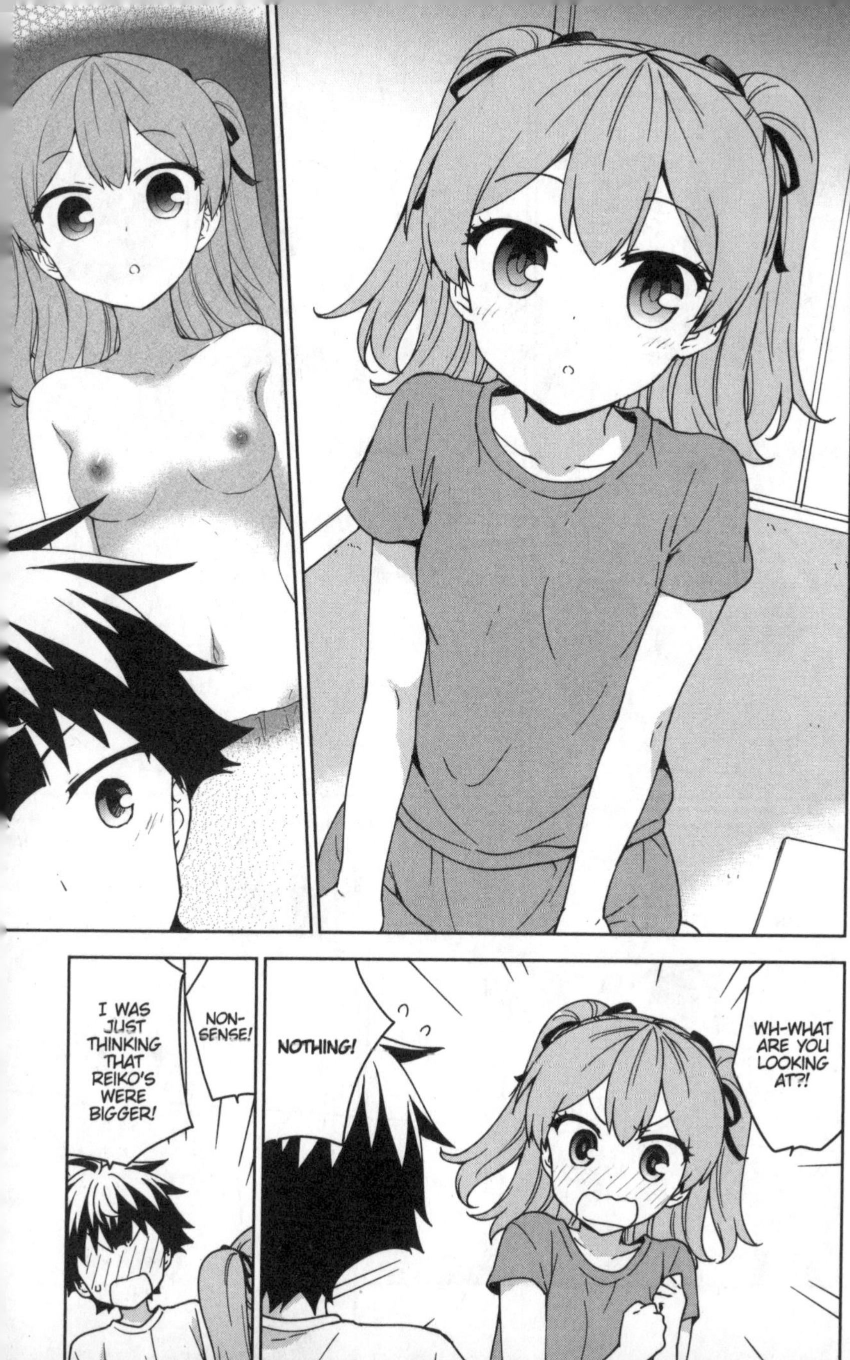
WH-WHAT ARE YOU LOOKING AT?!
NOTHING!
NON-SENSE!
I WAS JUST THINKING THAT REIKO'S WERE BIGGER!

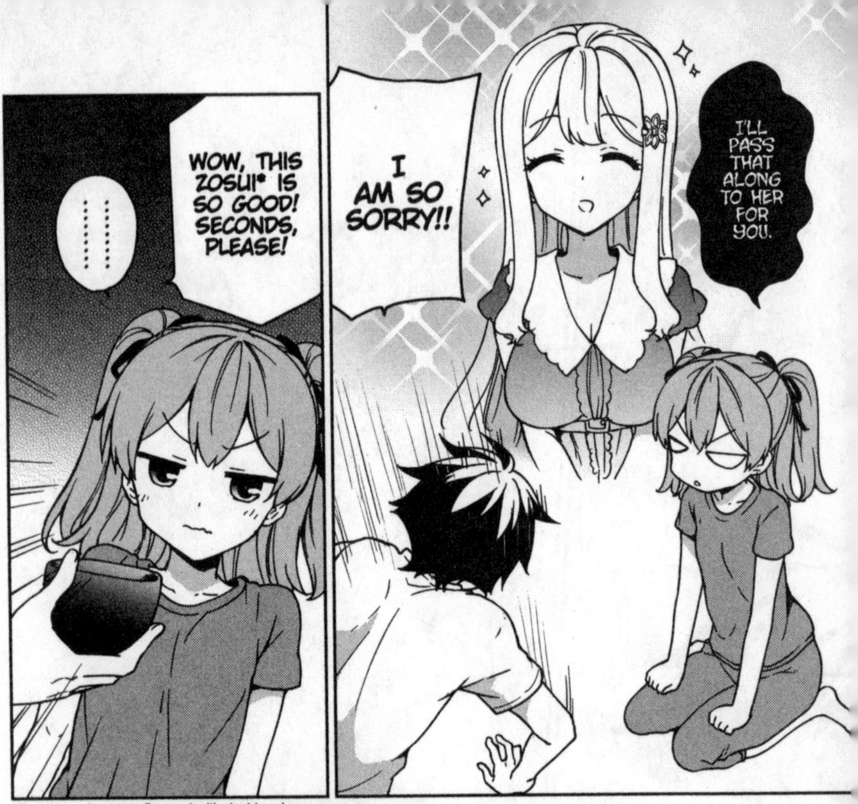
I'LL PASS THAT ALONG TO HER FOR YOU.
I AM SO SORRY!!
WOW, THIS ZOSUI* IS SO GOOD! SECONDS, PLEASE!
......

*Zosui is a rice soup flavored with dashi and soy sauce.

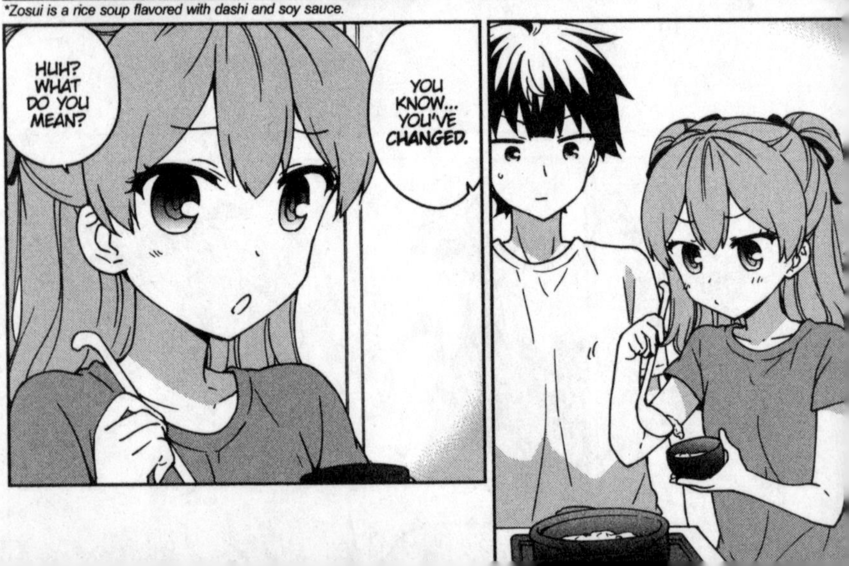
YOU KNOW... YOU'VE CHANGED.
HUH? WHAT DO YOU MEAN?

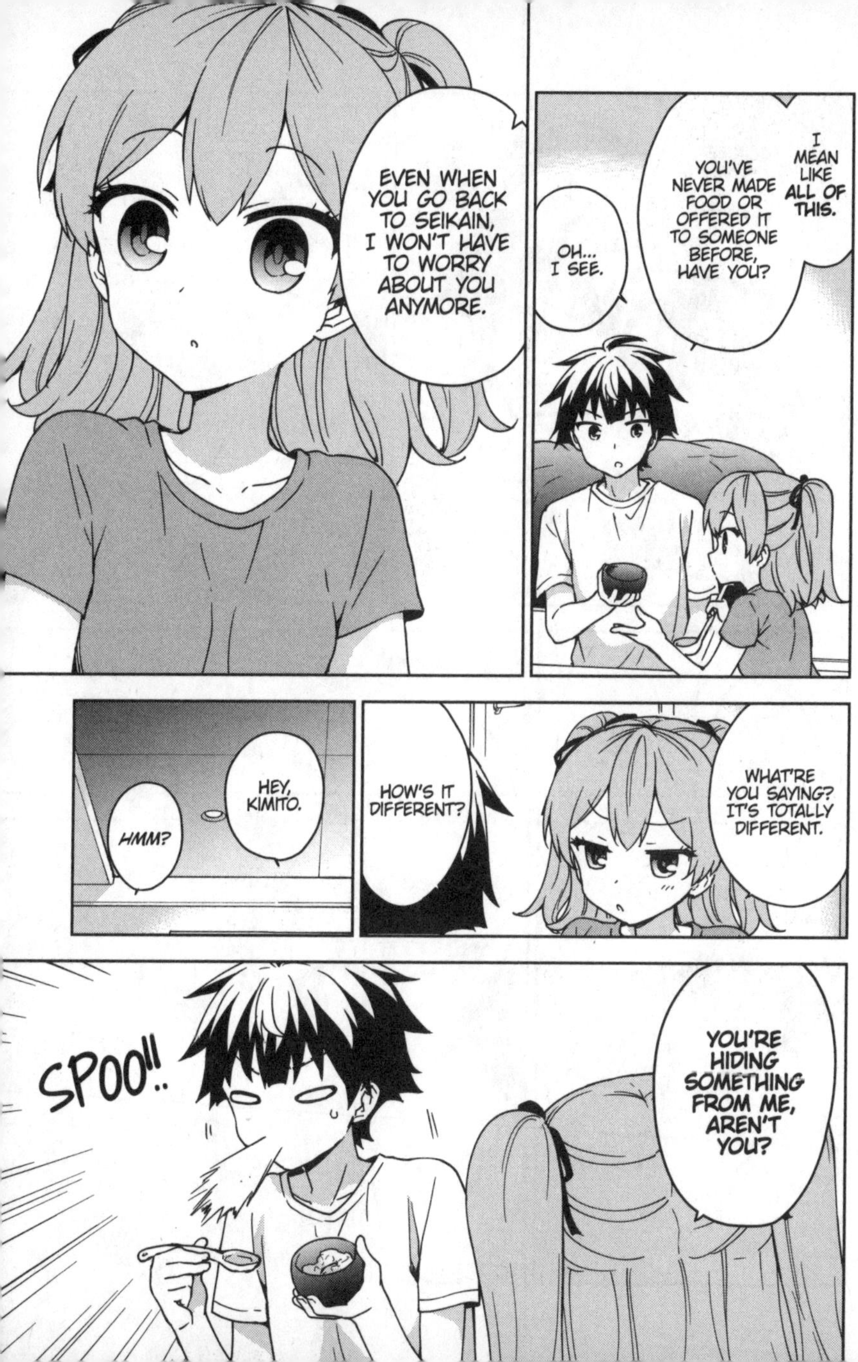
I MEAN LIKE ALL OF THIS.
YOU'VE NEVER MADE FOOD OR OFFERED IT TO SOMEONE BEFORE, HAVE YOU?
OH... I SEE.
EVEN WHEN YOU GO BACK TO SEIKAIN, I WON'T HAVE TO WORRY ABOUT YOU ANYMORE.
WHAT'RE YOU SAYING? IT'S TOTALLY DIFFERENT.
HOW'S IT DIFFERENT?
HEY, KIMITO.
HMM?
YOU'RE HIDING SOMETHING FROM ME, AREN'T YOU?
SPOO!!..

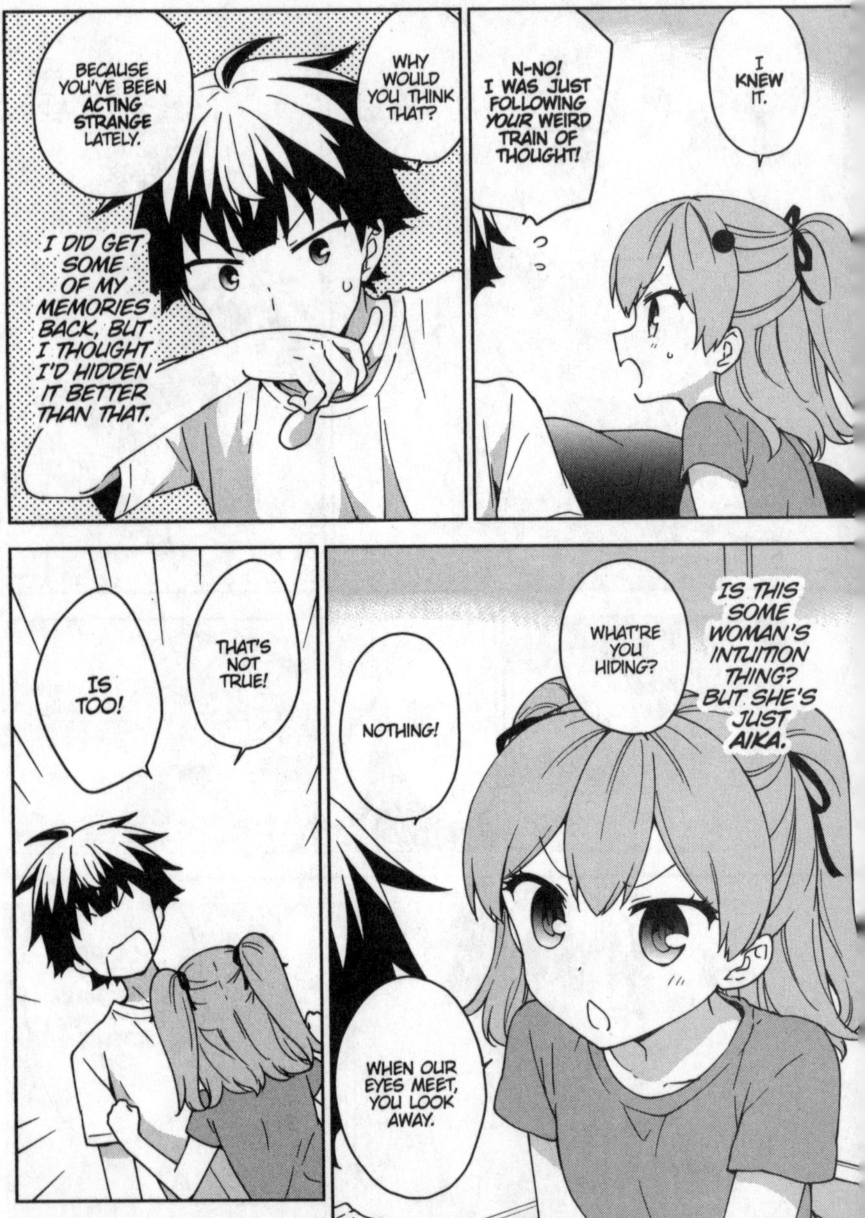
I KNEW IT.
N-NO! I WAS JUST FOLLOWING YOUR WEIRD TRAIN OF THOUGHT!
WHY WOULD YOU THINK THAT?
BECAUSE YOU'VE BEEN ACTING STRANGE LATELY.
I DID GET SOME OF MY MEMORIES BACK, BUT I THOUGHT I'D HIDDEN IT BETTER THAN THAT.
IS THIS SOME WOMAN'S INTUITION THING? BUT SHE'S JUST AIKA.
WHAT'RE YOU HIDING?
NOTHING!
WHEN OUR EYES MEET, YOU LOOK AWAY.
THAT'S NOT TRUE!
IS TOO!

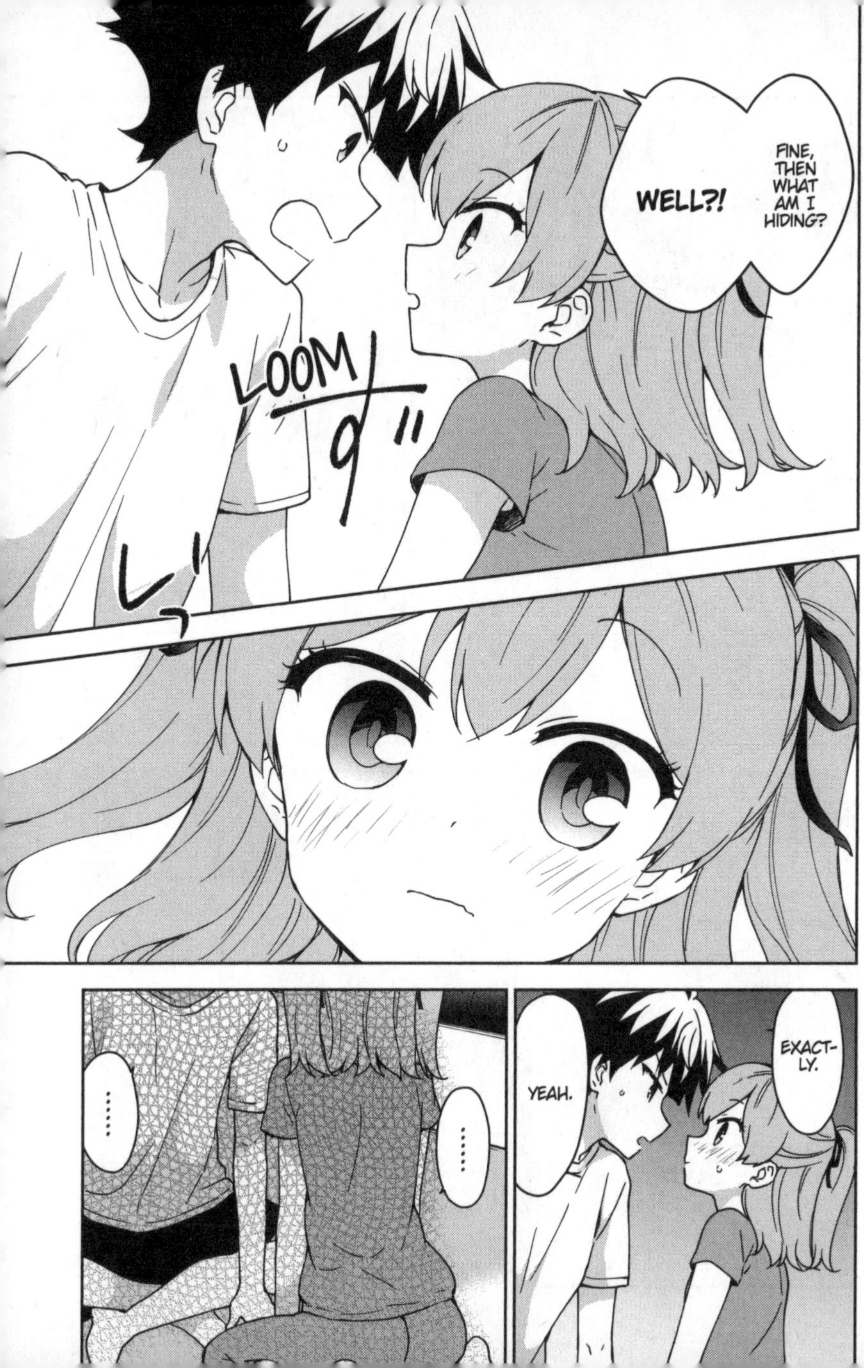
FINE, THEN WHAT AM I HIDING?
WELL?!
LOOM
EXACT-LY.
YEAH.
......
......

I WONDER WHY...

I CAN'T LOOK AWAY.

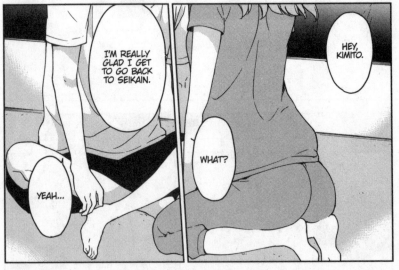

I'M REALLY GLAD I GET TO GO BACK TO SEIKAIN.

HEY, KIMITO.

WHAT?

YEAH...

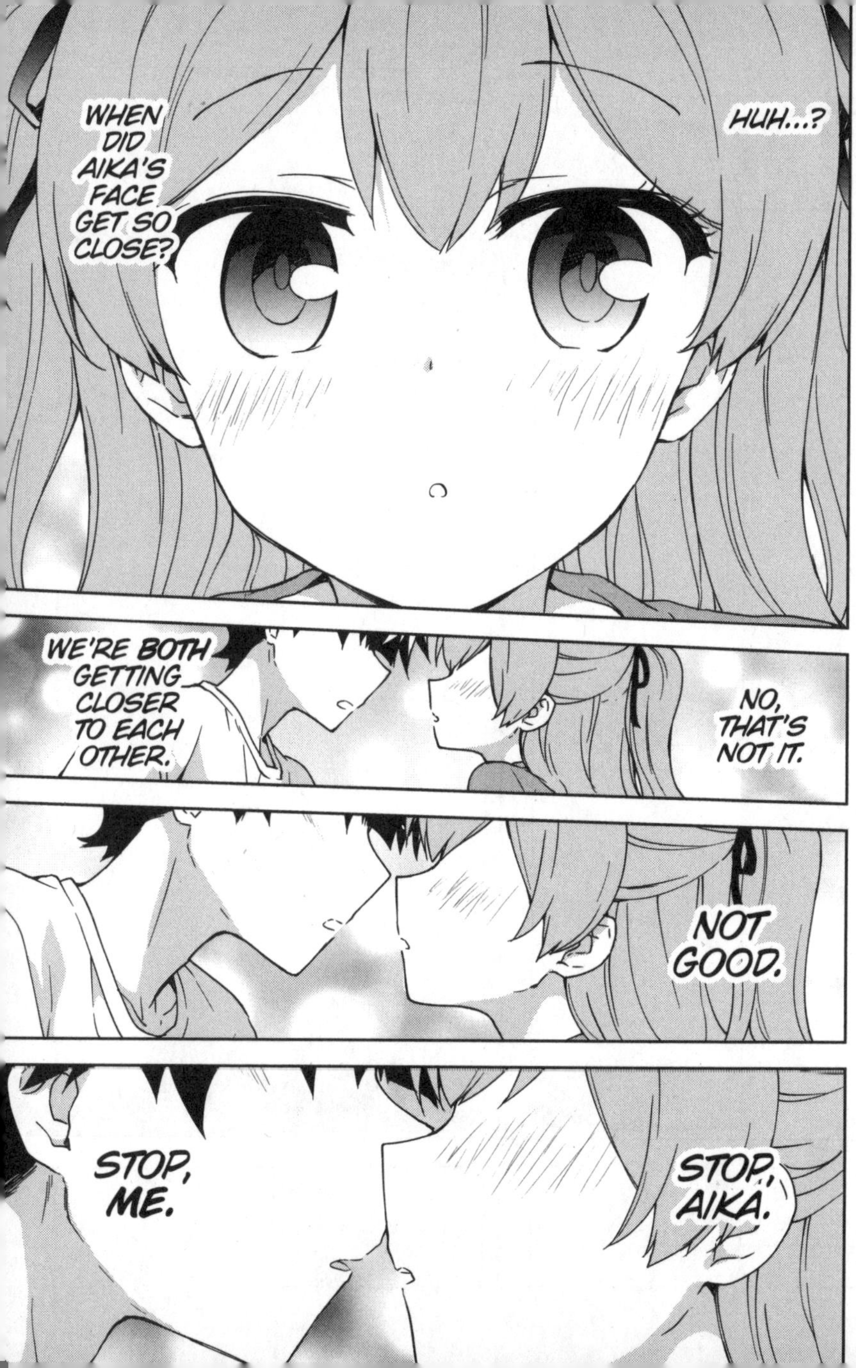
HUH...?
WHEN DID AIKA'S FACE GET SO CLOSE?
NO, THAT'S NOT IT.
WE'RE BOTH GETTING CLOSER TO EACH OTHER.
NOT GOOD.
STOP, AIKA.
STOP, ME.

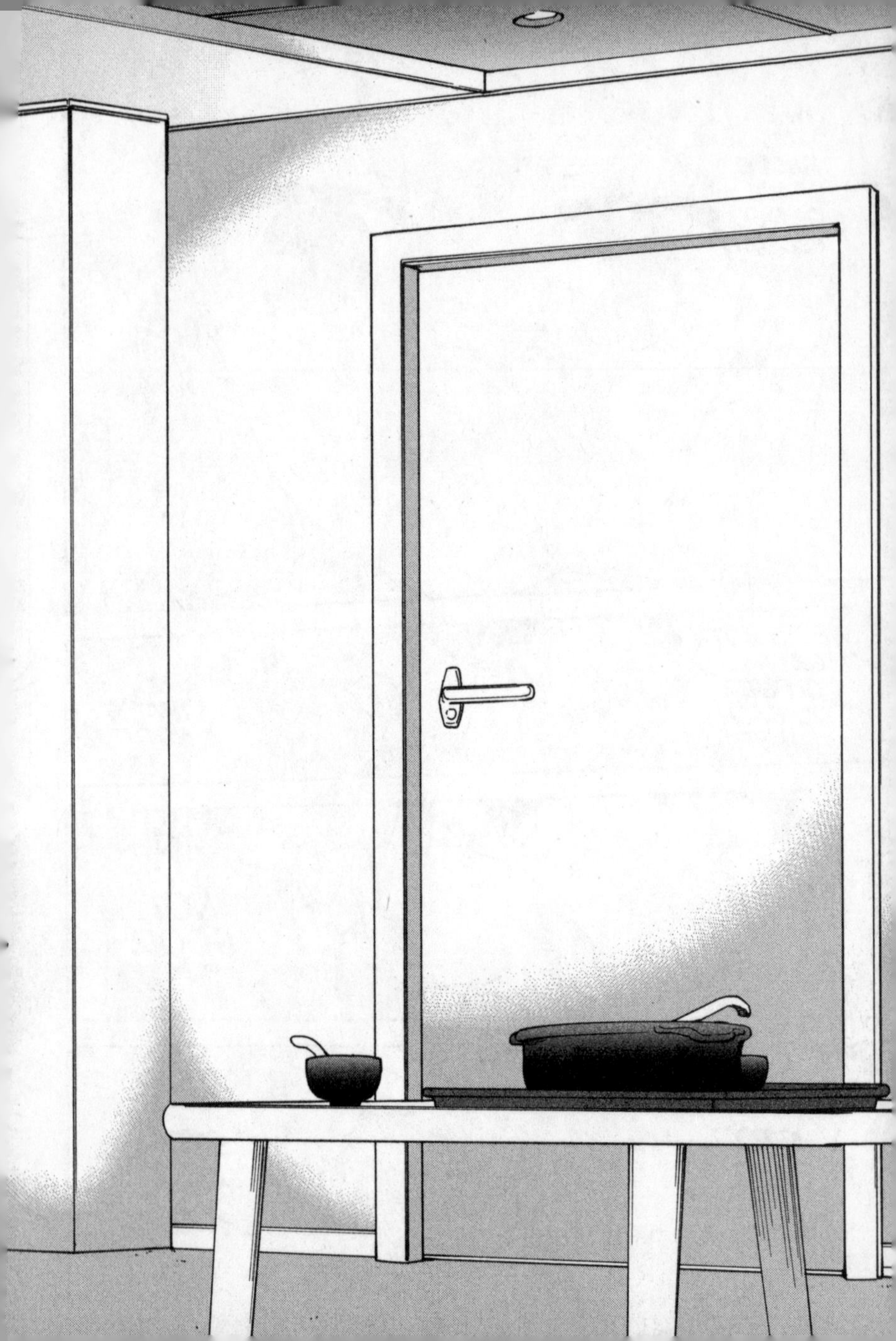

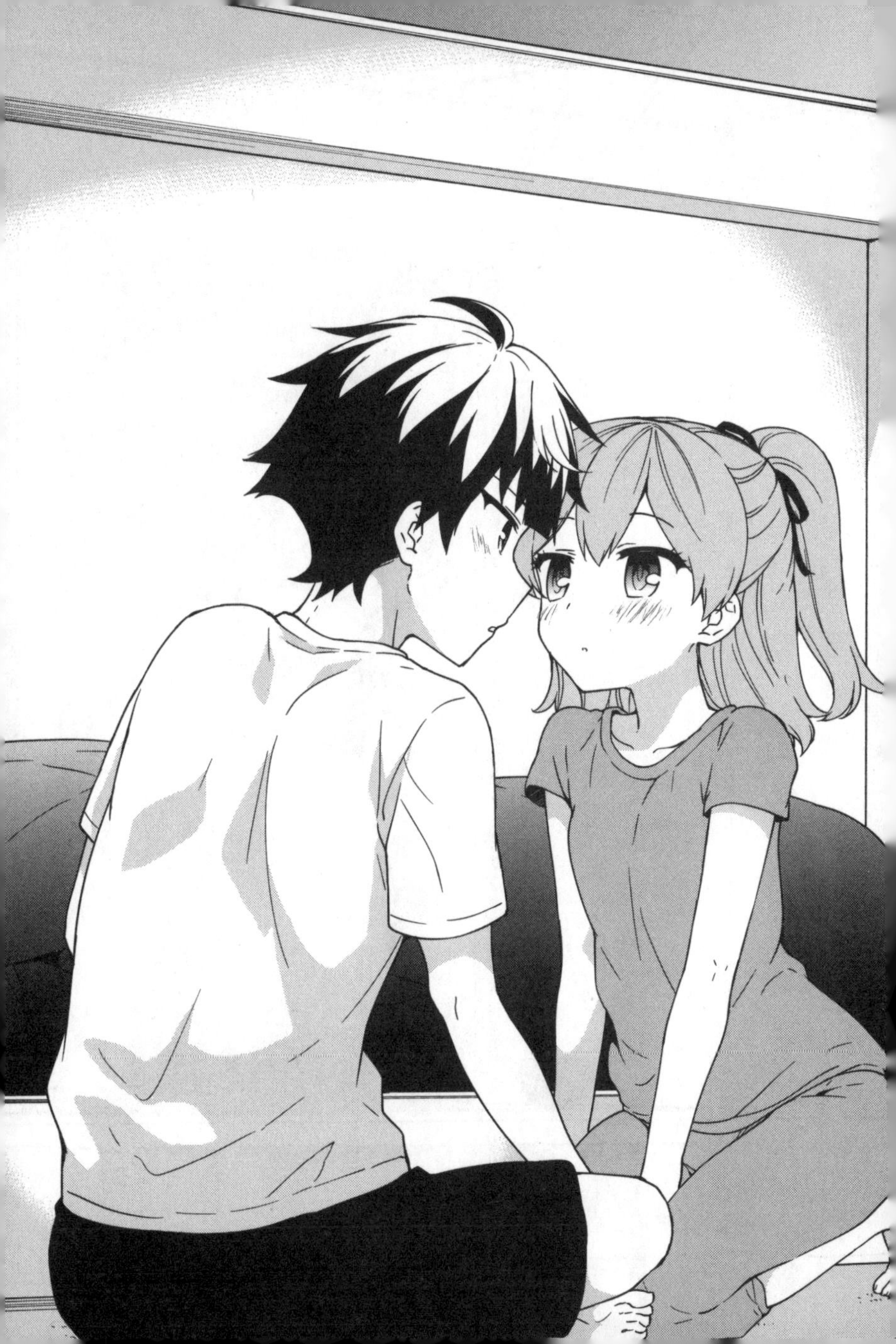

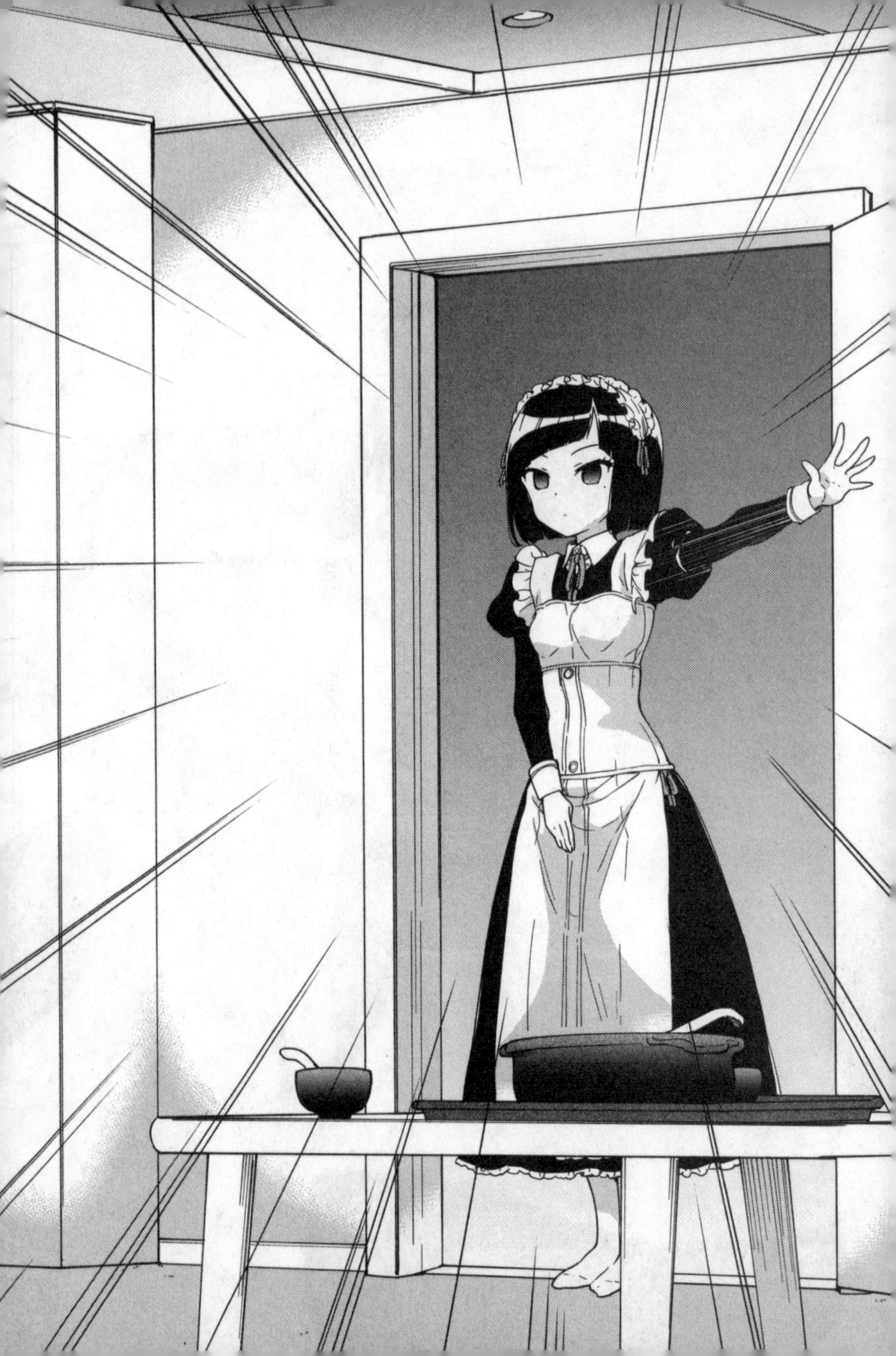

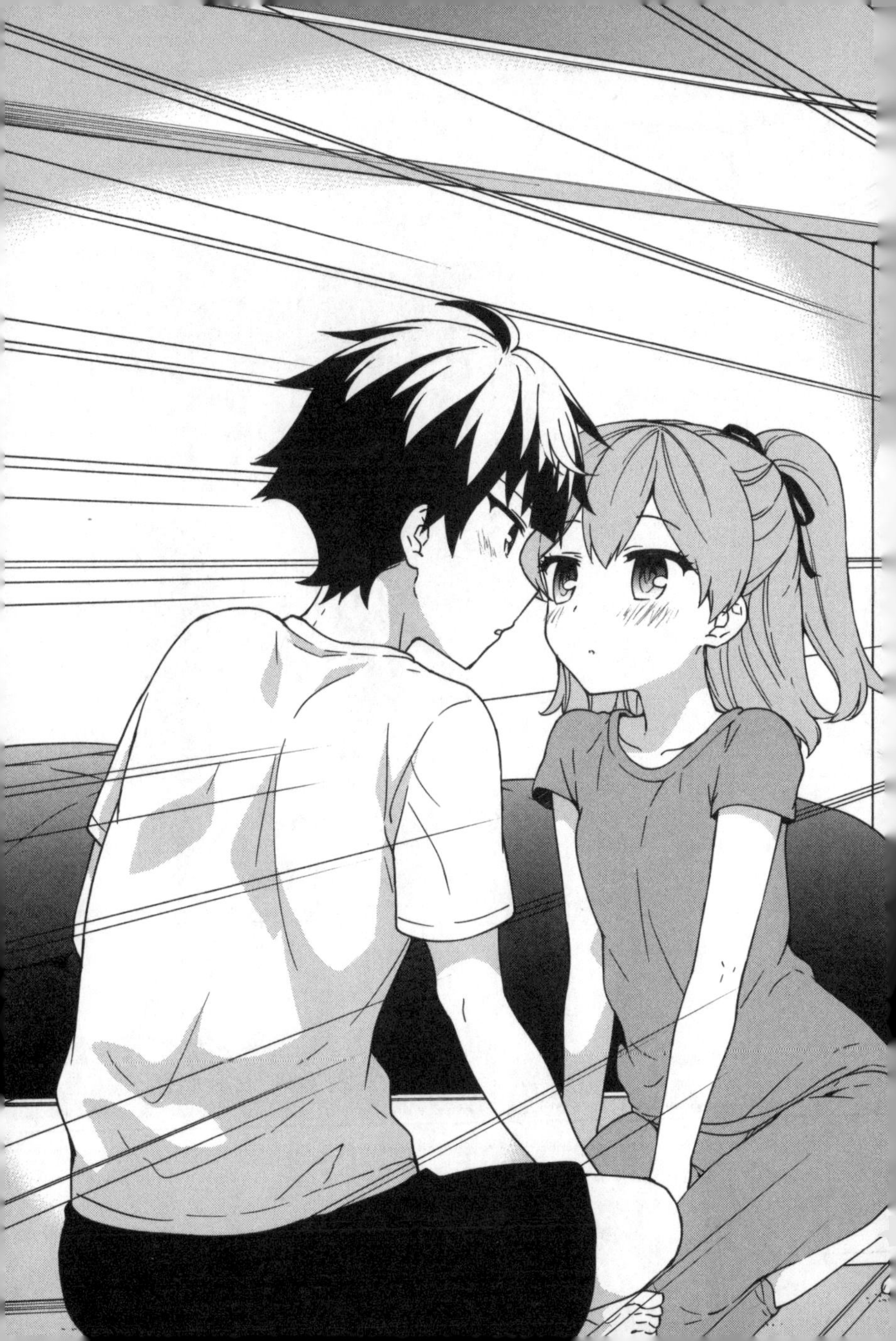

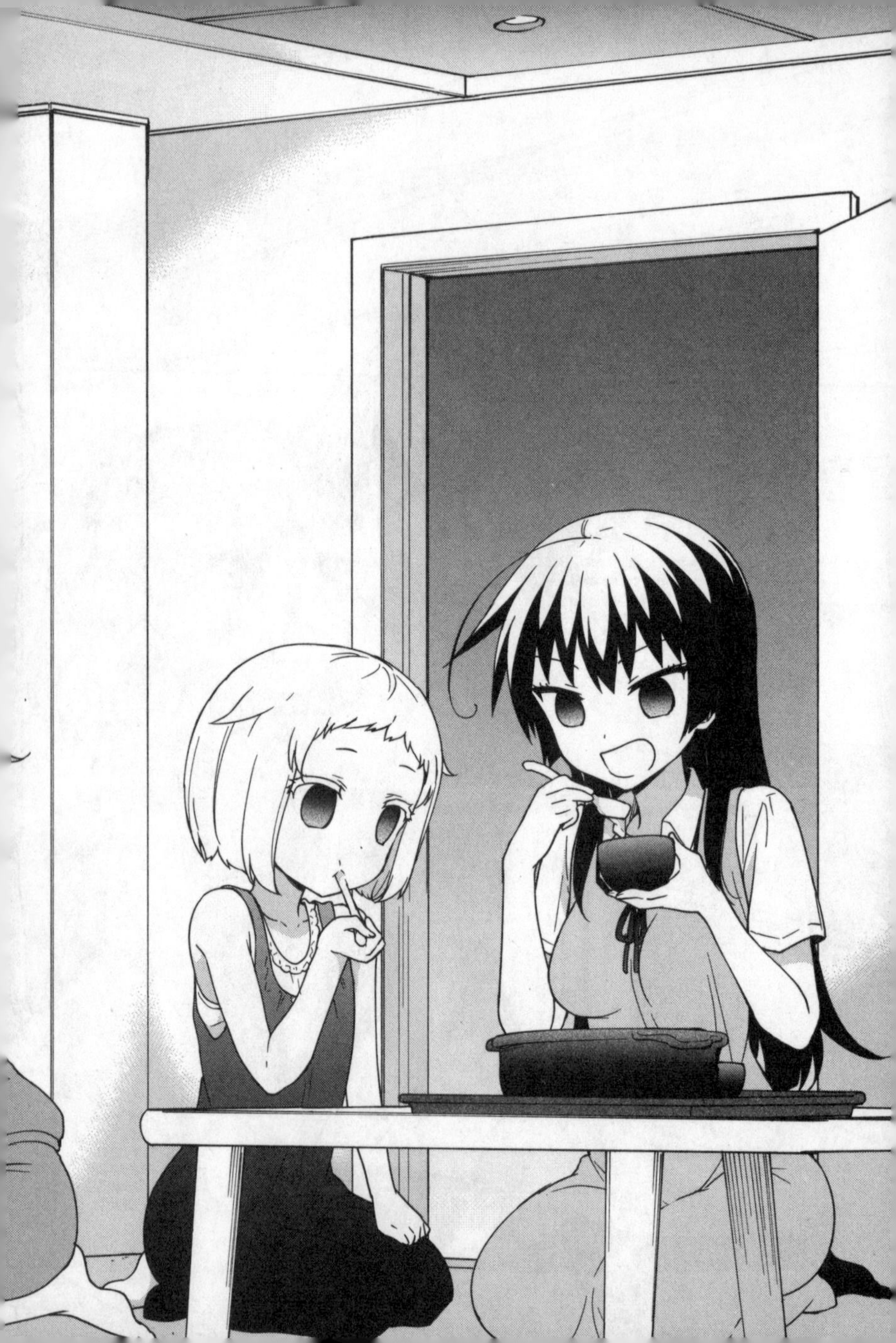

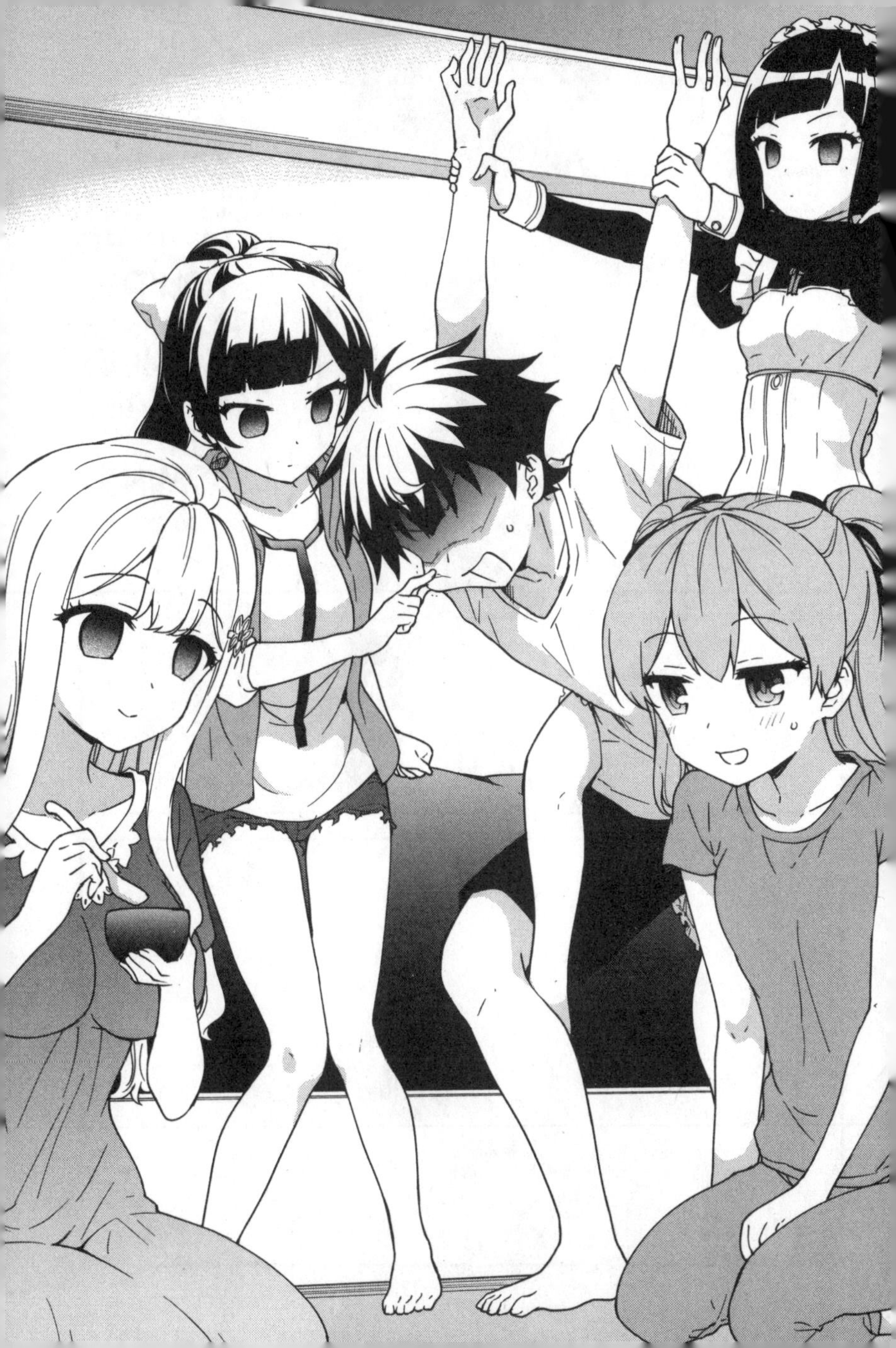

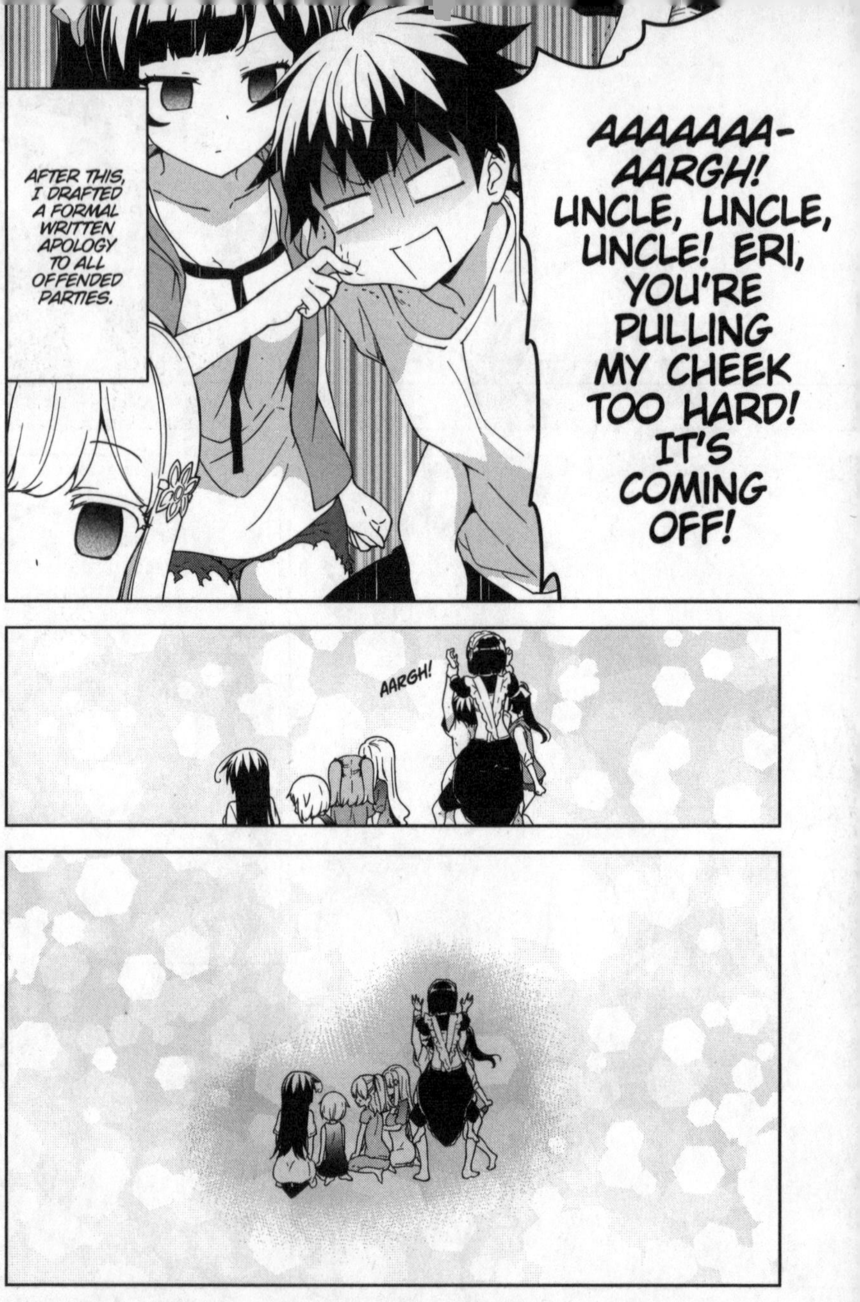
AAAAAAA-AARGH! UNCLE, UNCLE, UNCLE! ERI, YOU'RE PULLING MY CHEEK TOO HARD! IT'S COMING OFF!
AFTER THIS, I DRAFTED A FORMAL WRITTEN APOLOGY TO ALL OFFENDED PARTIES.
AARGH!

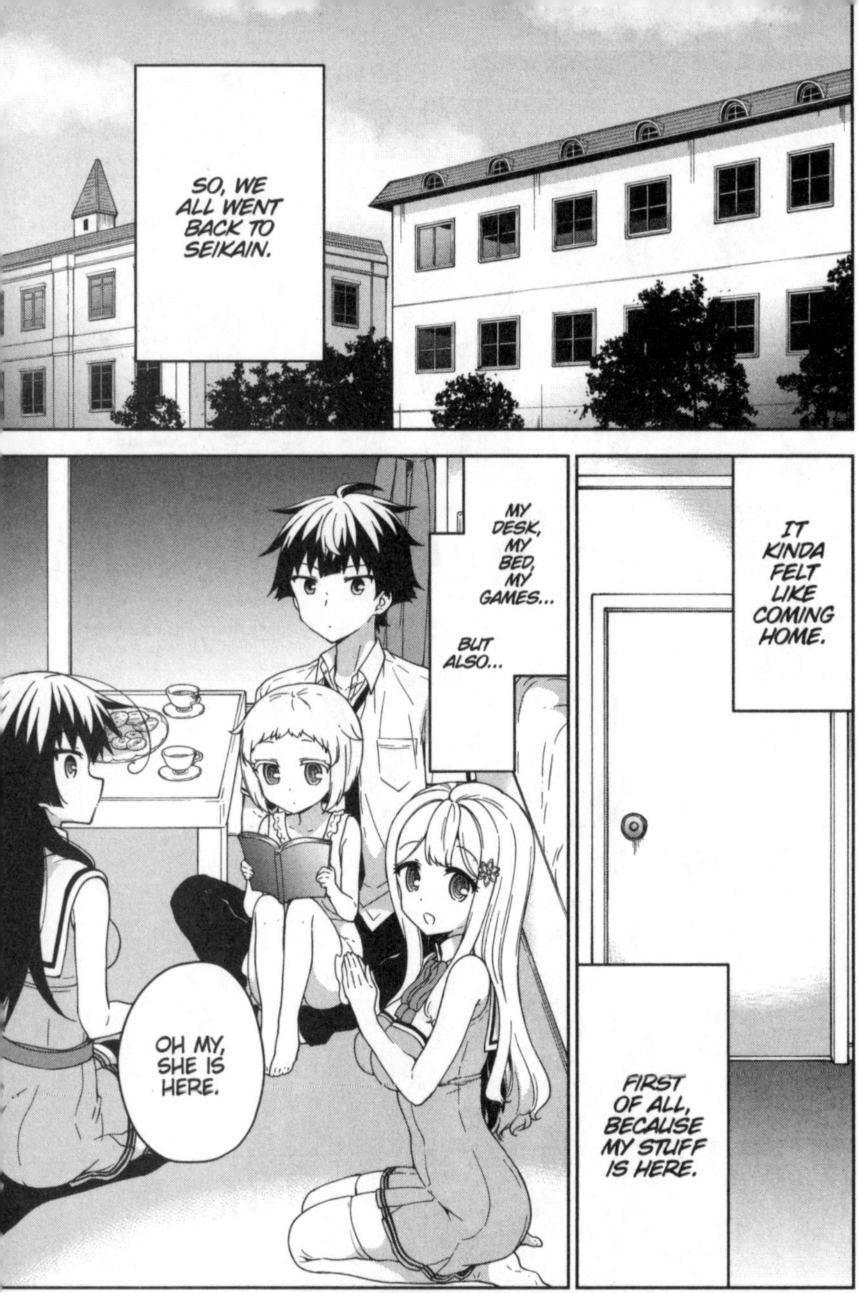
SO, WE ALL WENT BACK TO SEIKAIN.
IT KINDA FELT LIKE COMING HOME.
FIRST OF ALL, BECAUSE MY STUFF IS HERE.
MY DESK, MY BED, MY GAMES...
BUT ALSO...
OH MY, SHE IS HERE.

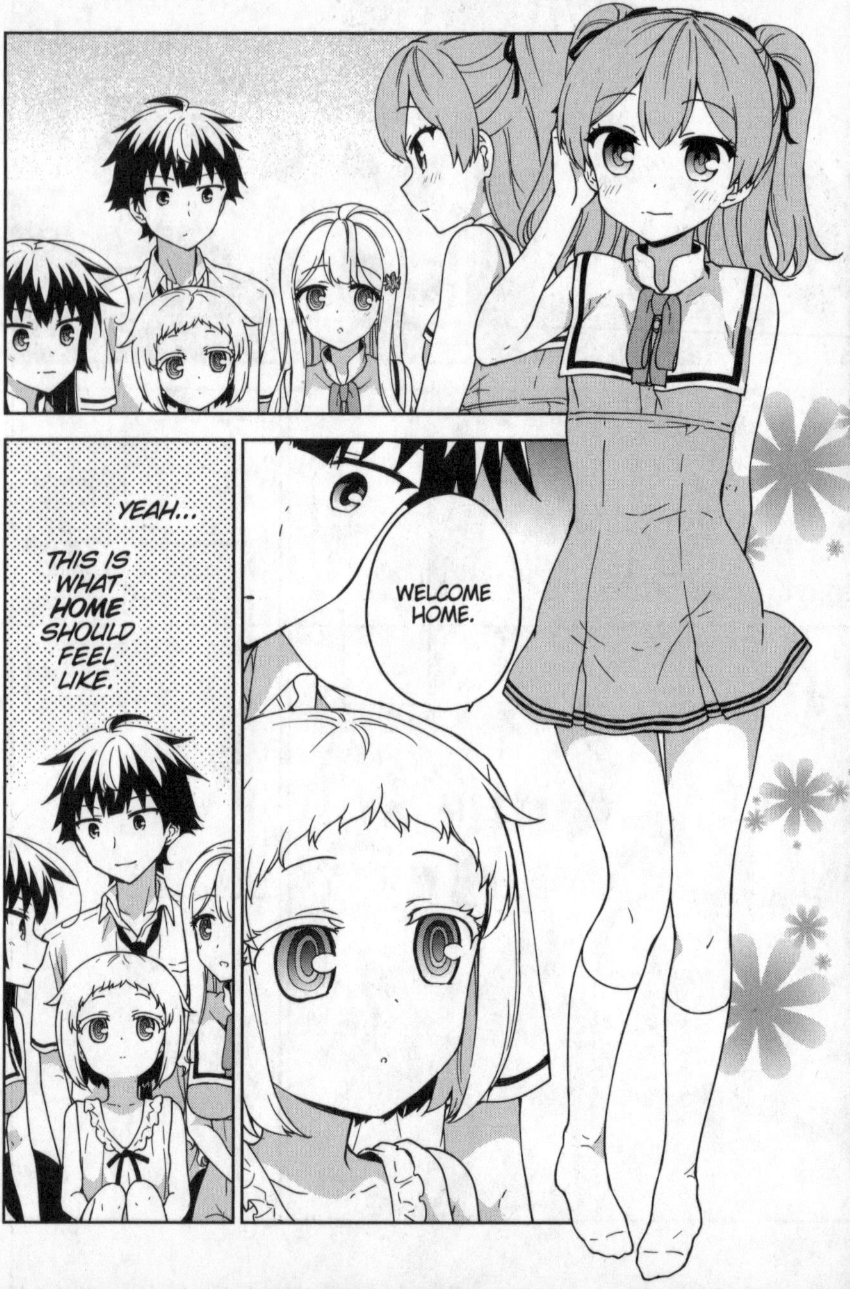
WELCOME HOME.
YEAH...
THIS IS WHAT HOME SHOULD FEEL LIKE.

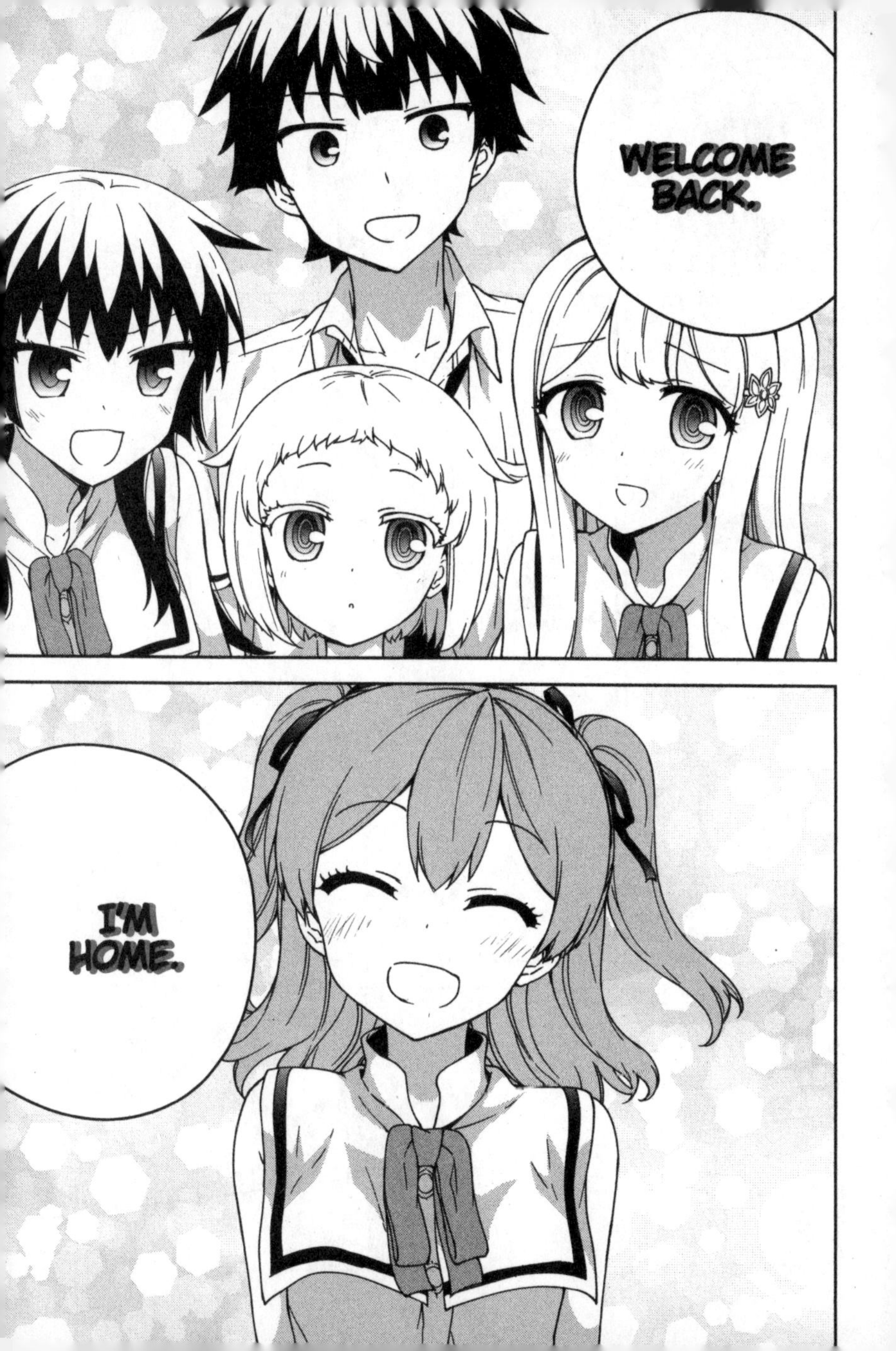
WELCOME BACK.
I'M HOME.

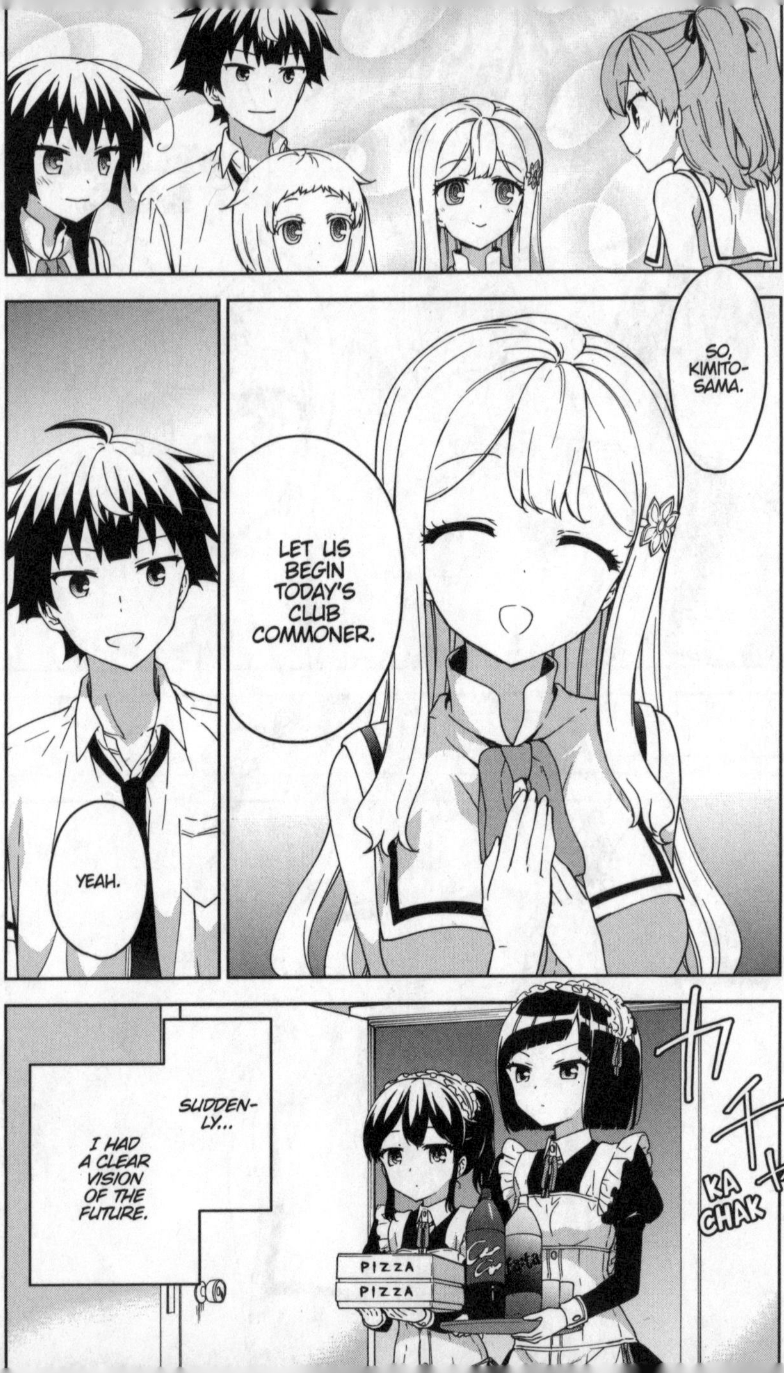
SO, KIMITO-SAMA.
LET US BEGIN TODAY'S CLUB COMMONER.
YEAH.
KA CHAK
SUDDEN-LY...
I HAD A CLEAR VISION OF THE FUTURE.
PIZZA
PIZZA

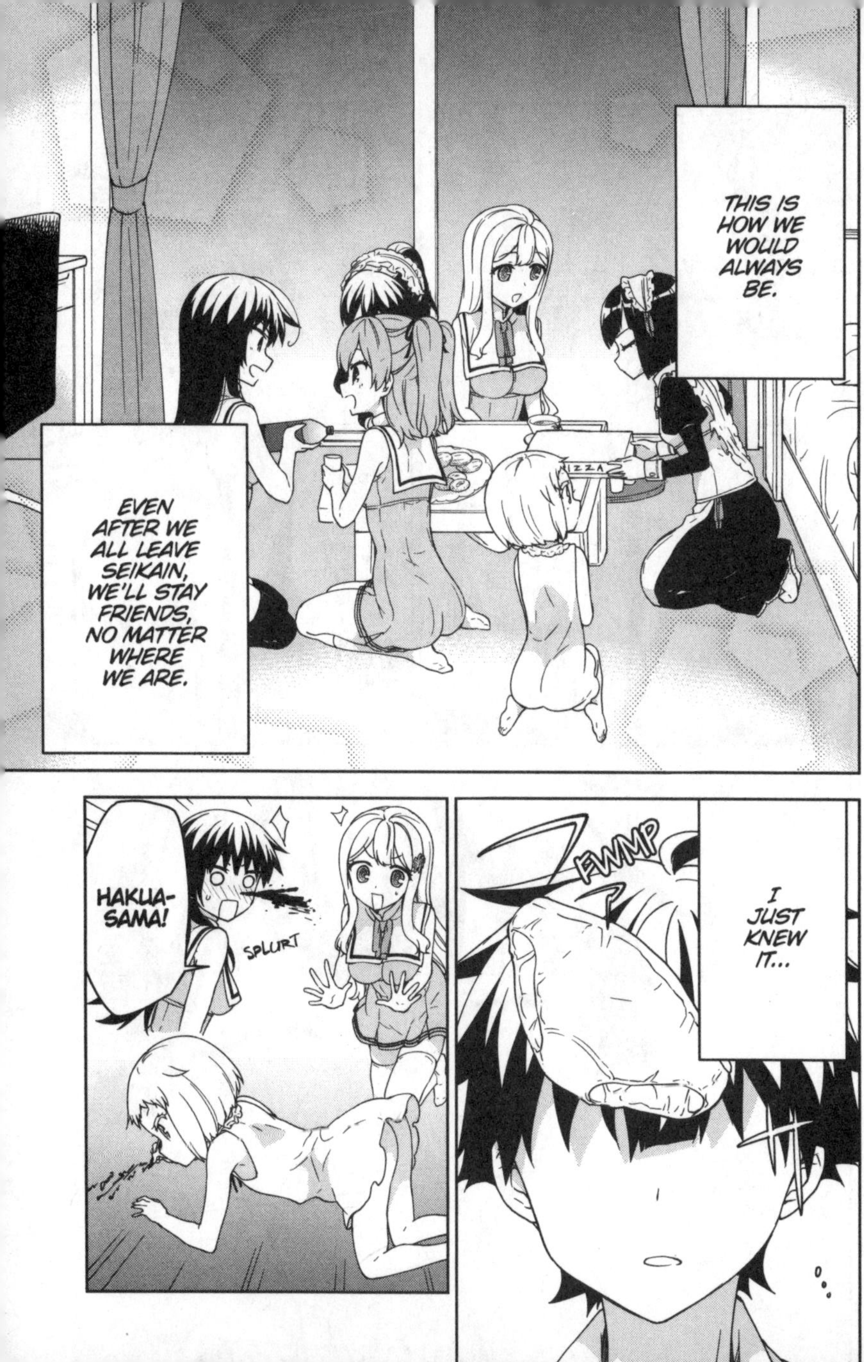
THIS IS HOW WE WOULD ALWAYS BE.
EVEN AFTER WE ALL LEAVE SEIKAIN, WE'LL STAY FRIENDS, NO MATTER WHERE WE ARE.
PIZZA
FWMP
I JUST KNEW IT...
HAKUA-SAMA!
SPLURT

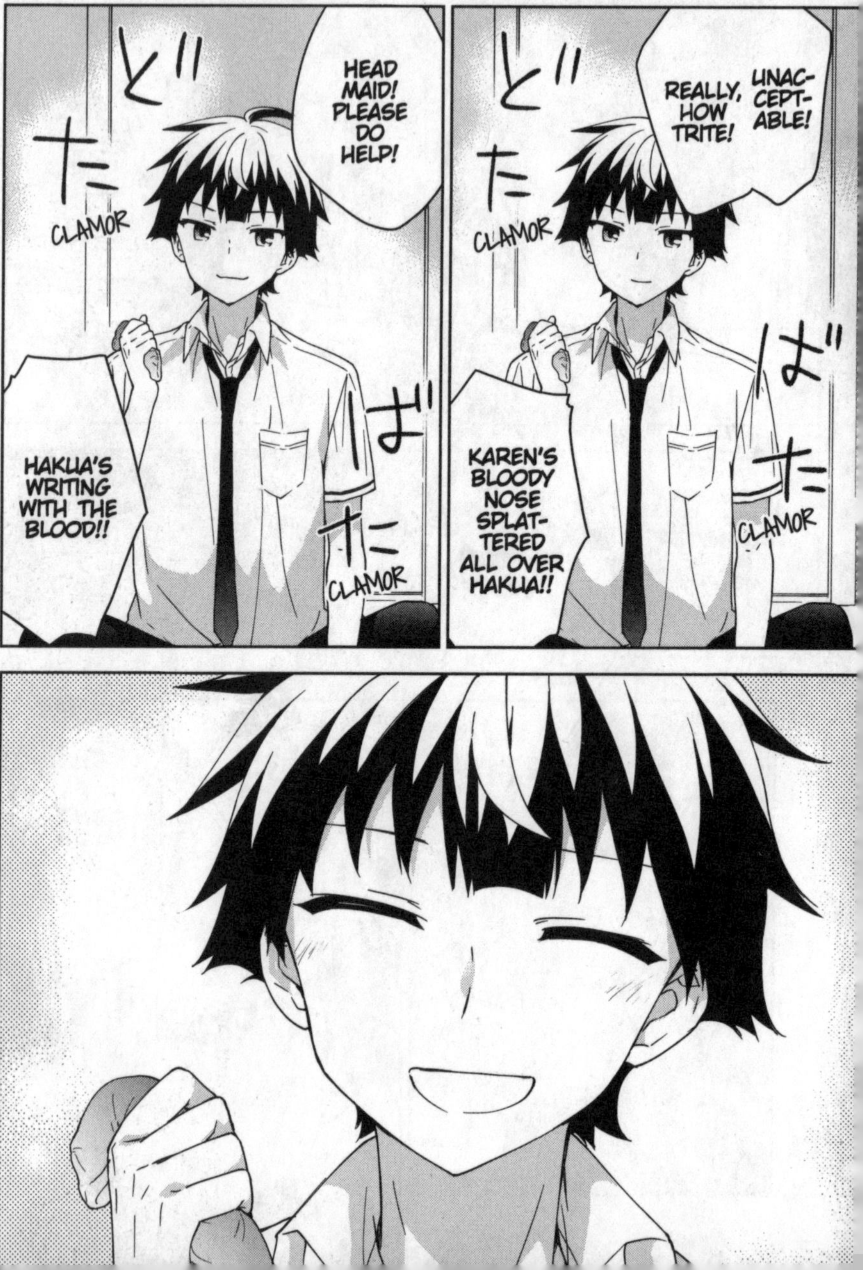
どだ
CLAMOR
UNACCEPTABLE!
REALLY, HOW TRITE!
ばた
CLAMOR
KAREN'S BLOODY NOSE SPLATTERED ALL OVER HAKUA!!
どだ
CLAMOR
HEAD MAID! PLEASE DO HELP!
ばた
CLAMOR
HAKUA'S WRITING WITH THE BLOOD!!

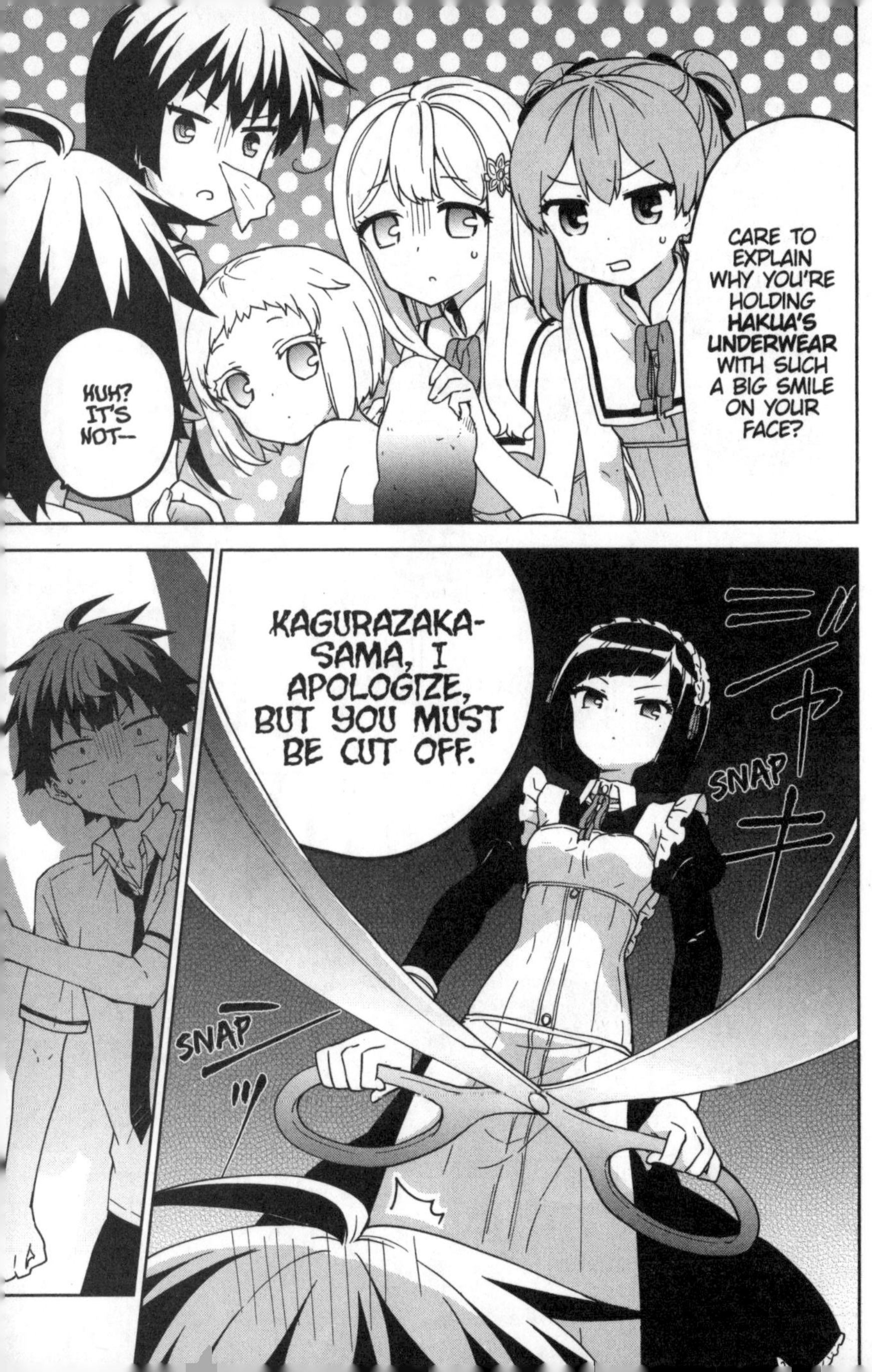
CARE TO EXPLAIN WHY YOU'RE HOLDING HAKUA'S UNDERWEAR WITH SUCH A BIG SMILE ON YOUR FACE?
HUH? IT'S NOT--
SNAP
KAGURAZAKA-SAMA, I APOLOGIZE, BUT YOU MUST BE CUT OFF.
SNAP

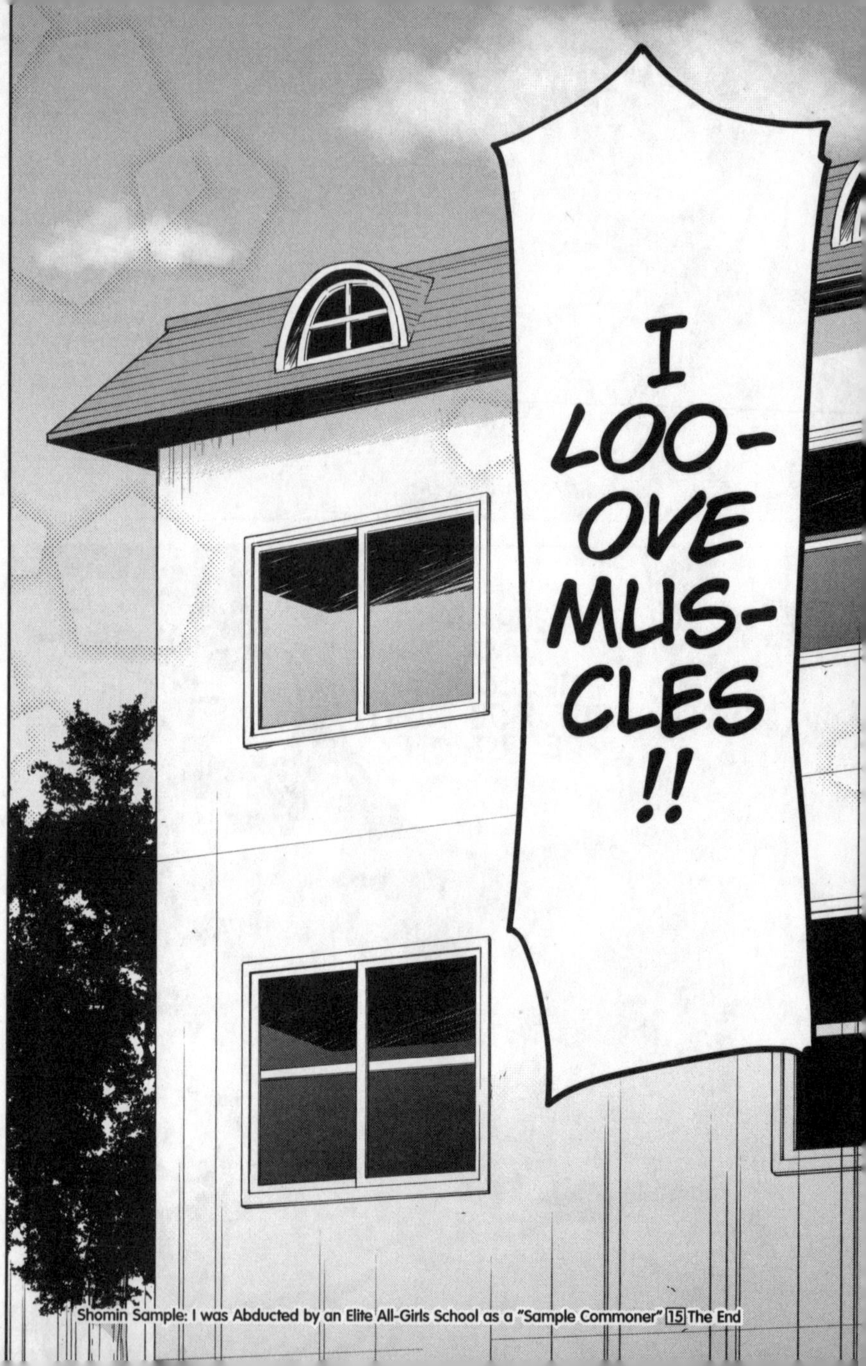
I LOO-OVE MUS-CLES!!
Shomin Sample: I was Abducted by an Elite All-Girls School as a "Sample Commoner" 15 The End

SHOMIN SAMPLE 15

I Was Abducted by an Elite All-Girls
School as a Sample Commoner

SEVEN SEAS ENTERTAINMENT PRESENTS

SHOMIN SAMPLE

I Was Abducted by an Elite All-Girls School as a Sample Commoner VOL. 15

story by **TAKAFUMI NANATSUKI** / art by **RISUMAI** / character design by **GEKKA URUU**

TRANSLATION
Beni Axia Conrad

ADAPTATION
Patrick King

LETTERING AND LAYOUT
Alexandra Gunawan

COVER DESIGN
Kris Aubin

PROOFREADER
Janet Houck, Dawn Davis

EDITOR
Shanti Whitesides

PREPRESS TECHNICIAN
Rhiannon Rasmussen-Silverstein

PRODUCTION MANAGER
Lissa Pattillo

MANAGING EDITOR
Julie Davis

ASSOCIATE PUBLISHER
Adam Arnold

PUBLISHER
Jason DeAngelis

SHOMIN SAMPLE: I WAS ABDUCTED BY AN ELITE ALL-GIRLS SCHOOL AS A SAMPLE COMMONER VOL. 15

Seven Seas press and purchase enquiries can be sent to Marketing Manager Lianne Sentar at press@gomanga.com. Information regarding the distribution and purchase of digital editions is available from Digital Manager CK Russell at digital@gomanga.com.

ISBN: 978-1-64505-997-4

Printed in Canada

First Printing: June 2021

10 9 8 7 6 5 4 3 2 1

READING DIRECTIONS

This book reads from ***right to left***, Japanese style. If this is your first time reading manga, you start reading from the top right panel on each page and take it from there. If you get lost, just follow the numbered diagram here. It may seem backwards at first, but you'll get the hang of it! Have fun!!

1
2
3
4
5
6
7
8
9

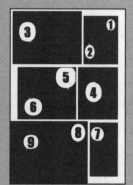